SolidWorks 2007:
The Basics
with Multimedia CD

A Working Knowledge of SolidWorks using a Step-by-Step Project Based Approach

David C. Planchard & Marie P. Planchard

ISBN: 978-1-58503-352-2

SDC

PUBLICATIONS

Schroff Development Corporation

www.schroff.com
www.schroff-europe.com

Trademarks and Disclaimer

SolidWorks and its family of products are registered trademarks of the Dassault Système. Microsoft Windows, Microsoft Office and its family of products are registered trademarks of the Microsoft Corporation. Other software applications and parts described in this book are trademarks or registered trademarks of their respective owners.

Dimensions of parts are modified for illustration purposes. Every effort is made to provide an accurate text. The authors and the manufacturers shall not be held liable for any parts or drawings developed or designed with this book or any responsibility for inaccuracies that appear in the book. World Wide Web and company information was valid at the time of the printing.

Examination Copies

Books received as examination copies are for review purposes only and may not be made available for student use. Resale of examination copies is prohibited.

Electronic Files

Any electronic files associated with this book are licensed to the original user only. These files may not be transferred to any other party.

INTRODUCTION

SolidWorks 2007: The Basics is a subset of **Engineering Design with SolidWorks 2007**. The book is designed for instructors that require a comprehensive hands-on, step-by-step text book approach to teach students using SolidWorks during a 6 - 12 week semester.

The book provides a sound foundation on using SolidWorks in an engineering design environment. The book supplies a general introduction to the User interface, CommandManager, menus, toolbars, etc. and design modeling techniques to create and modify parts, assemblies, and drawings.

Follow the step-by-step instructions in 60 activities to develop eight parts, four sub-assemblies, three drawings, and six document templates. Formulate the skills to create and modify solid features to model a Flashlight assembly. The following features are used in this book: Extruded Base, Extruded Boss, Extruded Cut, Fillet, Chamfer, Revolved Base, Revolved Thin Boss, Revolved Thin Cut, Dome, Shell, Hole Wizard, Circular Pattern, Sweep Base, Sweep Boss, Loft Base, Loft Boss, Mirror, Draft, Shape, Rib, and Linear Pattern.

Learn the techniques to reuse sketches and features through symmetry, patterns, and design tables. The following geometric relations are addressed: Vertical, Coincident, Pierce, Tangent, Equal, Intersection, Midpoint, Symmetric, Intersection, and Perpendicular.

Work between multiple documents, features, commands, and properties that represent how engineers and designers utilize SolidWorks in industry. Review individual features, commands, and tools for each project with the book's Multimedia CD and SolidWorks Help. The project exercises analyze and examine usage competencies based on the project objectives.

The book is designed to compliment the Online Tutorials contained within SolidWorks. Each section explores the SolidWorks Online User's Guide to build your working knowledge of SolidWorks.

The authors developed the industry scenarios by combining their own industry experience with the knowledge of engineers, department managers, vendors and manufacturers. These professionals are directly involved with SolidWorks everyday. Their responsibilities go far beyond the creation of just a 3D model.

About the Cover

Displayed on the front cover is the
FLASHLIGHT Assembly drawing. The
FLASHLIGHT Assembly contains eight
parts, and four sub-assemblies.

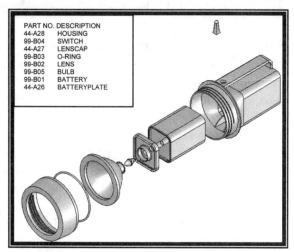

PART NO.	DESCRIPTION
44-A28	HOUSING
99-B04	SWITCH
44-A27	LENSCAP
99-B03	O-RING
99-B02	LENS
99-B05	BULB
99-B01	BATTERY
44-A26	BATTERYPLATE

The following features were used to create
the FLASHIGHT Assembly: Extruded
Base, Extruded Boss, Extruded Cut, Fillet,
Chamfer, Revolved Base, Revolved Thin
Boss, Revolved Thin Cut, Dome, Shell,
Hole Wizard, Circular Pattern, Sweep Base,
Sweep Boss, Loft Base, Loft Boss, Mirror,
Draft, Shape, Rib, and Linear Pattern.

The FLASHIGHT Assembly used the
following Assembly tools: Insert Component, Hide/Show, Change Suppression, Mate,
Move Component, Rotate Component, Exploded View, and Interference Detection.

The FLASHIGHT Assembly drawing contains a Bill of Materials.

About the Authors

Marie Planchard is the Director of Education Marketing at SolidWorks Corporation.
Before she joined SolidWorks, Marie spent over 10 years as an engineering professor at
Mass Bay College in Wellesley Hills, MA. She has 13 plus years of industry software
experience and held a variety of management and engineering positions including Beta
Test Manager for CAD software at Computervision Corporation. As a Certified
SolidWorks Professional (CSWP), she presented at SolidWorks World. Marie was the
founder of the New England SolidWorks Users Group.

David Planchard is the President of D&M Education, LLC. Before starting D&M
Education LLC, he spent over 23 years in industry and academia holding various
Engineering, Marketing, and teaching positions and degrees. He has five U.S. patents
and one International patent. He has published and authored numerous papers on
equipment design. David is also a technical editor for Cisco Press. He is a member of
the New England Pro/Users Group, New England SolidWorks Users Group, and the
Cisco Regional Academy Users Group. David Planchard is an active industry and
education consultant. David is a SolidWorks Research Partner and SolidWorks Solution
Partner.

David and Marie Planchard are co-authors of the following books:

- **A Commands Guide Reference Tutorial for SolidWorks 2007.**

- **Engineering Design with SolidWorks 1999, 2000, 2001, 2001Plus, 2003, 2004, 2005, 2006, and 2007.**

- **SolidWorks Tutorial with Multimedia CD 2001/2001Plus, 2003, 2004, 2005, 2006, and 2007.**

- **SolidWorks: The Basics, with Multimedia CD 2004, 2005, 2006, and 2007.**

- **Assembly Modeling with SolidWorks 2001Plus, 2003, 2004-2005, and 2006.**

- **Drawing and Detailing with SolidWorks 2001/2001Plus, 2002, 2003, 2004, and 2006.**

- **Applications in Sheet Metal Using Pro/SHEETMETAL & Pro/ENGINEER.**

- **An Introduction to Pro/SHEETMETAL.**

Dedication

A special acknowledgment goes to our loving daughter Stephanie Planchard who supported us during this intense and lengthy project. Stephanie continues to support us with her patience, love, and understanding.

Contact the Authors

This book is a subset of the 8th edition of Engineering Design with SolidWorks. We realize that keeping software application books current is imperative to our customers. We value the hundreds of professors, students, designers, and engineers that have provided us input to enhance our book. We value your suggestions and comments. Please contact us with any comments, questions, or suggestions on this book or any of our other SolidWorks books. David and Marie Planchard, D & M Education, LLC, dplanchard@msn.com.

Note to Instructors

Please contact the publisher **www.schroff.com** for additional materials: PowerPoint presentations, solution models, and the Instructor's Guide with tips that support the usage of this text in a classroom environment.

Trademarks, Disclaimer, and Copyrighted Material

SolidWorks and its family of products are registered trademarks of the Dassault Systemes Corporation. Microsoft Windows, Microsoft Office and its family of products are registered trademarks of the Microsoft Corporation. Pro/ENGINEER is a registered trademark of PTC. AutoCAD is a registered trademark of Autodesk. Other software applications and parts described in this book are trademarks or registered trademarks of their respective owners.

Dimensions of parts are modified for illustration purposes. Every effort is made to provide an accurate text. The authors and the manufacturers shall not be held liable for any parts or drawings developed or designed with this book or any responsibility for inaccuracies that appear in the book. World Wide Web and company information was valid at the time of this printing.

The Y14 ASME Engineering Drawing and Related Documentation Publications utilized in this text are as follows: ASME Y14.1 1995, ASME Y14.2M-1992 (R1998), ASME Y14.3M-1994 (R1999), ASME Y14.41-2003, ASME Y14.5-1982, ASME Y14.5M-1994, and ASME B4.2. Note: By permission of The American Society of Mechanical Engineers, Codes and Standards, New York, NY, USA. All rights reserved.

References

- SolidWorks Users Guide, SolidWorks Corporation, 2007.
- ASME Y14 Engineering Drawing and Related Documentation Practices.
- Beers & Johnson, Vector Mechanics for Engineers, 6th ed. McGraw Hill, Boston, MA.
- Betoline, Wiebe, Miller, Fundamentals of Graphics Communication, Irwin, 1995.
- Earle, James, Engineering Design Graphics, Addison Wesley, 1999.
- Hibbler, R.C, Engineering Mechanics Statics and Dynamics, 8th ed, Prentice Hall, Saddle River, NJ.
- Hoelscher, Springer, Dobrovolny, Graphics for Engineers, John Wiley, 1968.
- Jensen, Cecil, Interpreting Engineering Drawings, Glencoe, 2002.
- Jensen & Helsel, Engineering Drawing and Design, Glencoe, 1990.
- Olivo C., Payne, Olivo, T, Basic Blueprint Reading and Sketching, Delmar, 1988.
- Planchard & Planchard, Drawing and Detailing with SolidWorks, SDC Pub., Mission, KS 2006.
- Walker, James, Machining Fundamentals, Goodheart Wilcox, 1999.
- 80/20 Product Manual, 80/20, Inc., Columbia City, IN, 2006.
- Reid Tool Supply Product Manual, Reid Tool Supply Co., Muskegon, MI, 2006.
- Simpson Strong Tie Product Manual, Simpson Strong Tie, CA, 2006.
- Ticona Designing with Plastics – The Fundamentals, Summit, NJ, 2006.
- SMC Corporation of America, Product Manuals, Indiana, 2006.
- Gears Educational Design Systems, Product Manual, Hanover, MA, 2006.
- Emhart – A Black and Decker Company, On-line catalog, Hartford, CT, 2006.

TABLE OF CONTENTS

What is SolidWorks?

SolidWorks is a design automation software package used to produce parts, assemblies and drawings. SolidWorks is a Windows native 3D solid modeling CAD program. SolidWorks provides easy to use, highest quality design software for engineers and designers who create 3D models and 2D drawings ranging from individual parts to assemblies with thousands of parts.

The SolidWorks Corporation, headquartered in Concord, Massachusetts, USA develops and markets innovative design solutions for the Microsoft Windows platform. Additional information on SolidWorks and its family of products can be obtained at their URL, www.SolidWorks.com.

In SolidWorks, you create 3D parts, assemblies and 2D drawings. The part, assembly, and drawing documents are related.

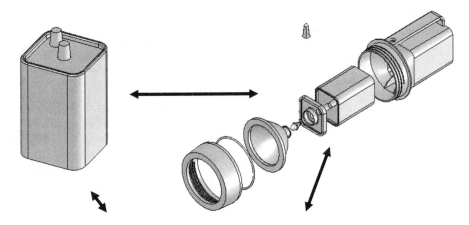

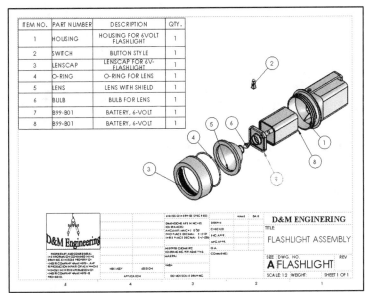

Features are the building blocks of parts. Use features to create parts, such as: Extruded Boss and Extruded Cut. Extruded features begin with a 2D sketch created on a Sketch plane.

The 2D sketch is a profile or cross section. Sketch tools such as: lines, arcs, and circles are used to create the 2D sketch. Sketch the general shape of the profile. Add geometric relationships; Coincident, Pierce, Tangent, Equal, Intersection, Midpoint, etc. and dimensions to control the exact size of the geometry.

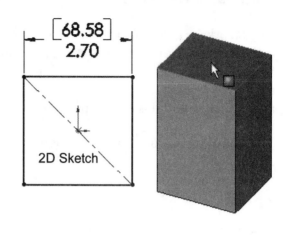

Create features by selecting edges or faces of existing features, such as a Fillet. The Fillet feature rounds sharp corners.

Dimensions drive features. Change a dimension, and you change the size of the part.

Use Geometric relationships: Vertical, Horizontal, Parallel, etc. to maintain Design intent.

Create a hole that penetrates through a part. SolidWorks maintains relationships through the change.

The step-by-step approach used in this text allows you to create parts, assemblies, and drawings.

The text allows you to modify and change all components of the model. Change is an integral part of design.

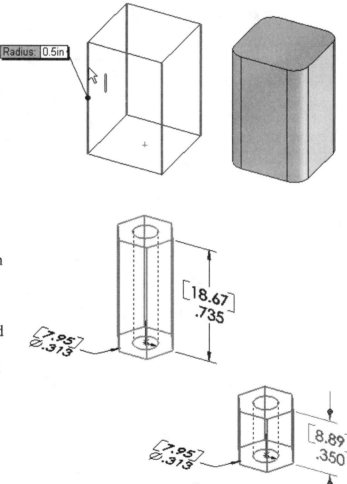

Design Intent

The SolidWorks definition of design intent is the process in which the model is developed to accept future changes.

Models behave differently when design changes occur. Design for change.

Utilize geometry for symmetry, reuse common features and reuse common parts.

Build change into the following areas:

1. Sketch.

2. Feature.

3. Part.

4. Assembly.

5. Drawing.

1. Design Intent in the Sketch.

Build the design intent in the sketch as the profile is created.

A profile is determined from the sketch tools, Example: rectangle, circle, and arc.

Build symmetry into the profile through a sketch centerline, mirror entity and position about the Reference planes and Origin.

Build design intent as you sketch with automatic relationships.

A rectangle contains horizontal, vertical, and perpendicular automatic relations.

Build design intent using added geometric relations. Example: horizontal, vertical, coincident, midpoint, intersection, tangent, and perpendicular.

Example A: Develop a square profile.

Build the design intent to create a square profile.

Sketch a rectangle. Insert a centerline. Add a midpoint relation. Add an equal relation between the two perpendicular lines. Insert a dimension to define the width of the square.

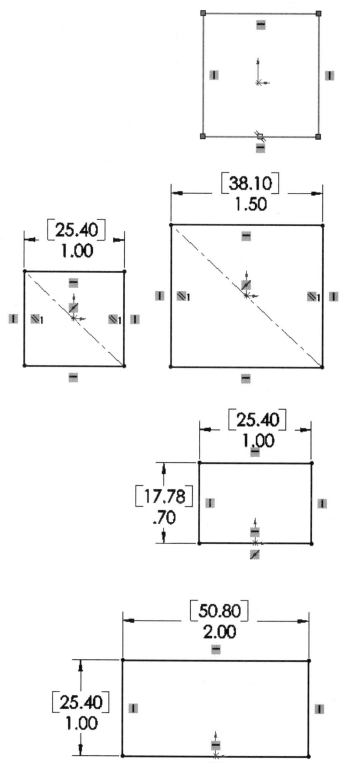

Example B: Develop a rectangular profile.

The bottom horizontal midpoint of the rectangular profile is located at the Origin.

Sketch a rectangle.

Add a midpoint relation between the horizontal edge of the rectangle and the Origin.

Insert two dimensions to define the width and height of the rectangle.

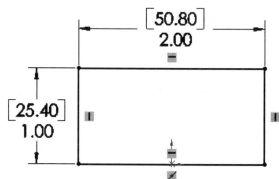

2. Design Intent in the Feature.

Build design intent into a feature by addressing symmetry, feature selection and the order of feature creations.

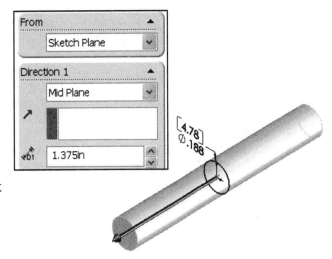

Example A: Extruded feature remains symmetric about a plane.

Utilize the Mid Plane End Condition. Change the depth and the feature remains symmetric about the Front Plane.

Example B: Create six holes for a pattern.

Do you create six separate Extruded Cuts? No. Create one hole with the Hole Wizard.

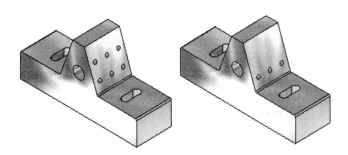

Insert a Linear Pattern.

Modify the number of holes from six to three.

3. Design Intent in the Part.

Utilize symmetry, feature order and reusing common features to build design intent into the part.

Example A: Feature order.

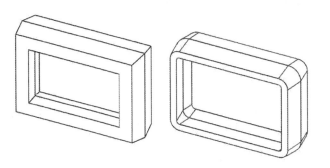

Is the entire part symmetric?

Feature order affects the part. Apply the Shell feature before the Fillet feature and the inside corners remain perpendicular.

4. Design Intent in the Assembly.

Utilizing symmetry, reusing common parts and using the Mate relationship between parts builds the design intent into an assembly.

Example A: Reuse Geometry in an assembly.

The PNEUMATIC-TEST-MODULE Assembly contains a Linear Pattern of holes. Insert one SCREW into the first Hole. Utilize Component Pattern to copy the SCREW part to the other holes.

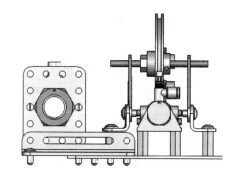

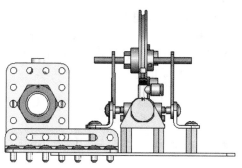

5. Design Intent in the Drawing.

Utilize dimensions, tolerance and notes in parts and assemblies to build the design intent into the Drawing.

Example A: Tolerance and material in the drawing.

Insert an outside diameter tolerance +.000/-.002 into the TUBE part. The tolerance propagates to the drawing.

Define the Custom Property MATERIAL in the Part. The MATERIAL Custom Property propagates to the drawing.

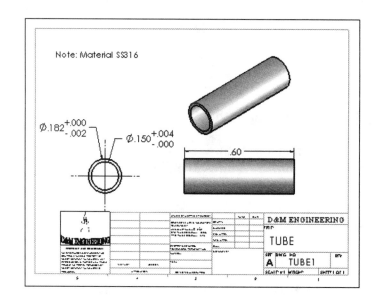

Additional information on the design process and design intent is available in Online Help.

Overview of Projects

Project 1: Extruded Boss/Base Features

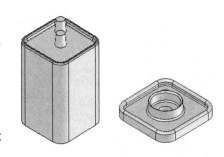

How do you start a model in SolidWorks? What is the design intent? How do you take a customer's requirements and covert them into a model? Project 1 introduces the basic concepts behind SolidWorks. In Project 1 you create two parts: BATTERY and BATTERYPLATE. You apply the following features: Extruded Boss, Extruded Base, Extruded Cut, Fillet, and Chamfer.

Project 2: Revolved Boss/Base Features

In Project 2 you create two parts: LENS and BULB. You apply the following features: Extruded Base, Extruded Boss, Extruded Cut, Revolved Base, Revolved Boss Thin, Revolved Thin Cut, Dome, Shell, Hole Wizard, and Circular Pattern along with the following Geometric relations: Equal, Coincident, Symmetric, Intersection, and Perpendicular.

Project 3: Sweep and Loft Boss/Base Features

In Project 3, you create four parts: O-RING, SWITCH, LENSCAP, and HOUSING. Project 3 covers the development of the Sweep Base, Sweep Boss, Loft Base, Loft Boss, Mirror, Draft, Shape, Rib, and Linear Pattern features and strengthens the use of the previously applied features.

Project 4: Assembly Fundamentals - Bottom-up

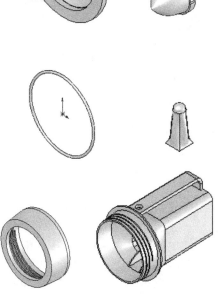

In Project 4, you learn about the Bottom-up assembly technique and create four assemblies: LENSANDBULB, CAPANDLENS, BATTERYANDPLATE, and the FLASHLIGHT assembly.

You insert the following Standard Mate types: Coincident, Concentric, and Distance and use the following Assembly tools: Insert Component, Hide/Show, Change Suppression, Mate, Move Component, Rotate Component, Exploded View, and Interference Detection.

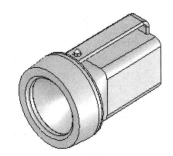

Project 5: Drawing Fundamentals

Project 5 covers the development of a customized drawing template. Develop a Company logo. Create a BATTERY drawing with five views. Develop and incorporate a Bill of Materials into the FLASHLIGHT assembly drawing.

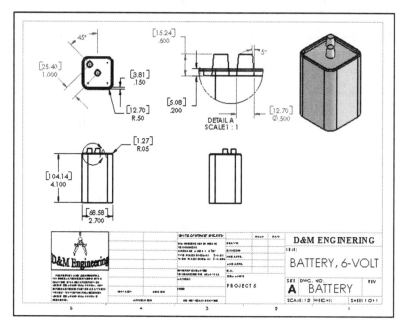

Project 5 introduces Design Tables and configurations in the drawing. Create three configurations of the O-RING part. Display the three configurations in the O-RING-TABLE drawing.

About the Book

The following conventions are used throughout this book:

- The term document is used to refer a SolidWorks part, drawing, or assembly file.

- The list of items across the top of the SolidWorks interface is the Main menu. Each item in the Main menu has a pull-down menu. When you need to select a series of commands from these menus, the following format is used; Click **Insert**, **Reference Geometry**, **Plane** from the Main menu. The Plane PropertyManager is displayed.

- The book is organized into 5 Projects. Each Project is focused on a specific subject or feature.

- Use the enclosed Multimedia CD to obtain parts, and models that are used in this book and to view the features created in Projects.

The following command syntax is used throughout the text. Commands that require you to perform an action are displayed in **Bold** text.

Format:	Convention:	Example:
Bold	• All commands actions. • Selected icon button. • Selected geometry: line, circle. • Value entries.	• Click **Tools**, **Options** from the Main menu. • Click **Rectangle** ⬚ from the Sketch toolbar. • Select the **centerpoint**. • Enter **3.0** for Radius.
Capitalized	• Filenames. • First letter in a feature name.	• Save the **FLATBAR** assembly. • Click the **Fillet** feature.

Windows Terminology in SolidWorks

The mouse buttons provide an integral role in executing SolidWorks commands. The mouse buttons execute commands, select geometry, display Shortcut menus and provide information feedback.

A summary of mouse button terminology is displayed below:

Item:	Description:
Click	Press and release the left mouse button.
Double-click	Double press and release the left mouse button.
Click inside	Press the left mouse button. Wait a second, and then press the left mouse button inside the text box. Use this technique to modify Feature names in the FeatureManager design tree.
Drag	Point to an object, press and hold the left mouse button down. Move the mouse pointer to a new location. Release the left mouse button.
Right-click	Press and release the right mouse button. A Shortcut menu is displayed. Use the left mouse button to select a menu command.
ToolTip	Position the mouse pointer over an Icon (button). The tool name is displayed below the mouse pointer.
Large ToolTip	Position the mouse pointer over an Icon (button). The tool name and a description of its functionality are displayed below the mouse pointer.
Mouse pointer feedback	Position the mouse pointer over various areas of the sketch, part, assembly or drawing. The cursor provides feedback depending on the geometry.

A mouse with a center wheel provides additional functionality in SolidWorks. Roll the center wheel downward to enlarge the model in the Graphics window. Hold the center wheel down. Drag the mouse in the Graphics window to rotate the model. Review various Windows terminology that describes: menus, toolbars, and commands that constitute the graphical user interface in SolidWorks.

Project 1

Introduction to Part Modeling

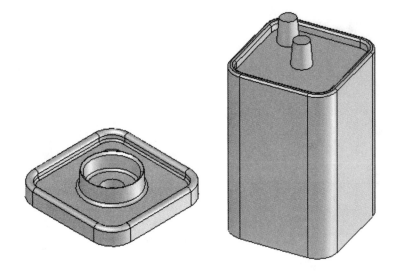

Below are the desired outcomes and usage competencies based on the completion of Project 1.

Project Desired Outcomes:	Usage Competencies:
• A comprehensive understanding of the SolidWorks 2007 User Interface.	• Ability to establish a SolidWorks session. Use the SolidWorks User Interface: CommandManager, Toolbars, Task Pane, Search, Confirmation Corner, and more.
• Address File Management with file folders.	• Aptitude to create file folders for various Projects and Templates

• Two Part Templates:
   o PART-IN-ANSI.
   o PART-MM-ISO.
	• Skill to apply System Options and Document Properties.

• Two FLASHLIGH Parts:
   o BATTERY.
   o BATTERYPLATE.
	• Specific knowledge and understanding of the following features: Extruded Boss, Extruded Base, Extruded Cut, Fillet, and Chamfer.

Notes:

Project 1-Introduction to Part Modeling

Project Overview

SolidWorks is a 3D design software application used to model and produce parts, assemblies, and drawings. Project 1 introduces you to the SolidWorks 2007 User Interface, CommandManager, and Toolbars.

A template is the foundation for a SolidWorks document. A template contains settings for units, dimensioning standards, and other properties. Create two part templates:

- PART-IN-ANSI.

- PART-MM-ISO.

Create two parts for the FLASHLIGHT assembly in this project:

- BATTERY.

- BATTERYPLATE.

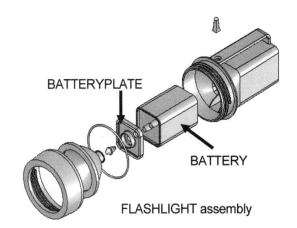

BATTERYPLATE

BATTERY

FLASHLIGHT assembly

Part models consist of 3D features. Features are the building blocks of a part.

A sketch is required to create an Extruded Base feature. Utilize the sketch geometry and sketch tools to create the following features:

- Extruded Base.

- Extruded Boss.

- Extruded Cut.

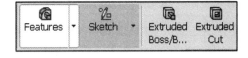

Utilize existing faces and edges to create the following features:

- Fillet.

- Chamfer.

On the completion of this project, you will be able to:

- Establish a SolidWorks Session.

- Comprehend the SolidWorks 2007 User Interface.

- Recognize default Reference Planes.

- Insert a new sketch and add sketch geometry with the following tools: Line, Circle, Rectangle, Tangent Arc, and Centerline.

- Establish Geometric Relations, dimensions, and determine the status of the sketch.

- Manipulate existing geometry with the following Sketch tools: Line, Rectangle, Circle, Convert Entities, Offset Entities, and Mirror Entities.

- Use the following features: Extruded Boss/Base, Extruded Cut, Fillet, and Chamfer.

- Create two part templates: PART-IN-ANSI and PART-MM-ISO.

- Create two parts for the FLASHLIGHT assembly: BATTERY and BATTERPLATE.

File Management

File management organizes parts, assemblies, drawings, and templates. Why do you require file management? Answer: A top level assembly has hundreds or even thousands of documents that requires organization. Utilize folders to organize projects, vendor components, templates, and libraries. Create the folders. The first folder is named SOLIDWORKS-MODELS. Create two sub-folders named MY-TEMPLATES and PROJECTS.

Activity: File Management

Create a new folder in Windows.
1)   Click **Start** from the Windows Taskbar.

2)   Click **My Documents** in Windows.

3)   Click **File**, **New**, **Folder** ⬜ Folder from the Main menu.

Enter the new folder name.
4)   Enter **SOLIDWORKS-MODELS 2007**.

Note: Select the Microsoft Windows commands from the Main menu, toolbar icons and with the right mouse button.

Create the first sub-folder.
5)   Double-click the **SOLIDWORKS-MODELS 2007** folder.

6)   Click **File**, **New**, **Folder** from the Main menu. A New Folder icon is displayed. Enter **MY-TEMPLATES** for the folder name.

Create the second sub-folder.
7)   Click the **SOLIDWORKS-MODELS 2007** folder.

8)   Click **File**, **New**, **Folder** from the Main menu.

9)   Enter **PROJECTS** for the second sub-folder name.

Return to the SOLIDWORKS-MODELS 2007 folder.
10)   Click the **SOLIDWORKS-MODELS 2007** folder.

Utilize the MY-TEMPLATES folder and the PROJECTS folder throughout the text.

Start a SolidWorks session

The SolidWorks application is located in the Programs folder. By default, SolidWorks displays a Tip of the Day box. Read the Tip of the Day every day to obtain additional information on using SolidWorks.

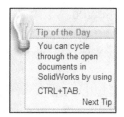

Open a new part. Select File, New from the Main menu. There are two options for new documents: Novice and Advanced. Select the Advanced option. Select the Part document.

Activity: Start SolidWorks

Start a SolidWorks 2007 session.

11) Click **Start** on the Windows Taskbar. Click **All Programs**. Click the **SolidWorks 2007** folder.

12) Click **SolidWorks 2007** ⬛ SolidWorks 2007 application. The SolidWorks program window opens. Note: Do not open a document at this time.

Read the Tip of the Day dialog box.

13) Click the **Collapse arrow** ≫ in the Task Pane to close the Tip of the Day. Note: If you do not see this screen, click the SolidWorks **Resources** 🏠 icon on the right side of the Graphics window.

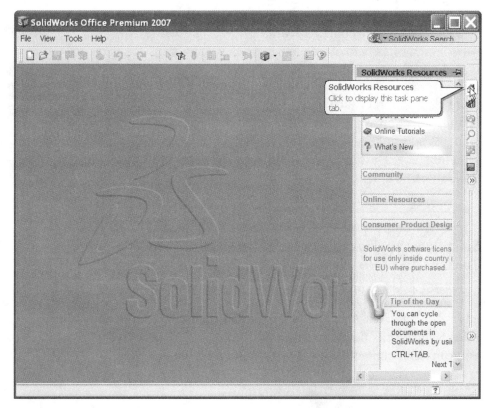

The SolidWorks 2007 Task Pane is displayed when a SolidWorks session starts. The Task Pane can be displayed in the following states: visible or hidden, expanded or collapsed, pinned or unpinned, docked or floating. The Task Pane contains the following standard tabs: SolidWorks Resources, Design Library, File Explorer, Search, View Palette, and PhotoWorks Items.

SolidWorks Resources

Utilize the left/right arrows ⟫ to expand or collapse the Task Pane options. The basic SolidWorks Resources menu displays the following default selections:

- Getting Started.

- Community.

- Online Resources.

- Tip of the Day.

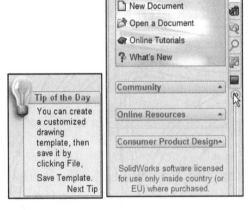

Other user interfaces are available to be displayed during the initial software installation selection: Machine Design, Mold Design, or Consumer Products Design. The illustration displays the Consumer Product Design user interface.

Design Library

The Design Library contains reusable parts, assemblies, and other elements, including library features.

The Design Library tab contains four default selections. Each default selection contains additional sub-categories. The selections are: Design Library, Toolbox, 3D ContentCentral, and SolidWorks Content.

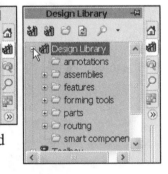

🔆 Click Tools, Add-Ins.., SolidWorks Toolbox and SolidWorks Toolbox Browser to active the SolidWorks Toolbox.

To access the Design Library folders in a non-network environment, click Add File Location 🏠, then enter: C:\Program Files\SolidWorks\data\design library. Click OK. In a network environment, contact your IT department for system details.

File Explorer

File Explorer in the Task Pane duplicates the function of Windows Explorer from your local computer and displays the Recent and Open documents in the SolidWorks directories.

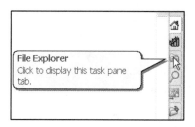

Search

Microsoft Windows Search is installed with SolidWorks and indexes the resources once before searching begins, either after installation, or when you initiate the first search.

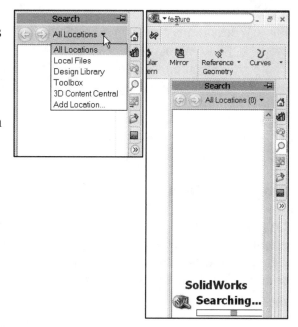

The SolidWorks Search box is displayed in the upper right corner of the SolidWorks Graphics window. Enter the text or key words to search. Click the drop down arrow to view the last 10 recent searches.

The Search tool $\mathcal{P}$ in the Task Pane searches the following locations:

- All locations.

- Local Files.

- Design Library.

- SolidWorks Toolbox.

- 3D ContentCentral.

- Added location.

Select any or all of the above locations. If you do not select a file location, all locations are searched.

View Palette

Use the View Palette, located in the Task Pane, to insert drawing views of an active part, or click the Browse button to locate the desired model. Click and drag the view from the View Palette into an active drawing sheet to create a drawing view.

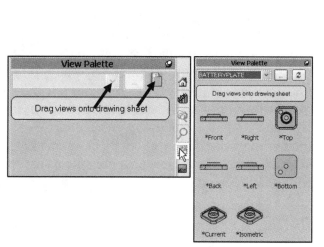

Auto Recovery

If auto recovery is initiated in the System Options section and the system terminates unexpectedly with an active document, the saved information files are available on the Task Pane Document Recovery tab.

PhotoWorks

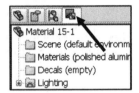

PhotoWorks Items create photo-realistic images of SolidWorks models. PhotoWorks provides many professional rendering effects. PhotoWorks contains the following default folders: Scene, Materials, Decals, and Lighting.

Click Tools, Add-Ins.., PhotoWorks from the Main menu to active the PhotoWorks feature.

Drop-Down Menu

SolidWorks takes advantage of the familiar Microsoft® Windows® graphical user interface. Communicate with SolidWorks either through the drop-down menus or through the application toolbars. A command is an instruction that informs SolidWorks to perform a task.

To close a SolidWorks drop-down menu, press the Esc key. You can also click any other part of the SolidWorks Graphics window, or click another drop-down menu. The drop-down menu options perform three basic functions. They are: displays a SolidWorks dialog box, submits a command to create or modify a drawing, or offers an expanded set of tools located in the SolidWorks toolbars.

Fly-out FeatureManager

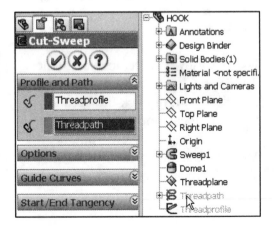

The fly-out FeatureManager design tree allows you to view and select items in the PropertyManager and the FeatureManager design tree at the same time. The fly-out FeatureManager provides the ability to select items which may be difficult to view or select from the Graphics window. You can hide, modify the transparency of, go to, or zoom to selected items. You cannot suppress items or roll back the build.

Throughout the book, you will select commands and command options from the drop-down menu, fly-out FeatureManager, or from the SolidWorks toolbar.

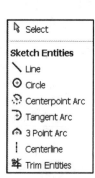

Another method for accessing a command is to use an accelerator key. Accelerator keys are special keystrokes which activates the drop-down menu options. Some commands in the menu bar and items in the drop-down menus have an underlined character. Pressing the Alt key followed by the corresponding key to the underlined character activates that command or option.

Right Click Pop-up menus

Right-click in the Graphics window to display a context-sensitive shortcut menu. If you are in the middle of a command, this menu displays a list of options specifically related to that command. Example: if you right-click your mouse before picking the first point of the Rectangle tool, a menu is displayed in the Graphics window. The menu displays Sketch Entities, Selected Entity, and other Relations and menu options.

FeatureManager design tree

The FeatureManager design tree is located on the left side of the SolidWorks Graphics window. The FeatureManager design tree provides a summarized view of the active part, assembly, or drawing. The FeatureManager displays the details on how your part, assembly, or drawing is created.

Understand the FeatureManager design tree to troubleshoot your model. The FeatureManager is used extensively throughout this book. Expand, collapse, and roll back the FeatureManager design tree.

To collapse all items in the FeatureManager, right-click and select Collapse items, or press the Shift +C keys.

Confirmation Corner

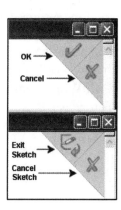

When numerous SolidWorks commands are active, a symbol or a set of symbols is displayed in the upper right corner of the Graphics window. This area is called the Confirmation Corner.

When you activate or open a sketch, the confirmation corner box displays two symbols. The first symbol is the sketch tool icon. The second symbol is a large red X. These two symbols supply a visual reminder that you are in an active sketch.

There are two modes in the New
SolidWorks Document dialog
box: Novice and Advanced.
The Novice option is the default
option with three templates.
The Advanced option contains
access to additional templates.

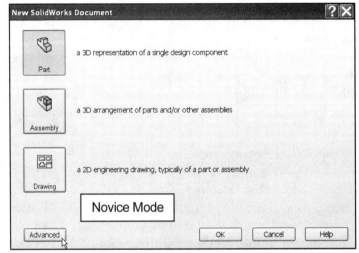

Create a new part.

14) Click **File**, **New** ⬜ from the
Main menu.

Select Advanced Mode.

15) Click the **Advanced** button to
display the New SolidWorks
Document dialog box in
Advanced mode.

16) The Templates tab is the
default tab. Part is the
default template from the
New SolidWorks Document
dialog box. Click **OK**.

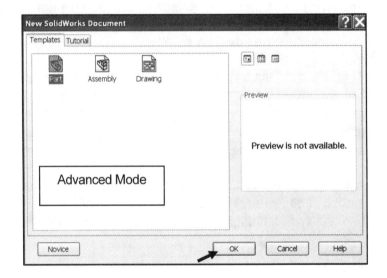

The Advanced mode remains selected for all new documents in the current SolidWorks
session. When you exit SolidWorks, the Advanced mode setting is saved.

The default SolidWorks installation contains two tabs in the New SolidWorks Document
dialog box, Templates and Tutorial. The Templates tab corresponds to the default
SolidWorks templates. The Tutorial tab corresponds to the templates utilized in the SW
Tutorials.

SolidWorks User Interface and CommandManager

The SolidWorks user interface combines the menus, toolbars, and commands with graphic display and Microsoft Windows properties.

Part1 is displayed. Part1 is the new default part name. The Main menu, Standard toolbar, View toolbar, and CommandManager are displayed above the Graphics window.

The part Origin ⌞ is displayed in blue in the center of the Graphics window. The Origin represents the intersection of the three default Reference planes: Front Plane, Top Plane, and Right Plane. The positive X-axis is horizontal and points to the right of the Origin in the Front view. The positive Y-axis is vertical and point upward in the Front view.

The FeatureManager contains a list of features, reference geometry, and settings utilized in the part.

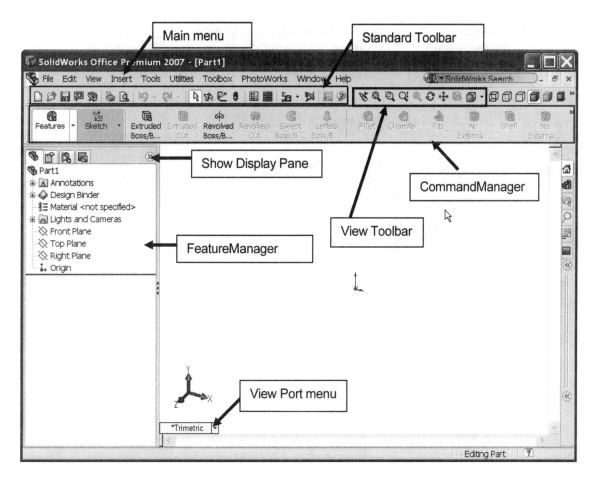

The CommandManager is divided into the Control Area and an expanded toolbar. Select a Control Area icon to display the corresponding toolbar. The Features icon and Features toolbar are selected by default in Part mode.

Features Toolbar

Sketch Toolbar

The CommandManager is utilized in this text. Control the CommandManager display. Right-click in the gray area to the right of the Help entry in the Main menu. A complete list of toolbars is displayed. Check CommandManager if required.

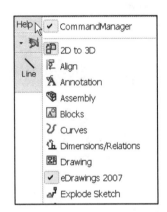

Select individual toolbars from the toolbar list to display in the Graphics window. Reposition toolbars by moving their drag handles.

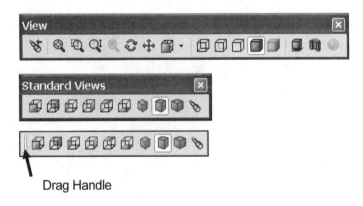

Drag Handle

Activity: User Interface and CommandManager

Maximize the Graphics window.
17) Click the **Maximize** button in the top right corner of the SolidWorks window.

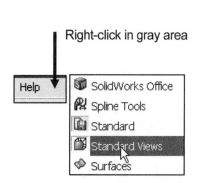

Right-click in gray area

Display the Standard Views toolbar.
18) Right-click in the **gray area** of the Main menu to the right of Help as illustrated. The SW toolbars are displayed.

19) Activate the Standard Views toolbar. Click **Standard Views**. The Standard Views toolbar is displayed in the SolidWorks window.

Display Tools and Toolbars.
20) Position the **mouse pointer** on the Standard Views icon. View the Tool tip.

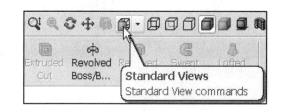

21) Click **Standard Views** 🗗 from the View toolbar to list the default views. The down arrow ▾ icon indicates additional information.

Display the Features tools.
22) Click **Features** Features from the Control Area of the CommandManager.

23) Position the mouse pointer over the **Extruded Boss/Base** Boss/B... feature. Do not select the feature at this time. A Tool tip displays the Extruded Boss/Base feature name and a short description.

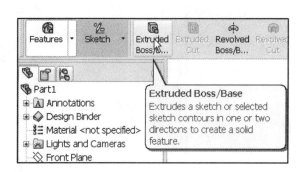

Display the Sketch tools.

24) Click **Sketch** Sketch from the Control Area of the
CommandManager.

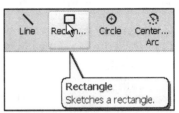

25) Position the mouse pointer over the **Rectangle** Rectan... tool
in the Sketch toolbar. Do not select.

Display Help for a rectangle.

26) Click **Help** from the Main menu.

27) Click **SolidWorks Help Topics**. The SolidWorks 2007
Online User's Guide dialog box is displayed.

28) Click the **Index** tab.

29) Enter **rectangles**. The description is displayed in the right
window. Review the provided information.

Close the Help window.

30) Click **Close** ☒ from the SolidWorks 2007 Online User's
Guide dialog box.

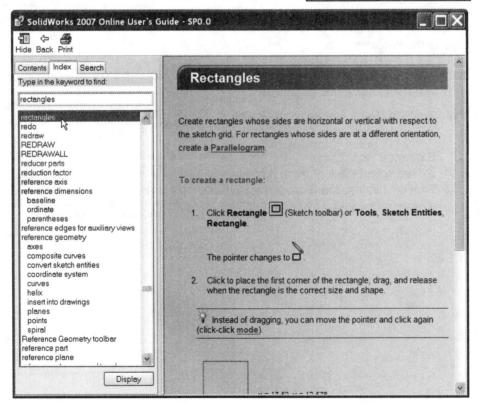

The Help option contains tools to assist the user. The SolidWorks Help Topics contains:

- **Contents** tab: Contains the SolidWorks Online User's Guide documents.

- **Index** tab: Contains additional information on key words.

- **Search** tab: To locate information.

Display the SolidWorks Tutorials.

31) Click **Help** from the Main menu.

32) Click **SolidWorks Tutorials**. The SolidWorks Tutorials are displayed. Review Lesson 1. This is a great location for additional information.

33) Click **Close** ☒ from the Online Tutorial dialog box. Return to the Graphics window.

Design Intent

The SolidWorks definition of design intent is the process in which the model is developed to accept future changes. Models behave differently when design changes occur. Design for change. Utilize geometry for symmetry, reuse common features and reuse common parts.

Build change into the following areas:

1. Sketch.

2. Feature.

3. Part.

4. Assembly.

5. Drawing.

1. Design Intent in the Sketch.

Build design intent in the sketch as the profile is created.

A profile is determined from the Sketch tools. Example: Rectangle, Circle, or Arc.

Build symmetry into the profile through a Sketch Centerline, or Mirror entity and position about the Reference planes and Origin.

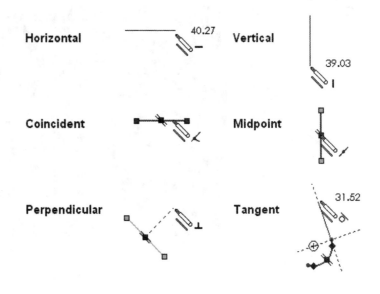

A rectangle contains horizontal, vertical, and perpendicular, automatic relations.

Build design intent using added Geometric relations. Example: Horizontal, Vertical, Coincident, Midpoint, Intersection, Tangent, and Perpendicular.

Example A: Develop a square profile. Build design intent to create a square profile.

Sketch a rectangle. Insert a centerline. Add a Midpoint relation. Add an Equal relation between the two perpendicular lines. Insert a dimension to define the width of the square.

Example B: Develop a rectangular profile.

The bottom horizontal Midpoint of the rectangular profile is located at the Origin.

Sketch a rectangle.

Add a Midpoint relation between the horizontal edge of the rectangle and the Origin.

Insert two dimensions to define the width and height of the rectangle.

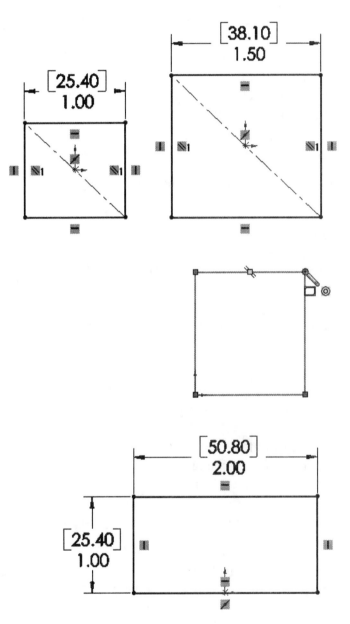

2. Design Intent in the Feature.

Build design intent into a feature by addressing symmetry, feature selection, and the order of the feature creations.

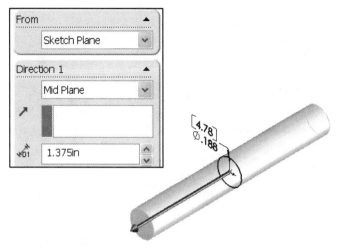

Example A: An Extruded Base feature remains symmetric about a plane.

Utilize the Mid Plane End Condition for Direction 1. Modify the depth and the feature remains symmetric about the Front Plane.

Example B: Create six holes for a pattern.

Do you create six separate Extruded Cuts? No. Create a single hole with the Hole Wizard feature.

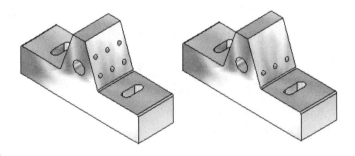

Insert a Linear Pattern feature.

Edit the LPattern1 feature from six to three holes.

3. Design Intent in the Part.

Utilize symmetry, feature order, and reusing common features to build design intent into the part.

Example A: Feature order.

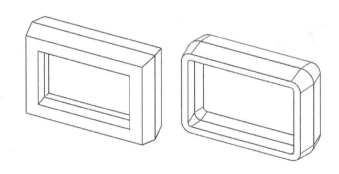

Is the entire part symmetric? Feature order affects the part. Apply the Shell feature before the Fillet feature and the inside corners remain perpendicular.

4. Design Intent in the Assembly.

Utilizing symmetry, reusing common parts, and using the Mate relationships between parts builds design intent into an assembly.

Example A: Reuse Geometry in an assembly.

The assembly contains a Linear Pattern of holes.

Insert a single SCREW into the first hole. Utilize Component Pattern to copy the SCREW to the other holes.

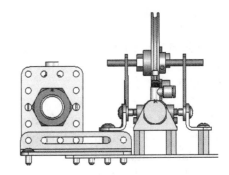

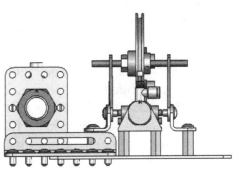

5. Design Intent in the Drawing.

Utilize dimensions, tolerance, and Parametric notes in parts and assemblies to build design intent into a Drawing.

Example A: Tolerance and material in the drawing.

Insert an outside diameter tolerance +.000/-.002 into the TUBE part. The tolerance propagates to the drawing.

Define the Custom Property MATERIAL in the Part. The MATERIAL Custom Property propagates to the drawing.

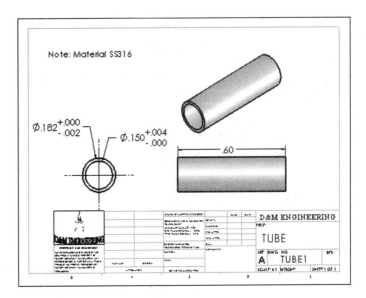

Additional information on the design process and design intent is available in SolidWorks Help.

Part Template

The Part Template is the foundation for a SolidWorks part. Part1 was created with the default Part Template in the New SolidWorks dialog box.

Document properties contain the default settings for the Part Template. The document properties include the dimensioning standard, units, dimension decimal display, grids, note font, and line styles. There are hundreds of document properties. You will modify the following document properties in this Project: Dimensioning standard, Unit, and Decimal Places.

The Dimensioning standard determines the display of dimension text, arrows, symbols, and spacing. Units are the measurement of physical quantities. MMGS, (millimeter, gram, second) and IPS, (inch, pound, second) are the two most common unit systems specified for engineering parts and drawings.

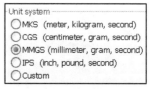

Document properties are stored with the document. Apply the document properties to the Part Template. Create two Part Templates: PART-IN-ANSI and PART-MM-ISO. Save the Part Templates in the MY-TEMPLATE folder.

System Options are stored in the registry of your computer. The File Locations option controls the file folder location of SolidWorks documents. Utilize the File Locations option to reference your Part Templates in the MY-TEMPLATES folder. Add the SOLIDWORKS-MODELS 2007\MY-TEMPLATES folder path name to the Document Templates File Locations list.

Activity: Part Template

Set the Dimensioning standard to ANSI.
34) Click **Tools**, **Options**, **Document Properties** tab from the Main menu.

35) Select **ANSI** from the Dimensioning standard box.

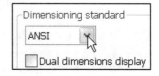

Set the Part units.
36) Click **Units**. Select **IPS, (inch, pound, second)** for Unit system.

37) Select **3** for Length units Decimal places.

38) Select **0** for Angular units Decimal places.

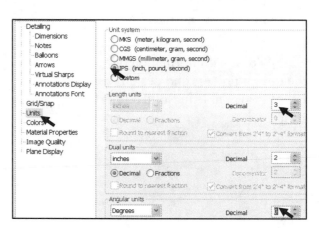

Set the Grid/Snap option.
39) Click **Grid/Snap**. Uncheck the **Display grid** option.

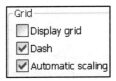

Return to the SolidWorks Graphics window.
40) Click **OK** from the Document Properties Grid/Snap dialog box.

Save the Part Template.
41) Click **File**, **Save As** from the Main menu.

42) Select the **SOLIDWORKS-MODELS 2007/MY-TEMPLATES** folder.

43) Select **Part Templates (*.prtdot)** from the Save as type box.

44) Enter **PART-IN-ANSI** in the File name box.

45) Click **Save**.

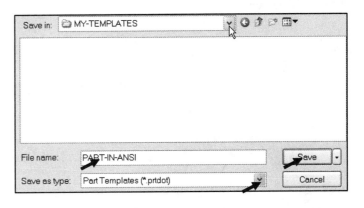

Set the Dimensioning standard to ISO.
46) Click **Tools**, **Options, Document Properties** tab from the Main menu.

47) Select **ISO** from the Dimensioning standard box.

Set the Part units.
48) Click **Units**.

49) Select **MMGS, (millimeter, gram, second)** for Unit system.

50) Select **2** for Length units Decimal places.

51) Select **0** for Angular units Decimal places.

52) Click **OK**.

Save the Part Template.
53) Click **File**, **Save As** from the Main menu.

54) Select **Part Templates (*.prtdot)** from the Save as type box.

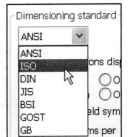

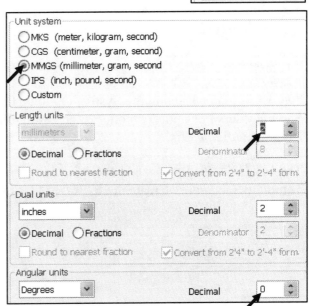

55) Select the **SOLIDWORKS-MODELS 2007/MY-TEMPLATES** folder.

56) Enter **PART-MM-ISO** in the File name box.

57) Click **Save**.

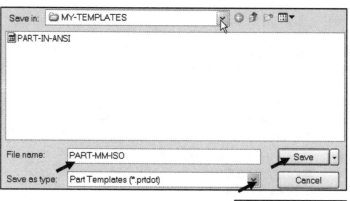

Set the System Options.
58) Click **Tools**, **Options** from the Main menu.

59) Click **File Locations** from the System Options tab.

60) Select **Document Templates** from Show folders for.

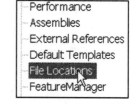

61) Click the **Add** button.

62) Select the **MY-TEMPLATES** folder.

63) Click **OK** from the Browse for Folder.

64) Click **OK** from the System Options.

```
:\Program Files\SolidWorks\data\templates\
:\Program Files\SolidWorks\lang\english\Tutorial
:\SOLIDWORKS-MODELS 2007\MY-TEMPLATES
```

Close All documents.
65) Click **Windows**, **Close All** from the Main menu.

Display the MY-TEMPLATES folder and templates.

66) Click **File**, **New** ⬚ from the Main menu.

67) Click the **MY-TEMPLATES** tab. View the two new Part Templates.

68) Click **Cancel**.

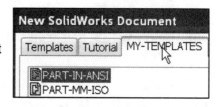

Each folder listed in the System Options, File Locations, Document Templates, Show Folders For option produces a corresponding Tab in the New SolidWorks Document dialog box.

The MY-TEMPLATES tab is only visible when the folder contains a SolidWorks Template document. Create the PART-MM-ANSI template as an exercise.

The PART-IN-ANSI Template contains document properties settings for the parts contained in the FLASHLIGHT assembly. Substitute the PART-MM-ISO or PART-MM-ANSI template to create the identical parts in millimeters.

The primary units in this book are IPS, (inch, pound, second). The optional secondary units are MMGS, (millimeter, gram, second) and are indicated in brackets [ ]. Illustrations are provided in both inches and millimeters.

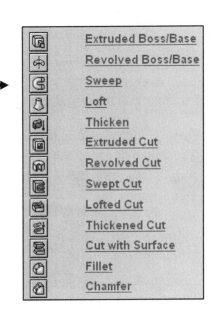

Input toolbars, click Features in SolidWorks Help Topics to review the function of each tool in the Features toolbar.

Additional information on System Options, Document Properties, File Locations, and Templates is found in SolidWorks Help Topics. Keywords: Options (detailing, units), templates, Files (locations), menus and toolbars (features, sketch).

 Review of the User Interface and Part Templates

The SolidWorks user interface consists of the following: Drop-down menus, toolbars, CommandManager, FeatureManager, Task Pane, and Graphics window. The CommandManager controls the display of the Sketch toolbar and Features toolbar.

You created two Part Templates: PART-MM-ISO and PART-IN-ANSI. The document properties dimensioning standard, units and decimal places were stored in the Part Templates. The File Locations System Option, Document Templates option controls the reference to the MY-TEMPLATES folder.

Note: In some network locations and school environments, the File Locations option must be set to MY-TEMPLATES for each session of SolidWorks. You can exit SolidWorks at any time during this project. Save your document. Select File, Exit from the Main menu.

BATTERY Part

The BATTERY is a simplified representation of a purchased OEM part. Represent the BATTERY terminals as cylindrical extrusions. The BATTERY dimensions are obtained from the ANSI standard 908D.

A 6-Volt BATTERY weighs approximately 1.38 pounds, (0.62kg). Locate the center of gravity closest to the center of the BATTERY. Create the BATTERY part.

Use features to create parts. Features are building blocks that add or remove material.

Utilize the Extruded Base feature. The Extrude Base feature adds material. The Base feature is the first feature of the part.

Utilize symmetry. Sketch a rectangle profile on the Top

Plane, centered at the Origin ⌞. Extend the profile perpendicular (⊥) to the Top Plane.

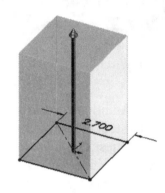

Utilize the Fillet feature to round four vertical edges.

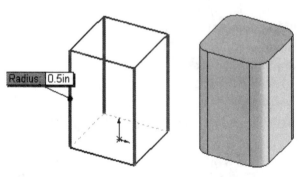

The Extruded Cut feature removes material from the top face. Utilize the top face for the Sketch plane. Utilize the Offset Entity Sketch tool to create the profile.

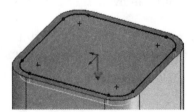

Utilize the Fillet feature to round the top narrow face.

The Extruded Boss feature adds material. Conserve design time. Represent each of the terminals as a cylindrical Extruded Boss feature.

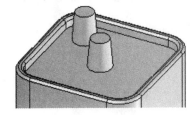

BATTERY Part-Extruded Base Feature

The Extruded Base feature requires:

- Sketch plane (Top).
- Sketch Profile (Rectangle).
  - o Geometric relations and dimensions.
- End Condition (Blind is the default End Condition).

Create a new part named, BATTERY. Insert an Extruded Base feature. Extruded features require a Sketch plane. The Sketch plane determines the orientation of the Extruded Base feature. The Sketch plane locates the Sketch Profile on any plane or face.

The Top Plane is the Sketch plane. The Sketch Profile is a rectangle. The rectangle consists of 2 horizontal lines and 2 vertical lines. Geometric relations and dimensions constrain the sketch in 3D space. The Blind End Condition requires a depth value to extrude the 2D Sketch Profile and to complete the 3D feature.

Note: Alternate between Feature and Sketch in the Control Area to display the Features toolbar and Sketch toolbar or display the individual toolbars outside the Graphics window.

Activity: BATTERY Part

Create a new part.

69)   Click **File**, **New** ⬜ from the Main menu.

70)   Click the **MY-TEMPLATES** tab.

71)   Double-click **PART-IN-ANSI**, [**PART-MM-ISO**] from the New SolidWorks Document dialog box.

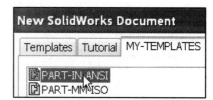

Save the part.

72)   Click **Save** 💾 .

73)   Select the **SOLIDWORKS-MODELS 2007\PROJECTS** folder.

74)   Enter **BATTERY** for file name.

75)   Enter **BATTERY, 6-VOLT** for Description.

76)   Click **Save**. The BATTERY FeatureManager is displayed.

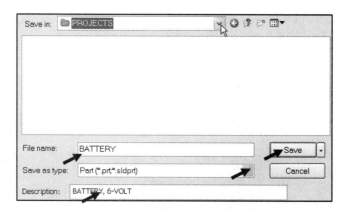

Select the Sketch plane.
77)   Click **Top Plane** from the FeatureManager.

Sketch the profile.

78)   Click **Sketch** ✏️ Sketch from the CommandManager.

79)   Click **Rectangle** ⬜ Rectan... from the Sketch toolbar.

80)   Click the **first point** in the lower left quadrant.

81)   Drag and click the **second point** in the upper right quadrant as illustrated. The

Origin ⌊ is approximately in the middle of the rectangle.

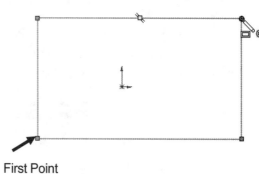

First Point

Sketch the Centerline.

82) Click **Centerline** Centerl... from the Sketch toolbar.

83) Sketch a diagonal centerline from the **upper left corner** to the **lower right corner** as illustrated. The endpoints of the centerline are coincident with the corner points of the rectangle.

84) Right-click **Select** Select .

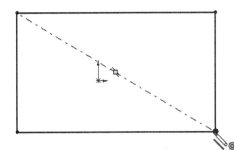

Add a Midpoint relation between the centerline and the Origin.

85) Click the **centerline**.

86) Hold the **Ctrl** key down.

87) Click the **Origin**. The Properties PropertyManager is displayed.

88) Release the **Ctrl** key.

89) Click **Midpoint** from the Add Relations box.

90) Click **OK** from the Properies PropertyManager.

Note: Your Line# may be different than the line numbers displayed. The Line# is dependent on the line number order creation. To clear entities from the Selected Entities box, Right-click Clear Selections.

Create a square. Add an Equal relation.

91) Click the **top horizontal line**.

92) Hold the **Ctrl** key down.

93) Click the **left vertical line**.

94) Release the **Ctrl** key.

95) Click **Equal** from the Add Relations box.

96) Click **OK** from the Properties PropertyManager.

Add a dimension.

97) Click **Smart Dimension** Smart Dimens... from the Sketch toolbar.

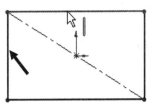
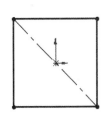

98) Select the **top horizontal line**.

99) Click a **position** above the horizontal line. Enter **2.700**in, **[68.58]** for width.

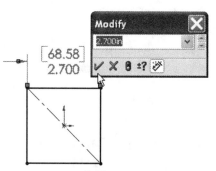

100) Click the **Green Check mark** in the Modify dialog box. The black sketch status is fully defined.

View the sketch relations.

101) Click **Display/Delete Relations**  Relations from the Sketch toolbar. The Distance1 relation was created from the dimension.

102) Click **OK** from the Display/Delete Releaions PropertyManager.

Activity: BATTERY Part-Extruded Base Feature

Insert an Extruded Base feature.

103) Click **Features** Features, **Extruded**

Boss/Base Boss/B... from the Features toolbar. The Extrude PropertyManager is displayed. Blind is the default End Condition for Direction 1.

104) Enter **4.100**in, **[104.14]** for Depth.

105) Click **OK** from the Extrude PropertyManager. Extrude1 is displayed in the FeatureManager.

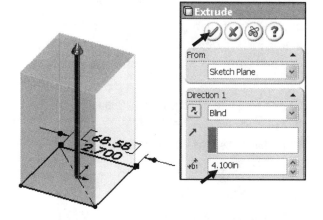

Fit the part to the Graphics window.
106) Press the **f** key.

Rename the Extrude1 feature.
107) Click **Extrude1** in the FeatureManager.

108) Enter **Base Extrude**.

Save the BATTERY part.

109) Click **Save**.

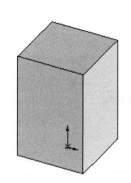

Utilize an Equal relation versus two linear dimensions when a rectangular profile is square.

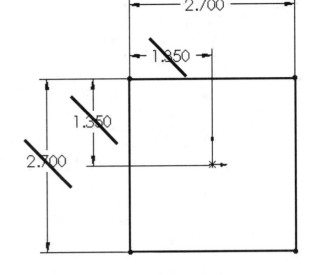

One dimension controls the size. The 6-Volt manufacturing standard determines the square profile.

The Midpoint relation centers the square profile about the Origin. One relation eliminates two dimensions to locate the profile with respect to the Origin.

The color of the sketch indicates the sketch status.

- Green: – Currently selected.

- Blue: – Under defined, requires additional Geometric relations and dimensions.

- Black: – Fully defined.

- Red: – Over defined, requires Geometric relations or dimensions to be deleted or redefined to solve the sketch.

Short Cuts save time. Right-click Select ⟋ Select to choose geometry. Click inside the Graphics window to close the Properties PropertyManager or Dimension PropertyManager. Tools are located on the right mouse button and the toolbars. The Select icon is also located in the Standard toolbar.

Fillet Feature

Fillets remove sharp edges. Use the Hidden Lines Visible view option to display hidden edges of a model.

An edge Fillet requires:

- Edge.

- Fillet radius.

Select a vertical edge. Select the Fillet feature from the Features toolbar. Enter the Fillet radius. Add the other vertical edges to the Items to Fillet option. The order of selection for the Fillet feature is not predetermined.

The Fillet feature uses the Fillet PropertyManager. The Fillet PropertyManager for 2007 has had a major interface enhancement, and provides the ability to select either the Manual or FilletXpert tab. Each tab has a separate menu and option selections. The Fillet PropertyManager displays the appropriate selections based on the type of fillet you create.

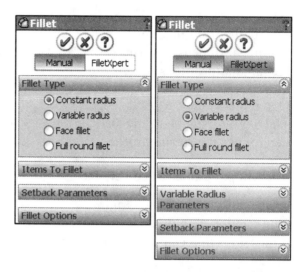

The FilletXpert automatically manages, organizes, and reorders your fillets in the FeatureManager design tree.

The FilletXpert PropertyManager provides the ability to add or change fillets using the Add or Change tabs. Use the Add tab to create new constant radius fillets. The PropertyManager remembers its last used state.

Activity: BATTERY Part-Fillet Feature

Display the hidden edges.

110) Click **Hidden Lines Visible** ⬚ from the View toolbar.

Insert the Fillet feature.

111) Click the **left vertical edge** of the Base Extrude feature.

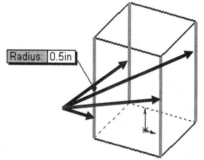

112) Click **Fillet** ⬔ Fillet from the Features toolbar. The Fillet PropertyManager is displayed. Edge<1> is displayed in the Items To Fillet box.

113) Click the remaining **3 vertical edges**. The four selected edges are displayed in the Items To Fillet box.

114) Enter .500in, [**12.7**] for Radius. Accept the default settings.

115) Click **OK** ⬤ from the Fillet PropertyManager. Fillet1 is displayed in the FeatureManager.

116) Rename **Fillet1** to **Side Fillet**.

117) Click **Shaded With Edges** ⬛.

118) Click **Save** 💾.

Note: Select edges to produce the correct result.

Extruded Cut Feature

An Extruded Cut feature removes material. An Extruded Cut requires:

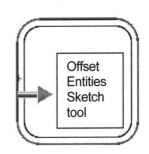

- Sketch plane, (top face).

- Sketch Profile, (Offset Entities).

- End Condition, (Blind is the default End Condition).

The Offset Entities Sketch tool uses existing geometry, extracts an edge or face and locates the geometry on the selected Sketch plane. Offset the existing Top face for the 2D sketch. Utilize the Blind End Condition in Direction 1.

Activity: Battery Part-Extruded Cut Feature-Edge

Select the Sketch plane.
119) Click the **Top face** of the BATTERY as illustreated.

Create the Sketch.

120) Click **Sketch** Sketch from the Sketch toolbar.

Display the face.

121) Click **Top view** from the Standards View toolbar.

Offset the existing geometry from the boundary of the Sketch plane.

122) Click **Offset Entities** Offset from the Sketch toolbar. The Offset Entities PropertyManager is displayed.

123) Enter **.150**in, [**3.81**] for the Offset Distance.

124) Click the **Reverse** box. The new Offset yellow profile is displayed inside the original profile.

125) Click **OK** from the Offset Entities PropertyManager.

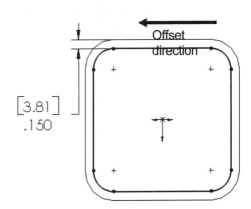

☀ A leading zero is displayed in the spin box. For inch dimensions less than 1, the leading zero is not displayed in the part dimension under the ANSI standard.

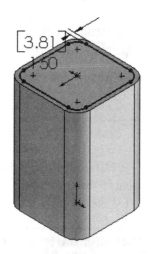

Display the profile.

126) Click **Isometric view** 🔲.

Insert an Extruded Cut feature.

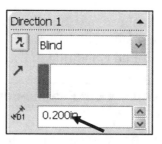

127) Click **Extruded Cut** 🔳 Cut from the Features toolbar. The Cut-Extrude PropertyManager is displayed. Blind is the default End Condition in Direction 1.

128) Enter .200in, [5.08] for Depth.

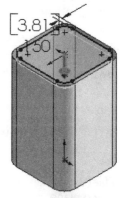

129) Click **OK** ✅ from the Cut-Extrude PropertyManager. Cut-Extrude1 is displayed in the FeatureManager.

130) Rename **Cut-Extrude1** to **Top Cut**.

Save the BATTERY part.

131) Click **Save** 💾.

The Cut-Extrude PropertyManager contains numerous options. The Reverse Direction option determines the direction of the Extruded Cut. The Extruded Cut is valid when the direction arrow points into material to be removed.

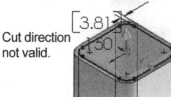

Cut direction not valid.

The Flip side to cut option determines if the cut is to the inside or outside of the Sketch Profile. The Flip side to cut arrow points outward. The Extruded Cut occurs on the outside.

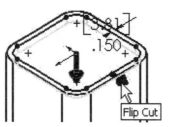

Extruded Cut with Flip side to cut option checked

Fillet Feature

The Fillet feature rounds sharp edges with a constant radius by selecting a face. A Fillet requires a:

- Face.

- Fillet Radius.

Activity: BATTERY Part-Fillet Feature

Insert the Fillet feature on the top face.

132) Zoom in 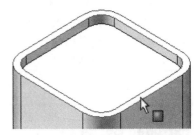 on the Top face of the BATTERY.

133) Click the **top thin face** of the BATTERY as illustrated.

134) Click **Fillet** Fillet from the Features toolbar. The Fillet PropertyManager is displayed. Face<1> is displayed in the Items To Fillet box.

135) Enter **.050**in, [**1.27**] for Radius. Accept the default settings.

136) Click **OK** from the Fillet PropertyManager. Fillet2 is displayed in the FeatureManager.

137) Rename **Fillet2** to **Top Face Fillet**.

138) Click **Save** .

View the mouse pointer for feedback to select Edges or Faces for the Fillet.

Do not select a Fillet radius which is larger then the surrounding geometry. Example: The top edge face width is .150in, [3.81]. The Fillet is created on both sides of the face. A common error is to enter a Fillet too large for the existing geometry. A minimum face width of .200in, [5.08] is required for a Fillet radius of .100in, [2.54].

The following error occurs when the Fillet radius is too large for the existing geometry:

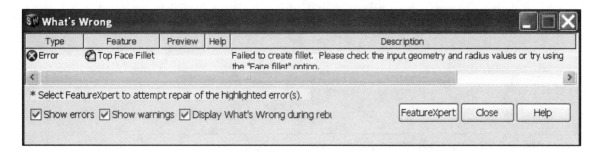

Avoid the Fillet Rebuild error. Reduce the fillet size or increase the face width. The FeatureXpert is a new option in 2007. The FeatureXpert can change the feature order in the FeatureManager design tree or adjust the tangent properties so you can successfully rebuild the part. The FeatureXpert can also, to a lesser extent, repair reference planes that have lost their references. See SolidWorks Help for additional information.

Extruded Boss Feature

The Extruded Boss requires a truncated cone shape to represent the geometry of the BATTERY terminals. The draft angle option creates the tapered shape. Sketch the first circle on the top face. Utilize the Ctrl key to copy the first circle.

The dimension between the center points is critical. Dimension the distance between the two center points with an aligned dimension. The dimension text toggles between linear and aligned. An aligned dimension is created when the dimension is positioned between the two circles.

An angular dimension is required between the Right Plane and the centerline. Acute angles are less than 90°. Acute angles are the preferred dimension standard. The overall BATTERY height is a critical dimension. The BATTERY height is 4.500in, [114.30mm]. Calculate the depth of the extrusion:

For inches: 4.500in – (4.100in Base-Extrude height – .200in Offset cut depth) = .600in
The depth of the extrusion is .600in.

For millimeters: 114.3mm – (104.14mm Base-Extrude height – 5.08mm Offset cut depth) = 15.24mm. The depth of the extrusion is 15.24mm.

Activity: BATTERY Part-Extruded Boss Feature

Select the Sketch plane.
139) Click the **top face** of the Top Cut feature.

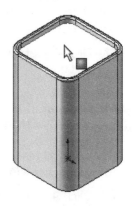

Create the Sketch.
140) Click **Sketch** Sketch from the Sketch toolbar.

Display the Sketch Plane.
141) Click **Top view** from the Standards View toolbar.

Sketch the profile.
142) Click **Circle** Circle from the Sketch toolbar. The Circle PropertyManager is displayed.

143) Click the **center point** of the circle coincident to the Origin.

144) Drag and click the **mouse pointer** to the right of the Origin.

Add dimensions.
145) Click **Smart Dimension** Dimens... from the Sketch toolbar.

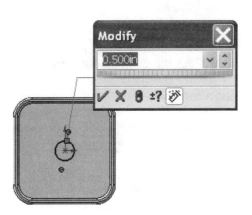

146) Click the **circumference** of the circle.

147) Click a **position** diagonally to the right.

148) Enter .500in, [12.7].

149) Click the **Green Check mark** . The black sketch is fully defined.

Copy the sketched circle.
150) Right-click **Select** Select .

151) Hold the **Ctrl** key down.

152) Click the **circumference** of the circle.

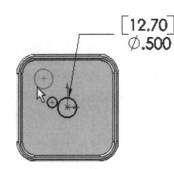

153) Drag the **circle** to the upper left quadrant.

154) Release the **mouse button**.

155) Release the **Ctrl** key. The second circle is selected and is displayed in green.

Add an Equal relation.

156) Hold the **Ctrl** key down. Click the **circumference of the first circle**. Both circles are selected. Release the **Ctrl** key.

157) Click **Equal** from the Add Relations text box

158) Click **OK** from the Properties PropertyManager.

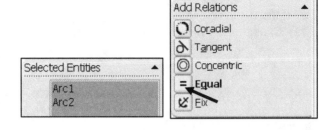

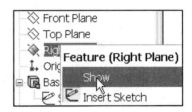

Show the Right Plane for the dimension reference.

159) Right-click **Right Plane** from the FeatureManager.

160) Click **Show**. The Right Plane is displayed.

Add a dimension.

161) Click **Smart Dimension** Dimens... from the Sketch toolbar.

162) Click the **two center points** of the two circles.

163) Click a **position** off the profile in the upper left corner.

164) Enter **1.000**in, **[25.4]** for the aligned dimension.

165) Click the **Green Check mark** ✓ .

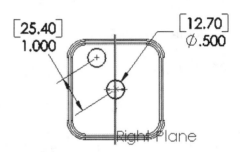

Add a centerline.

166) Click **Centerline** Centerl... from the Sketch toolbar.

167) Sketch a centerline between the **two circle center points**.

168) Right-click **End Chain** to end the line.

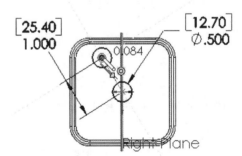

Add a dimension.

169) Click **Smart Dimension** Dimens....

170) Click the **centerline** between the two circles.

171) Click **Right Plane** from the fly-out FeatureManager. Click a **position** between the centerline and the Right Plane, off the profile as illustrated.

172) Enter **45**deg.

173) Click the **Green Check mark** ✓ .

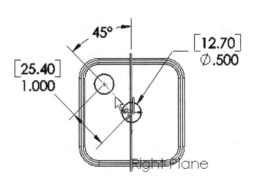

Create an angular dimension between three points or two lines. Sketch a centerline/construction line when an additional point or line is required.

Insert an Extruded Boss feature.

Extruded
174) Click **Extruded Boss/Base** Boss/B... from the Features toolbar. Blind is the default End Condition.

175) Enter **.600**in, [**15.24**] for Depth. Click the **Draft ON/OFF** button. Enter **5**deg in the Draft Angle box. Click **OK** from the Extrude PropertyManager.

176) Click **Isometric view** . Right-click **Right Plane** from the FeatureManager.

177) Click **Hide**.

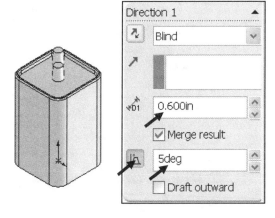

Rename the Feature and Sketch.
178) Rename **Extrude2** to **Terminals**.

179) **Expand** Terminals. Rename **Sketch3** to **Sketch-Terminals**.

Each time you create a feature of the same feature type, the feature name is incremented by one. Example: Extrude1 is the first Extrude feature. Extrude2 is the second Extrude feature. If you delete a feature, rename a feature or exit a SolidWorks session, the feature numbers will vary from those illustrated in this text.

Rename features with descriptive names. Standardize on feature names that are utilized in mating parts. Example: Mounting Holes.

Measure the overall BATTERY height.
180) Click **Right view** .

181) Click **Tools, Measure** Measure... from the Main menu. Click the **top edge** of the BATTERY terminal.

182) Click the **bottom edge** of the BATTERY. The overall height, Delta Y is 4.500in, [114.3].

183) Click **Close** from the Measure – BATTERY dialog box.

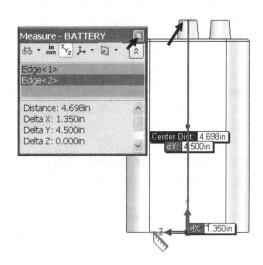

☀ Right-click Clear Selections in the Selected items block to measure the distance between various edges or faces.

Hide all planes and display a Trimetric view.
184) Click **View**; uncheck **Planes** from the Main menu.

185) Click **Trimetric view** 🗔 .

186) Click **Save** 💾.

🔍 Additional information on Extrude Boss/Base Extrude Cut and Fillets is located in SolidWorks Help Topics. Keywords: Extrude (Boss/Base, Cut), Fillet (constant radius fillet), Geometric relations (sketch, equal, midpoint), Sketch (rectangle, circle), Offset Entities and Dimensions (angular).

 Review of the BATTERY Part

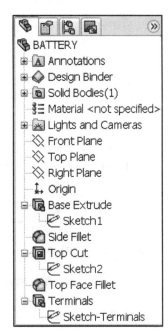

The BATTERY utilized an Extrude Base feature sketched on the Top Plane. The rectangle was sketched with a diagonal centerline to build symmetry into the part. A Midpoint Geometric relation centered the sketch at the Origin. The Equal relation created a square sketch.

The Fillet feature rounded sharp edges. All four edges were selected to combine common geometry into the same Fillet feature. The Fillet feature also rounded the top face. The Sketch Offset Entity created the profile for the Extruded Cut feature.

The Terminals were created with an Extruded Boss feature. You sketched a circular profile and utilized the Ctrl key to copy the sketched geometry. A centerline was required to locate the two holes with an angular dimension. The draft angle option tapered the Extruded Boss feature. All features were renamed.

BATTERYPLATE Part

The BATTERYPLATE is a critical FLASHLIGHT part. The BATTERYPLATE:

- Aligns the LENS assembly.

- Creates an electrical connection between the BATTERY and LENS.

Create the BATTERYPLATE. Utilize features from the BATTERY to develop the BATTERYPLATE. The BATTERYPLATE is manufactured as an injection molded plastic part. Build draft into the Extruded Boss\Base features.

Edit the BATTERY features. Create two holes from the original sketched circles. Use the Extruded Cut feature.

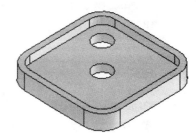

Modify the dimensions of the Base feature. Add a 3° draft angle.

Note: A sand pail contains a draft angle. The draft angle assists the sand to leave the pail when the pail is flipped upside down.

Insert an Extruded Boss feature. Offset the center circular sketch.

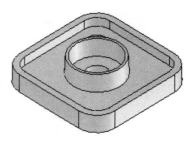

The Extruded Boss feature contains the LENS. Create an inside draft angle. The draft angle assists the LENS into the Holder.

Insert Face Fillet and a multi-radius Edge Fillet to remove sharp edges. Plastic parts require smooth edges. Group Fillet feature together into a Folder. Perform a Draft Analysis on this part.

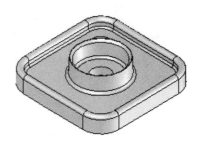

🔆 Group fillets together into a folder to locate quickly. Features listed in the FeatureManager must be continuous in order to be placed as a group into a folder.

Save As, Delete, Modify, and Edit Feature

Create the BATTERYPLATE from the BATTERY part. Utilize the File, Save As option to copy the BATTERY to the BATTERYPLATE.

Reuse existing geometry. Create two holes. Delete the Terminals feature and reuse the circle sketch. Select the sketch in the FeatureManager. Insert an Extruded Cut feature. The Through All End Condition option creates two holes that cut through the entire Extruded Base feature.

Right-click the Extruded Cut feature from the FeatureManager. Select the Edit Feature option. The Edit Feature option returns to the Cut-Extrude PropertyManager. Modify the End Condition from Blind to Through All. Modify the depth dimension. Sketch dimensions are displayed in black. Feature dimensions are displayed in blue. Select Rebuild to update the part.

Activity: Save As option and Delete, Modify, and Edit Feature

Create a new part.
187) Click **File**, **Save As** from the Main menu.

188) Select the **PROJECTS** folder.

189) Enter **BATTERYPLATE** for File name.

190) Enter **BATTERYPLATE FOR 6-VOLT** for Description.

191) Click **Save**. The BATTERYPLATE FeatureManager is displayed. The BATTERY part is closed.

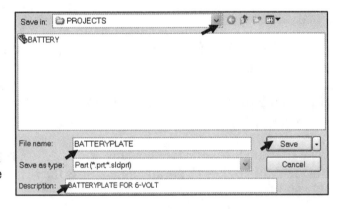

Delete the BATTERY Terminals.
192) Right-click **Terminals** from the FeatureManager.

193) Click **Delete** ✕ Delete...

194) Click **Yes** from the Confirm Delete box. Do not delete Sketch-Terminals.

Activity: BATTERYPLATE Part-Extruded Cut Feature

Create an Extruded Cut feature from the Sketch–Terminals.
195) Click **Sketch-Terminals** from the FeatureManager.

Extruded
196) Click **Extruded Cut** Cut from the Features toolbar. The Cut-Extrude PropertyManager is displayed.

197) Select **Through All** for End Condition.

198) Click **OK** ✅ from the Cut-Extrude PropertyManager. Cut-Exturde2 is displayed in the FeatureManager.

199) Rename **Cut-Extrude2** to **Holes**.

200) Click **Save** 💾 .

Edit the Base Extrude feature.
201) Right-click **Base Extrude** from the FeatureManager.

202) Click **Edit Feature**. The Base Extrude PropertyManager is displayed.

Modify the overall depth and draft.
203) Click the **4.100**in, **[104.14]** dimension.

204) Enter **.400**in, **[10.16]** for new Depth.

205) Click the **Draft ON/OFF** button.

206) Enter **1**deg in the Draft Angle box.

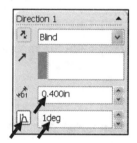

207) Click **OK** ✅ from the Base Extrude PropertyManager.

Fit the model to the Graphics window.
208) Press the **f** key.

Save the BATTERYPLATE part.
209) Click **Save** 💾 .

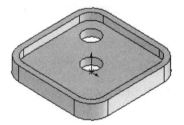

💡 Select the Also Delete Absorbed Feature check box to delete both the feature and the sketch at the same time.

Extruded Boss Feature

The Holder is created with a circular Extruded Boss feature. Utilize Offset Sketch Entity to create the second circle. Utilize a draft angle of 3° in the Extrude PropertyManager.

When applying the draft angle to the two concentric circles, the outside face tapers inwards and the inside face tapers outwards.

Draft Angle displayed at 5°

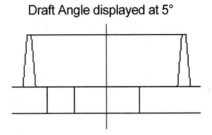

🔅 Plastic parts require a draft angle. A rule of thumb; 1deg to 5deg is the draft angle. The draft angle is created in the direction of pull from the mold. This is defined by geometry, material selection, mold production and cosmetics. Always verify the draft with the mold designer and manufacturer.

Activity: BATTERYPLATE Part-Offset Entities

Select the Sketch plane.
210) Click the **top face** of the BATTERYPLATE part.

Create the Sketch.

211) Click **Sketch** Sketch from the Sketch toolbar.

212) Click the **top circular edge** of the center hole as illustrated.

213) Click **Offset Entities** Offset from the Sketch toolbar.

214) Enter **.300**in, **[7.62]** for Offset Distance. Accept the default settings.

215) Click **OK** ✅ from the Offset Entities PropertyManager.

Create the second offset circle.
216) Click the **offset circle**.

217) Click **Top view** ⬜ .

218) Click **Offset Entities** Offset from the Sketch toolbar.

219) Enter **.100**in, **[2.54]** for the Offset Distance. Accept the default settings.

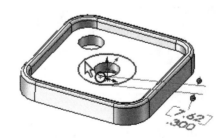

220) Click **OK** from the Offset Entities PropertyManager.

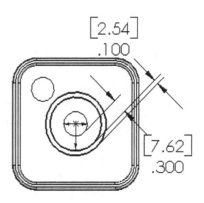

Activity: BATTERYPLATE Part-Extruded Boss Feature

Insert an Extruded Boss feature.

221) Click **Extruded Boss/Base** 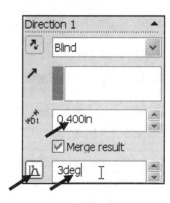 from the Features toolbar.

222) Enter **.400**in, [**10.16**] for Depth.

223) Click the **Draft ON/OFF** button.

224) Enter **3**deg in the Angle box.

225) Click **OK** 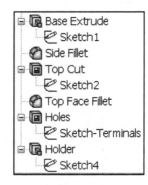 from the Extrude PropertyManager.

226) Rename **Extrude3** to **Holder**.

227) Click **Isometric view** 🔲.

Save the BATTERYPLATE part.

228) Click **Save** 💾 .

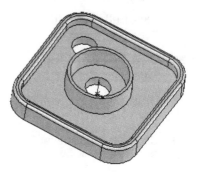

BATTERYPLATE Part-Fillet Features: Full Round, Multiple Radius Options

Fillet features are used to smooth rough edges. Plastic parts require fillets on sharp edges. Create two Fillets. Use two different techniques to create the Fillets.

The current Top Face Fillet produced a flat face. Delete the Top Face Fillet. The first Fillet is a Full Round Fillet. Insert a Full Round Fillet on the top face for a smooth rounded transition.

The second Fillet is a Multiple Radius Fillet. Select a different radius value for each edge in the set. Select the inside and outside edge of the Holder. Select all inside tangent edges of the Top Cut. A Multiple Radius Fillet is utilized next as an exercise. There are machining instances were radius must be reduced or enlarged to accommodate tooling. Note: There are other ways to create Fillets.

Group Fillets into a Fillet folder. Placing Fillets into a folder reduces the time spent for your mold designer or toolmaker to look for each Fillet in the FeatureManager.

Activity: BATTERYPLATE Part-Fillet Features: Full Round, Multiple Radius Options

---

Delete the Top Edge Fillet.

229) Right-click **Top Face Fillet** from the FeatureManager.

230) Click **Delete** ✕ Delete... . Click **Yes**.

231) Drag the **Rollback** bar below Top Cut in the FeatureManager.

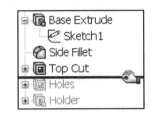

Insert a Full Round Fillet feature type .

232) Click **Hidden Lines Visible** 🔲 .

233) Click **Fillet** 🔘 Fillet from the Features toolbar. The Fillet PropertyManager is displayed.

234) Click **Full round fillet** in the Fillet Type box.

235) Click the **inside Top Cut face** for Side Face Set 1.

236) Click **inside** the Center Face Set box.

237) Click the **top face** for Center Face Set.

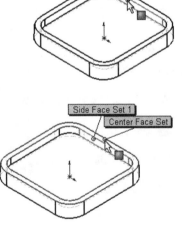

Rotate the part.

238) Press the **Left Arrow** key until you can select the outside Base Extrude face.

239) Click **inside** the Side Face Set 2 box.

240) Click the **outside Base Extrude face** for Side Face Set 2.

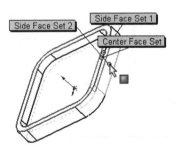

241) Click **OK** ✅ from the Fillet PropertyManager.

242) Rename **Fillet3** to **TopFillet**.

Save the BATTERYPLATE.

243) Click **Isometric view** 🔲 .

244) Click **Shaded With Edges** 🔲 .

245) Drag the **Rollback** bar back below Holder in the FeatureManager.

246) Click **Save** 💾 .

Note: The Rollback bar is placed at the bottom of the FeatureManager during a Rebuild.

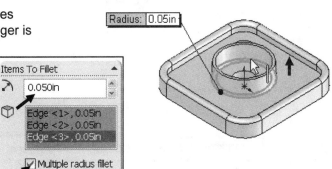

Insert a Multiple Radius Fillet feature.
247) Click the **bottom outside circular edge** of the Holder.

248) Click **Fillet** 🔘 Fillet from the Features toolbar. The Fillet PropertyManager is displayed.

249) Enter **.050**in, **[1.27]** for Radius.

250) Click the **bottom inside circular edge** of the Holder.

251) Click the **inside edge** of the Top Cut.

252) Check **Tangent Propagation**.

253) Check **Multiple radius fillet**.

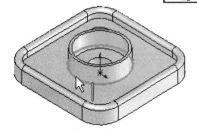

Modify the Fillet values.
254) Click the **Radius** box for the Holder outside edge.

255) Enter **0.060**in, **[1.52]**.

256) Click the **Radius** box for the Top Cut inside edge.

257) Enter **0.040**in, **[1.02]**.

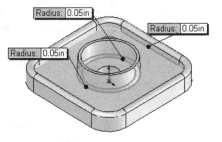

258) Click **OK** ✅ from the Fillet PropertyManager.

259) Rename **Fillet4** to **HolderFillet**.

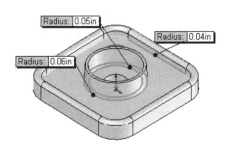

Group the Fillets into a folder.

260) Click **TopFillet** from the FeatureManager. Drag the **TopFillet** feature directly above the HolderFillet in the FeatureManager.

261) Click **HolderFillet** from the FeatureManager. Hold the **Ctrl** key down.

262) Click **Top Fillet** from the FeatureManager. Release the **Ctrl** key.

263) Right-click **Add to New Folder**. Rename **Folder1** to **FilletFolder**.

Save the BATTERYPLATE.

264) Click **Save** 💾.

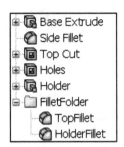

Chamfer Feature

A Chamfer feature bevels an edge or a face. There are three options for the Chamfer feature:

- Angle distance, (default setting).

- Distance distance.

- Vertex.

The Chamfer feature for the Holder requires:

- Edge or face.

- Angle and distance.

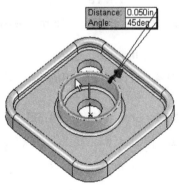

Activity: BATTERYPLATE Part-Chamfer Feature

Insert a Chamfer feature.

265) Click the **inside circular edge** of the Holder as illustrated.

266) Click **Chamfer** Chamfer from the Features toolbar. The Chamfer PropertyManager is displayed.

267) Enter **.050**in, **[1.27]** for Distance.

268) Enter **45**deg for Angle. Accept the default settings.

269) Click **OK** ✅ from the Chamfer PropertyManager. Chamfer1 is displayed in the FeatureManager.

270) Click **Isometric view** .

Save the BATTERYPLATE.

271) Click **Save** 💾.

Exit SolidWorks.
272) Click **File**, **Exit** from the Main menu.

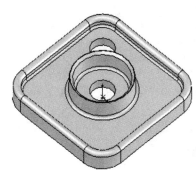

Multi-body Parts and Extruded Boss Feature

A Multi-body part has separate solid bodies within the same part document.

A WRENCH consists of two cylindrical bodies. Each extrusion is a separate body. The oval profile is sketched on the right plane and extruded with the Up to Body option.

The BATTERY consisted of a solid body with one sketched profile. The BATTERY is a single body part.

🔍 Additional information on Save, Extrude Boss/Base, Extrude Cut, Fillets, Copy Sketched Geometry and Multi-body are located in SolidWorks Help Topics. Keywords: Save (save as copy), Extruded (Boss/Base, Cut), Fillet (face blends, variable radius), Chamfer, Geometric Relations (sketch), Copy (sketch entities), Multi-body (extrude, modeling techniques).

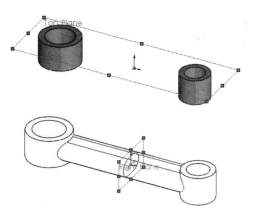

Multi-body part Wrench

Review of the BATTERYPLATE Part.

The File, Save As option was utilized to copy the BATTERY part to the BATTERYPLATE part. You modified and deleted features in the BATTERYPLATE.

The BATTERYPLATE is a plastic part. The Draft Angle option was added in the Extruded Base feature. The Holder Extruded Boss utilized a circular sketch and the Draft Angle option. The Sketch Offset tool created the circular ring profile.

Multi radius Edge Fillets and Face Fillets removed sharp edges. Similar Fillets were grouped together into a Folder. All features were renamed in the FeatureManager. The BATTERY and BATTERYPLATE utilized an Extruded Base feature.

Project Summary

SolidWorks is a 3D design software application utilized to create parts, assemblies, and drawings. You are designing a FLASHLIGHT assembly that is cost effective, serviceable, and flexible for future design revisions. The FLASHLIGHT assembly consists of various parts. The BATTERY and BATTERYPLATE parts were modeled in this project.

The SolidWorks Windows based user interface is divided into: Drop-down menus, toolbars, Pop-up menus, CommandManager, FeatureManager, Status bar, Task Pane, and the Graphics window.

Folders organized your models and templates. The Part Template is the foundation for all parts in the FLASHLIGHT assembly. You created the PART-IN-ANSI and PART-MM-ISO Part Template.

Project 1 concentrated on the Extruded Base feature. The Extruded Base feature required a Sketch plane, Sketch Profile and End Condition (Depth). The BATTERY and BATTERYPLATE parts incorporated an Extruded Base feature:

You addressed four major features in this project: Extruded Boss/Base, Extruded Cut, Fillet, and Chamfer. You addressed the following Sketch tools in this project: Smart Dimension, Sketch Entities, Line, Rectangle, Circle, and Centerline.

You addressed additional Sketch tools that utilized existing geometry: Add Relations, Display/Delete Relations, Mirror Entities, Convert Entities, and Offset Entities.

Geometric relations were utilized to build symmetry into the sketches. Practice these concepts with the project exercises.

Project Terminology

Assembly: An assembly is a document in which parts, features and other assemblies (sub-assemblies) are put together. The filename extension for a SolidWorks assembly file name is .SLDASM. The FLASHLIGHT is an assembly. The BATTERY is a part in the FLASHLIGHT assembly.

Chamfer: A feature that bevels sharp edges or faces by a specified distance and angle or by two specified distances.

Convert Entities: A sketch tool that extracts sketch geometry to the current Sketch plane.

Cursor Feedback: Feedback is provided by a symbol attached to the cursor arrow indicating your selection.

Dimension: A value indicating the size of feature geometry.

Dimensioning Standard: A set of drawing and detailing options developed by national and international organizations. A few key dimensioning standard options are: ANSI, ISO, DIN, JIS, BSI, GOST, and GB.

Draft angle: A draft angle is the degree of taper applied to a face. Draft angles are usually applied to molds or castings.

Drawing: A document containing a 2D representation of a 3D part or assembly. The filename extension for a SolidWorks drawing file name is .SLDDRW.

Edit Feature: A tool utilized to modify existing feature parameters. Right-click the feature in the FeatureManager. Click Edit Feature.

Edit Sketch: A tool utilized to modify existing sketch geometry. Right-click the feature in the FeatureManager. Click Edit Sketch.

Extruded Boss/Base: A feature that adds material utilizing a 2D sketch profile and a depth perpendicular to the sketch plane. The Base feature is the first feature in the part.

Extruded Cut: A feature that removes material utilizing a 2D sketch profile and a depth perpendicular to the sketch plane.

Features: Features are geometry building blocks. Features add or remove material. Features are created from sketched profiles or from edges and faces of existing geometry.

Fillet: A feature that rounds sharp edges or faces by a specified radius.

Geometric relationships: Relations between geometry that are captured as you sketch.

Menus: Menus provide access to the commands that the SolidWorks software offers.

Mirror Entities: A sketch tool that mirrors sketch geometry to the opposite side of a sketched centerline.

Mouse Buttons: The left and right mouse buttons have distinct meanings in SolidWorks. The left mouse button is utilized to select geometry. The right-mouse button is utilized to invoke commands.

Offset Entities: A sketch tool that offsets sketch geometry to the current sketch plane by a specific amount.

Part: A part is a single 3D object that consists of various features. The filename extension for a SolidWorks part is .SLDPRT.

Plane: Planes are flat and infinite. Planes are represented on the screen with visible edges. The reference plane in Project 1 is the Top Plane.

Relation: A relation is a geometric constraint between sketch entities or between a sketch entity and a plane, axis, edge or vertex. Utilize Add Relations to manually connect related geometry.

Sketch: The name to describe a 2D profile is called a sketch. 2D sketches are created on flat faces and planes within the model. Typical geometry types are lines, arcs, rectangles, circles, polygons and ellipses.

States of a Sketch: There are four key states that are utilized in this Project:

- Fully Defined: Has complete information, (Black).

- Over Defined: Has duplicate dimensions, (Red).

- Under Defined: There is inadequate definition of the sketch, (Blue).

- Selected: The current selected entity, (Green).

Template: A template is the foundation of a SolidWorks document. A Part Template contains the Document Properties such as: Dimensioning Standard, Units, Grid/Snap, Precision, Line Style and Note Font.

Toolbars: The toolbars provide shortcuts enabling you to access the most frequently used commands.

Units: Used in the measurement of physical quantities. Decimal inch dimensioning and Millimeter dimensioning are the two types of common units specified for engineering parts and drawings.

Questions

1. Identify and describe the function of the following features:

    - Extruded Boss/Base.
    - Fillet.
    - Chamfer.
    - Extruded Cut.

2. Explain the differences between a Template and a Part.

3. Explain the steps in opening a SolidWorks session.

4. Describe the procedure to develop a new sketch.

5. Explain the steps required to change part unit dimensions from inches to millimeters.

6. Identify the three default reference planes.

7. What is a Base feature? Provide two examples.

8. Describe the differences between an Extruded Base feature and an Extruded Cut feature.

9. The sketch color black indicates a sketch is _____ defined.

10. The sketch color blue indicates a sketch is _____ defined.

11. The sketch color red indicates a sketch is _____ defined.

12. True or False. Folders are utilized to only store part documents.

13. Describe a symmetric relation.

14. Describe an angular dimension.

15. What is a draft angle? Provide an example.

16. An arc requires _____ points?

17. Identify the properties of a Multi-body part.

Exercises

Exercise 1.1: Part Document Templates

Create a Metric part document template using an ANSI dimension standard.

Exercise 1.2: L-SHAPE Part

Create 3 parts: L-SHAPE-FRONT, L-SHAPE-TOP and L-SHAPE-RIGHT.

Utilize your own dimensions. Locate each profile on a different Sketch Plane.

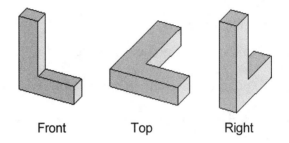

Front   Top   Right

Exercise 1.3: AXLE Part

Create the AXLE part. Utilize the Front Plane for the Sketch plane. Use the provided dimensions.

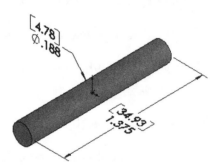

Exercise 1.4: SHAFT COLLAR Part

Create the SHAFT COLLAR part. Utilize the Front Plane for the Sketch plane. Use the provided dimensions.

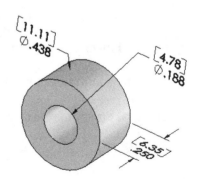

Exercise 1.5a -15.d: Create the following parts utilizing the Extrude Boss/Base, Extruded Cut, Fillet and Chamfer features. Dimensions are not provided. Utilize symmetry.

Exercise 1.5a: RING Part

Use the Top Plane as the sketch plane. Use the Offset Entities tool. Utilize a Tangent Arc Sketch tool. The part is symmetrical about the Front Plane. Utilize two diagonal centerlines to locate the centerpoints of the circles at the Midpoint of the centerline.

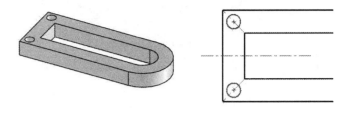

Exercise 1.5b: PLAQUE Part

Utilize the Offset Entities Sketch tool and Extruded Cut (Flip side) feature. The Base feature is symmetric about the Right Plane.

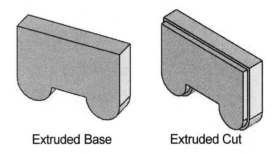

Extruded Base   Extruded Cut

Exercise 1.5c: CASTING Part

Utilize a 3° Draft Angle for the Extruded Base and Extrude Boss features. Add Fillets and Chamfers. Center the Base feature about the Origin.

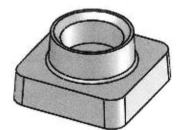

Exercise 1.5d: FITTING Part

Sketch the profile for the Extruded Base feature to the left of the Origin. Insert the Extruded Boss feature on the Right Plane. Utilize the Up to Surface option. Add an Extruded Cut utilizing Offset Entities.

Insert Fillets and Chamfers.

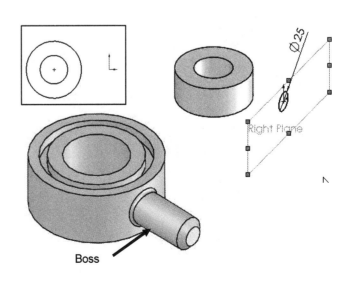

Boss

Notes:

Project 2

Revolved Features

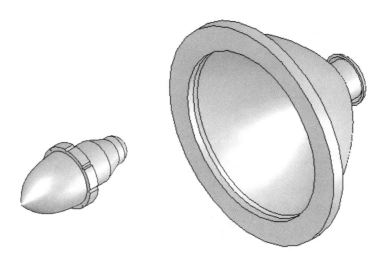

Below are the desired outcomes and usage competencies based on the completion of Project 2.

Project Desired Outcomes:	Usage Competencies:

• Two FLASHLIGHT parts:
    o LENS.
    o BULB.
	• Specific knowledge and understanding of the following Features: Extruded Base, Extruded Boss, Extruded Cut, Revolved Base, Revolved Boss Thin, Revolved Thin Cut, Dome, Shell, Hole Wizard, and Circular Pattern.

• Establish Geometric relations: Equal, Coincident, Symmetric, Intersection, and Perpendicular.	• Ability to apply multiple Geometric relations to a model. • Ability to apply Design Intent to Sketches, Features, Parts, and Assemblies.

Notes:

Project 2-Revolved Features

Project Overview

Project 2 introduces you to the Revolved Boss/Base feature. Create two parts for the FLASHLIGHT assembly in this project:

- LENS.

- BULB.

A Revolved Boss/Base feature requires a 2D sketch profile and a centerline. Utilize sketch geometry and sketch tools to create the following features:

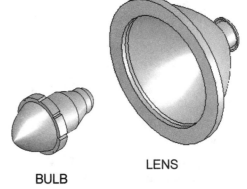

BULB   LENS

- Revolved Base.

- Revolved Boss.

- Revolved Boss Thin.

- Revolved Cut.

Utilize existing faces to create the following features:

- Shell.

- Dome.

- Hole Wizard.

Utilize the Extruded Cut feature to create a Circular Pattern.

After completing the activities in this project, you will be able to:

- Utilize the following Sketch tools: Circle, Line, 3 Point Arc, Centerpoint Arc, Spline, Mirror, Offset Entities, Trim, and Convert Entities.

- Establish Geometric relations: Equal, Coincident, Symmetric, Intersection, and Perpendicular.

- Develop Transparent Optical Properties.

- Create and edit the following features: Extruded Base, Extruded Boss, Extruded Cut, Revolved Base, Revolved Boss, Revolved Boss Thin, Revolved Thin Cut, Shell, Hole Wizard, Dome, and Circular Pattern.

- Create two parts for the FLASHLIGHT assembly: LENS and BULB.

LENS Part

Create the LENS. The LENS is a purchased part.

The LENS utilizes a Revolved Base feature.

Sketch a centerline and a closed
profile on the Right Plane. Insert a
Revolved Base feature. The
Revolved Base feature requires an
axis of revolution and an angle of
revolution.

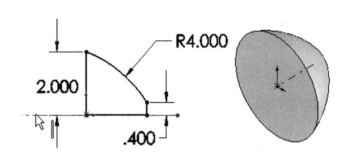

Insert the Shell feature. The Shell
feature provides uniform wall
thickness. Select the front face as
the face to be removed.

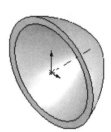

Utilize the Convert Entities sketch tool to extract
the back circular edge for the sketched profile.
Insert an Extruded Boss feature from the back of
the LENS.

Sketch a single profile. Insert a Revolved Thin feature to
connect the LENS to the BATTERYPLATE. The Revolved
Thin feature requires a thickness.

Insert a Counterbore hole with the Hole Wizard feature.

The BULB is located inside the Counterbore hole.

Insert the front Lens Cover with an Extruded Boss feature. The Extruded Boss feature is sketched on the Front Plane. Add a transparent Lens Shield with the Extruded Boss feature.

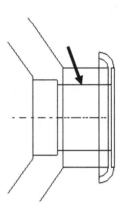

Activity: LENS Part

Create the new part.

1) Click **File, New** □ from the Main menu.

2) Click the **MY-TEMPLATES** tab.

3) Double-click **PART-IN-ANSI, [PART-MM-ISO]**.

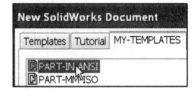

Save the part.

4) Click **Save** 🖫 .

5) Select the **PROJECTS** folder. Enter **LENS** for File name.

6) Enter **LENS WITH SHIELD** for Description. Click **Save**. The LENS FeatureManager is displayed.

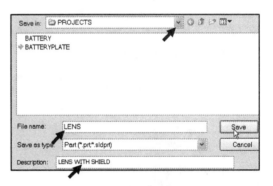

Create the Sketch.

7) Click **Right Plane** from the FeatureManager for the Sketch plane.

8) Click **Sketch** Sketch. Click **Centerline** Centerl... from the Sketch toolbar.

9) Sketch a horizontal **centerline** collinear to the Top Plane, through the Origin ↳ as illustrated.

0.017

Sketch the profile. Create three lines.

10)   Click **Line** Line from the Sketch toolbar.

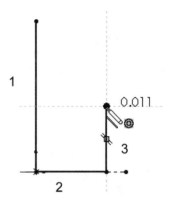

11)   Sketch a **vertical line** collinear to the Front plane coincident with the Origin.

12)   Sketch a **horizontal line** coincident with the Top plane.

13)   Sketch a **vertical line** approximately 1/3 the length of the first line.

14)   Right-click **End Chain**.

15)   Click **OK** from the Insert Line PropertyManager.

Create a 3 Point Arc.

16)   Click **3 Pt Arc** Arc from the Sketch toolbar.

17)   Click the **top point** on the left vertical line.

18)   Drag the **mouse pointer** to the right.

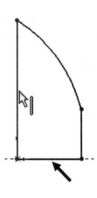

19)   Click the **top point** on the right vertical line.

20)   Drag the **mouse pointer** upward.

21)   Click a **position** on the arc.

Add an Equal relation.
22)   Right-click **Select**.

23)   Click the **left vertical line**.

24)   Hold the **Ctrl** key down.

25)   Click the **horizontal line**. The Properties PropertyManager is displayed. Release the **Ctrl** key. The selected sketch entities are displayed in the Selected Entities box.

26)   Click **Equal** = from the Add Relations box.

Add dimensions.

27)   Click **Smart Dimension** Dimens... from the Sketch toolbar.

28)   Click the **left vertical line**. Click a **position** to the left of the profile.

29) Enter **2.000**in, [**50.8**].

30) Click the **right vertical line**.

31) Click a **position** to the right of the profile.

32) Enter .**4000**in, [**10.16**].

33) Click the **arc**.

34) Click a **position** to the right of the profile.

35) Enter **4.000**in, [**101.6**].

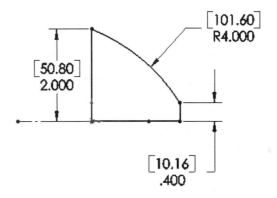

36) Click **OK**  from the Dimension PropertyManager. The black sketch is fully defined.

Utilize Tools, Sketch Tools, Check Sketch for Feature option to determine if a sketch is valid for a specific feature and to understand what is wrong with a sketch.

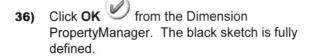

Activity: LENS Part-Revolved Base Feature

Insert a Revolved Base feature.

37) Click **Revolved Boss/Base** Boss/B... from the Feature toolbar. The Revolve PropertyManager is displayed. The centerline, Line1 is displayed in the Axis of Revolution box. The direction arrow points clockwise. Accept the default settings.

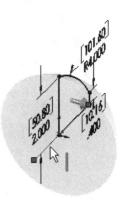

38) Click **OK** 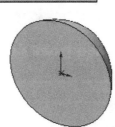 from the Revolve PropertyManager. Revolve1 is displayed in the FeatureManager.

39) Rename **Revolve1** to **BaseRevolve**.

40) Click **Save** 💾 .

Display the axis of revolution.
41) Click **View**; check **Temporary Axes** from the Main menu.

A Revolved Base feature contains an axis of revolution. The axis of revolution utilizes a sketched centerline, edge, or an existing feature/sketch or a Temporary Axis.

A solid Revolved feature contains a closed profile. A Revolved Boss Thin feature contains an open or closed profile.

Shell Feature

The Revolve1 feature is a solid. Utilize the Shell feature to create a constant wall thickness around the front face.

The Shell feature removes face material from a solid. The Shell feature requires a face and thickness. Use the Shell feature to create thin-walled parts.

Activity: LENS Part-Shell Feature

Insert the Shell feature.
42) Click the **front face** of the BaseRevolve feature as illustrated.

43) Click **Shell** Shell from the Features toolbar. The Shell1 PropertyManager is displayed.

44) Enter **.250**in, **[6.35]** for Thickness.

45) Click **OK** from the Shell1 PropertyManager. Shell1 is displayed in the FeatureManager.

46) Rename **Shell1** to **LensShell**.

47) Click **Save** 💾 .

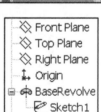

Apply fillets before the Shell feature. Select the Multi-thickness option to apply different thicknesses.

Extruded Boss Feature and Convert Entities Sketch tool

Create the LensNeck. The LensNeck houses the BULB base and is connected to the BATTERYPLATE. Use the Extruded Boss feature. The back face of the Revolved Base feature is the Sketch plane. Utilize the Convert Entities Sketch tool to extract the back circular face to the Sketch plane. The new curve develops an On Edge relation. Modify the back face, and the extracted curve updates to reflect the change. No sketch dimensions are required.

Activity: LENS Part-Extruded Boss Feature

Rotate the Lens.
48) Press the **left arrow** key approximately 8 times to view the back face.

Sketch the profile.
49) Click the **back face** for the Sketch plane.

50) Click **Sketch** Sketch. Click **Convert Entities** Convert from the Sketch toolbar.

Insert an Extruded Boss feature.

51) Click **Extruded Boss/Base** Boss/B... from the Features toolbar. The Extrude PropertyManager is displayed. Blind is the default End Condition for Direction 1.

52) Enter **.400**in, [**10.16**] for Depth.

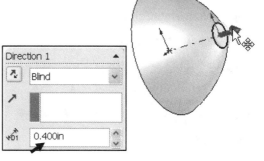

Direction 1	▲
Blind	▼
0.400in	

53) Click **OK** ✔ from the Extrude PropertyManager. Extrude1 is displayed in the FeatureManager.

54) Rename **Extrude1** to **LensNeck**. Click **Save** 🖫.

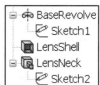

- ⊟ 🜨 BaseRevolve
- 🖉 Sketch1
- 🔲 LensShell
- ⊟ 🜀 LensNeck
- 🖉 Sketch2

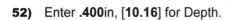

LENS Part-Hole Wizard

The LENS requires a Counterbore hole. Use the Hole Wizard. The Hole Wizard assists in creating complex and simple holes. Select the face or plane to locate the hole profile. Specify the user parameters for a custom Counterbore hole.

Insert a Coincident relation to position the hole center point. Dimensions for the Counterbore hole are provided in both inches and millimeters.

Activity: LENS Part-Hole Wizard Feature

Create a Counterbore hole.

55) Click **Front view** . Click the small **inside back face** of the LensShell feature. Do not select the Origin.

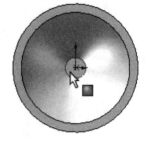

56) Click **Hole Wizard**  from the Features toolbar. The Hole Specification PropertyManager is displayed.

57) Click **Counterbore** in the Hole Specification box.

Note: For a metric hole, skip the next few steps.

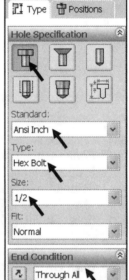

For inch Cbore Hole.
58) Select **Ansi Inch** for Standard.

59) Select **Hex Bolt** for Type.

60) Select **½** for Size.

61) Select **Through All** for End Condition.

62) **Expand** the Custom Sizing box.

63) Click the **Counterbore Diameter** value.

64) Enter **.600**in.

65) Click the **Counterbore Depth** value.

66) Enter **.200**in. Go to step **75**.

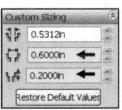

Note: For an inch hole, skip the next few steps.

For millimeter Cbore Hole.
67) Select **Ansi Metric** for Standard.

68) Select **Hex Bolt** for Type.

69) Select **M5** for Size.

70) Click **Through All** for End Condition.

71) Click the **Through Hole Diameter** value.

72) Enter **13.5**. Click the **Counterbore Diameter** value.

73) Enter **15.24**. Click the **Counterbore Depth** value.

74) Enter **5**.

75) Click the **Positions** tab.

76) Right-click **Select**.

Add a Coincident relation.

77) Click the **center point** of the Counterbore hole.

78) Hold the **Ctrl** key down.

79) Click the **Origin** ⌞. The Properties
PropertyManager is displayed.

80) Release the **Ctrl** key. The selected
sketch entities are displayed in the
Selected Entities box.

81) Click **Coincident** ⟋ from the Add
Relations box.

82) Click **OK** ✔ from the Properties
PropertyManager.

83) Click **OK** ✔ from the Hole Position PropertyManager.

Expand the Hole feature.
84) **Expand** the CBORE feature. Note: Sketch3 and Sketch4
created the CBORE feature.

Display the Section view.
85) Click **Right Plane** from the FeatureManager.

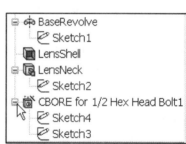

86) Click **Section view** ▥ from the View toolbar. The
Section View PropertyManager is displayed.

87) Click **Isometric view**. View the Section view of the
LENS.

88) Click **OK** ✔ from the Section View
PropertyManager.

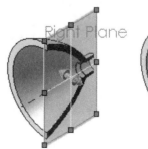

Display the Full view.

89) Click **Section view** 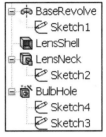.

90) Rename **CBORE for ½ Hex Head Bolt1** to **BulbHole**.

91) Click **Save** 🖫.

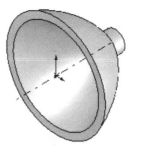

LENS Part-Revolved Boss Thin Feature

Create a Revolved Boss Thin feature. Rotate an open sketched profile around an axis. The sketch profile must be open and cannot cross the axis. A Revolved Boss Thin feature requires:

- Sketch plane, (Right Plane).

- Sketch Profile, (Center point arc).

- Axis of Revolution, (Temporary axis).

- Angle of Rotation, (360°).

- Thickness, .100in, [2.54].

Select the Right Plane for the Sketch plane. Sketch a center point arc. The sketched center point arc requires three Geometric relations: Coincident, Intersection, and Vertical.

The three Geometric relations insure that the 90° center point of the arc is coincident with the horizontal silhouette edges of the Revolved feature. A Revolved feature produces silhouette edges in 2D views. A silhouette edge represents the extent of a cylindrical or curved face. Utilize silhouette edges for Geometric relations.

Select the Temporary Axis for Axis of Revolution. Select the Revolved Boss feature. Enter .100in, [2.54] for Thickness in the Revolve PropertyManager. Enter 360° for Angle of Revolution.

Note: If you cannot select a silhouette edge in Shaded mode, switch to Wireframe mode.

Activity: LENS Part-Revolved Boss Thin Feature

Create the Sketch.

92) Click **Right Plane** from the FeatureManager.

93) Click **Sketch** Sketch from the Sketch toolbar.

94) Click **Right view** ⬚ .

95) **Zoom in** ⌕ on the LensNeck.

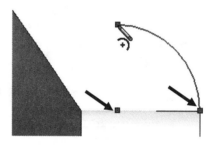

96) Click **Centerpoint Arc** Center... Arc from the Sketch toolbar.

97) Click the **top horizontal silhouette edge** of the LensNeck. Do not select the midpoint of the silhouette edge.

98) Click the **top right corner** of the LensNeck.

99) Drag the **mouse pointer** counterclockwise to the left.

100) Click a **position** above the center point.

Add a dimension.

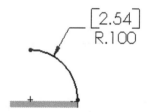

101) Click **Smart Dimension** Smart Dimens... from the Sketch toolbar.

102) Click the **arc**.

103) Click a **position** to the right of the profile.

104) Enter .**100**in, [**2.54**].

Add a Coincident relation.

105) Right-click **Select**.

106) Click the **arc center point**.

107) Hold the **Ctrl** key down.

108) Click the **top horizontal** line (silhouette edge) of the LensNeck feature.

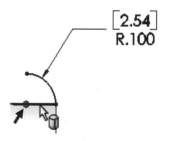

109) Release the **Ctrl** key.

110) Click **Coincident** ⦦ from the Add Relations box.

111) Click **OK** ✅ from the Properties PropertyManager.

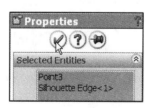

Add an Intersection relation.

112) Click the **arc start point**.

113) Hold the **Ctrl** key down.

114) Click the **right most vertical line** of the LensNeck feature.

115) Click the **top horizontal line** (silhouette edge) of the LensNeck feature.

116) Release the **Ctrl** key.

117) Click **Intersection** ✕ from the Add Relations box.

118) Click **OK** from the Properties PropertyManager.

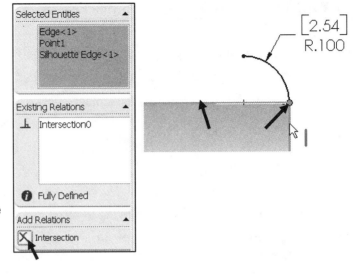

Add a Vertical relation.

119) Click the **arc center point**.

120) Hold the **Ctrl** key down.

121) Click the **arc end point**. Release the **Ctrl** key. Click **Vertical** from the Add Relations box.

122) Click **OK** from the Properties PropertyManager.

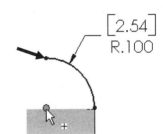

123) Click **Save** 💾.

Insert a Revolved Boss Thin feature.

124) Click **Revolved Boss/Base** Boss/B... from the Features toolbar. The Revolve PropertyManager is displayed.

125) Select **Mid-Plane** from the Thin Feature box.

126) Enter **.050**in, **[1.27]** for Direction1 Thickness.

127) Click the **Temporary Axis** for Axis of Revolution in the Graphics window.

128) Click **OK** from the Revolve PropertyManager.

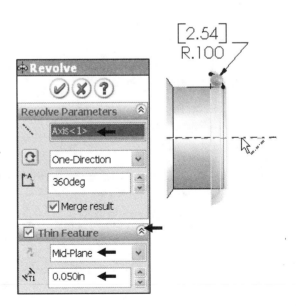

129) Rename **Revolve-Thin1** to **LensConnector**.

130) Click **Isometric view** .

131) Click **Save** .

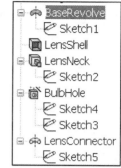

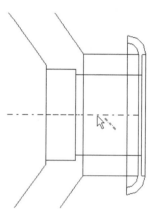 A Revolved sketch that remains open results in a Revolved

Thin feature ———. A Revolved sketch that is automatically closed, results in a line drawn from the start point to the end point of the sketch. The sketch is closed and results in a non

Revolved Thin feature ———.

LENS Part-Extruded Boss Feature and Offset Entities

Use the Extruded Boss feature to create the front LensCover. Utilize the Offset Entities Sketch tool to offset the outside circular edge of the Revolved feature. The Sketch plane for the Extruded Boss is the front circular face.

The Offset Entities Sketch tool requires an Offset Distance and direction. Utilize the Bi-direction option to create a circular sketch in both directions. The Extrude Direction is away from the Front Plane.

Activity: LENS Part-Extruded Boss Feature and Offset Entities

Create the Sketch.
132) Click the **front circular face** for the Sketch plane.

133) Click **Sketch** Sketch from the Sketch toolbar.

134) Click **Front view** .

Offset the selected edge.
135) Click the **outside circular edge** of the LENS as illustrated.

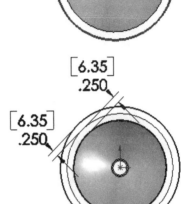

136) Click **Offset Entities** Offset from the Sketch toolbar.

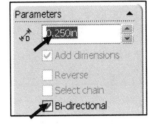

137) Click the **Bi-directional** box.

138) Enter **.250**, **[6.35]** for Offset Distance.

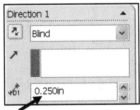

139) Click **OK** from the Offset Entities PropertyManager.

140) Click **Isometric view**.

Insert an Extruded Boss feature.

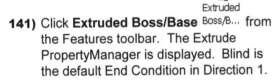

141) Click **Extruded Boss/Base** Boss/B... from the Features toolbar. The Extrude PropertyManager is displayed. Blind is the default End Condition in Direction 1.

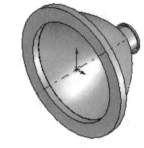

142) Enter **.250**, **[6.35]** for Depth.

143) Click **OK** from the Extrude PropertyManager. Extrude2 is displayed in the FeatureManager.

144) Rename **Extrude2** to **LensCover**.

145) Click **Isometric view**.

146) Click **Save**.

LENS Part-Extruded Boss Feature and Transparent Optical Property

Use an Extruded Boss feature to create the LensShield. Utilize the Convert Entities Sketch tool to extract the inside circular edge of the LensCover and place it on the Front Plane.

Apply the Transparent Optical property to the LensShield to control the ability for light to pass through the surface. Transparent is an Optical Property found in the Color PropertyManager. Control the following properties:

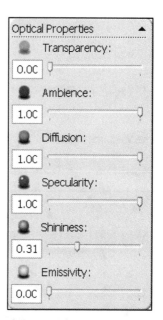

- **Transparency** - ability to pass light through the surface.

- **Ambience** - light reflected and scattered by other objects.

- **Diffusion** - light scattered equally in all directions on the surface.

- **Specularity** - ability to reflect light from a surface.

- **Shininess** - a glossy, highly reflective surface.

- **Emissivity** - ability to project light from the surface.

Activity: LENS Part-Extruded Boss Feature and Transparent Optical Property

Create the Sketch.
147) Click **Front Plane** from the FeatureManager.

148) Click **Sketch** Sketch from the Sketch toolbar.

149) Click the **front inner circular edge** of the LensCover (Extrude2) as illustrated.

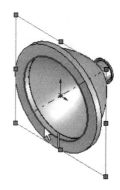

150) Click **Convert Entities** Convert from the Sketch toolbar. The circle is projected onto the Front Plane.

Insert an Extruded Boss feature.

Extruded
151) Click **Extruded Boss/Base** Boss/B... from the Features toolbar. The Extrude PropertyManager is displayed. Enter **.100**in, **[2.54]** for Depth.

152) Click **OK** from the Extrude PropertyManager. Extrude3 is displayed in the FeatureManager.

153) Rename **Extrude3** to **LensShield**.

154) Click **Save** 💾.

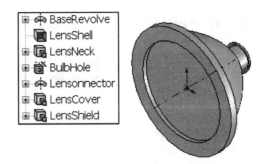

Add transparency to the LensShield.
155) Right-click **LensShield** from the FeatureManager.

156) Click **Appearance** under the Feature (LensShield).

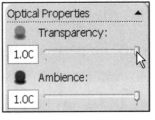

157) Click **Color** 🔲 Color....

158) Drag the **Transparency slider** to the far right side as illustrated.

159) Click **OK** ✅ from the Color and Optics PropertyManager.

160) Click **Save** 💾.

🔍 Additional information on Revolved Boss/Base, Shell, Hole Wizard and Appearance is located in SolidWorks Help Topics. Keywords: Revolved (features), Shell, Hole Wizard (Counterbore), and Color and Optics.

⚙️ Review of the LENS Part.

The LENS feature utilized a Revolved Base feature. A Revolved feature required an axis, profile, and an angle of revolution. The Shell feature created a uniform wall thickness. You utilized the Convert Entities Sketch tool to create the Extruded Boss feature for the LensNeck.

The Counterbore hole was created with the Hole Wizard. The Revolved Boss Thin feature utilized a single 3 Point Arc. Geometric relations were added to the Silhouette edge to define the arc.

The LensCover and LensShield utilized existing geometry to Offset and Convert the geometry to the sketch. The Color and Optics PropertyManager determined the LensShield transparency.

BULB Part

The BULB fits inside the LENS. Use the Revolved Base feature as the Base feature for the BULB.

Insert the Revolved Base feature from a sketched profile on the Right Plane.

Insert a Revolved Boss feature using a Spline sketched profile. A Spline sketched profile is a complex curve.

Insert a Revolved Thin Cut feature at the base of the BULB.

Insert a Dome feature at the base of the BULB.

Insert a Circular Pattern feature from an Extruded Cut.

BULB Part-Revolved Base Feature

Create a new part, BULB. The BULB utilizes a solid Revolved Base feature.

A solid Revolved Base feature requires a:

- Sketch plane, (Right Plane).

- Sketch Profile, (Lines).

- Axis of Revolution, (Centerline).

- Angle of Rotation, (360º).

Utilize the Centerline to create a diameter dimension for the profile. The flange of the BULB is located inside the Counterbore hole of the LENS. Align the bottom of the flange with the Front Plane. The Front Plane mates against the Counterbore face.

┌───┐
│ **Activity: BULB Part**   │
└───┘

Create a new Part.

161) Click **File**, **New** ⬛ from the Main menu. Click the **MY-TEMPLATES** tab.

162) Double-click **PART-IN-ANSI**, **[PART-MM-ISO]**.

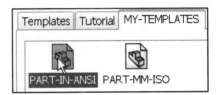

Save the part.

163) Click **Save** 🖫. Select the **PROJECTS** folder. Enter **BULB** for File name. Enter **BULB FOR LENS** for Description. Click **Save**.

Select the Sketch plane.
164) Click **Right Plane** from the FeatureManager.

Create the Sketch.

165) Click **Sketch** Sketch.

Sketch the Centerline.

166) Click **Centerline** Centerl... from the Sketch toolbar. Sketch a horizontal **centerline** through the Origin ⌞ as illustrated.

Create six profile lines.

167) Click **Line** Line from the Sketch toolbar.

168) Sketch a **vertical line** to the left of the Front Plane.

169) Sketch a **horizontal line** with the endpoint coincident to the Front Plane.

170) Sketch a short **vertical line** towards the centerline, collinear with the Front Plane.

171) Sketch a **horizontal line** to the right.

172) Sketch a **vertical line** with the endpoint collinear with the centerline.

173) Sketch a **horizontal line** to the first point to close the profile as illustrated.

Add dimensions.

174) Click **Smart Dimension** Dimens... from the Sketch toolbar. Click the **centerline**.

175) Click the **top right horizontal line**.

176) Click a **position** below the centerline and to the right.

177) Enter .400in, [**10.016**].

178) Click the **centerline**. Click the **top left horizontal line**.

179) Click a **position** below the centerline and to the left. Enter .590in, [**14.99**].

180) Click the **top left horizontal line**.

181) Click a **position** above the profile.

182) Enter .100in, [**2.54**].

183) Click the **top right horizontal line**.

184) Click a **position** above the profile.

185) Enter .500in, [**12.7**].

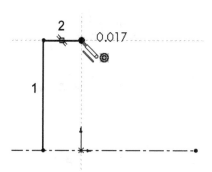

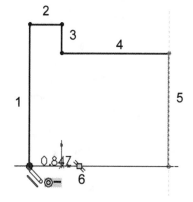

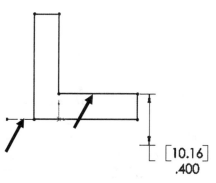

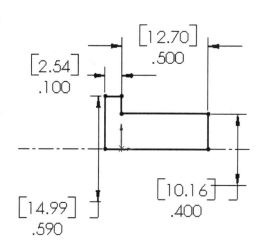

Fit the Model to the Graphics window.
186) Press the **f** key.

Activity: BULB Part-Revolved Base Feature

Insert a Revolved Base feature.

187) Click **Revolved Boss/Base** Boss/B... from the Feature toolbar. The Revolve PropertyManager is displayed. Accept the default settings.

188) Click **OK**  from the Revolve PropertyManager. Revolve1 is displayed in the FeatureManager.

189) Click **Isometric view** .

190) Click **Save** .

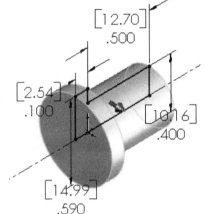

BULB Part-Revolved Boss Feature and Spline Sketch Tool

The BULB requires a second solid Revolved feature. The profile utilizes a complex curve called a Spline, (Non-Uniform Rational B-Spline or NURB). Draw Splines with control points. Adjust the shape of the curve by dragging the control points.

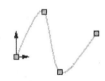

Activity: BULB Part-Revolved Boss Feature and Spline Sketch Tool

Create the Sketch.
191) Click **Right Plane** from the FeatureManager for the Sketch plane.

192) Click **View**; check **Temporary Axes** from the Main menu.

193) Click **Sketch** Sketch from the Sketch toolbar.

194) Click **Right view** . The Temporary Axis is displayed as a horizontal line.

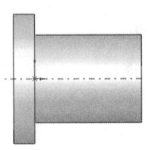

195) Press the **z** key approximately four times to view the top left vertical edge.

Sketch the profile.

196) Click **Spline**  Spline from the Sketch toolbar.

197) Click the **left vertical edge** of the Base feature for the start point.

198) Drag the **mouse pointer** to the left.

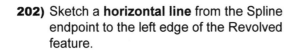

199) Click a **position** above the Temporary Axis for the Control point.

200) Double-click the **Temporary Axis** to create the End point and to end the Spline.

201) Click **Line** Line from the Sketch toolbar.

202) Sketch a **horizontal line** from the Spline endpoint to the left edge of the Revolved feature.

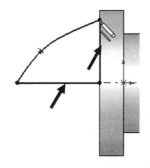

203) Sketch a **vertical line** to the Spline start point, collinear with the left edge of the Revolved feature. Note: Dimensions are not required to create a feature.

Insert a Revolved Boss feature.
204) Right-click **Select**.

205) Click the **Temporary Axis** in the Graphics window.

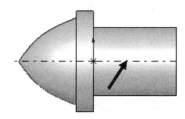

206) Click **Revolved Boss/Base** Boss/B... from the Features toolbar. The Revolve PropertyManager is displayed. Axis<1> is displayed in the Revolve Parameters box. Accept the default options.

207) Click **OK** from the Revolve PropertyManager. Revolve2 is displayed in the FeatureManager.

208) Click **Isometric view** . Click **Save** .

The points of the Spline dictate the shape
of the Spline. Edit control points in the
sketch to produce different results for the
Revolved Boss feature.

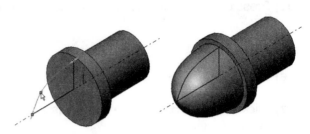

BULB Part-Revolved Thin Cut Feature

A Revolved Thin Cut feature removes material by rotating an open sketch profile around
an axis. Sketch an open profile on the Right Plane. Add a Coincident relation to the
silhouette and vertical edge. Insert dimensions.

Sketch a Centerline to create a diameter dimension for a revolved profile. The
Temporary axis does not produce a diameter dimension.

Note: If lines snap to grid intersections, uncheck Tools, Sketch Settings, Enable Snapping
for the next activity.

Activity: BULB Part-Revolved Thin Cut Feature

Create the Sketch.
209) Click **Right Plane** from the FeatureManager.

210) Click **Sketch** Sketch . Click **Right view** .

211) Click **Line** Line from the Sketch toolbar.

212) Click the **midpoint** of the top silhouette edge. Sketch a **line**
downward and to the right. Sketch a horizontal **line** to the
right vertical edge.

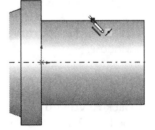

213) Right-click **Select**.

Add a Coincident relation.
214) Click the **end point** of the line.

215) Hold the **Ctrl** key down.

216) Click the right **vertical edge**.

217) Release the **Ctrl** key.

218) Click **Coincident** from the
Add Relations box.

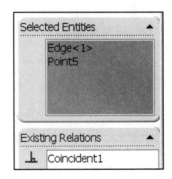

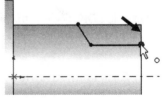

219) Click **OK**  from the Properties PropertyManager.

Sketch a Centerline.
220) Click **View**; uncheck **Temporary Axes** from the Main menu.

221) Click **Centerline** Centerl... from the Sketch toolbar.

222) Sketch a **horizontal centerline** through the Origin.

Add dimensions.

223) Click **Smart Dimension**  Dimens... from the Sketch toolbar.

224) Click the **horizontal centerline**. Click the **short horizontal line**. Click a **position** below the profile to create a diameter dimension.

225) Enter **.260**in, [**6.6**].

226) Click the **short horizontal** line.

227) Click a **position** above the profile to create a horizontal dimension.

228) Enter **.070**in, [**1.78**]. Click **OK** from the Dimension PropertyManager. The sketch is fully defined and is displayed in black.

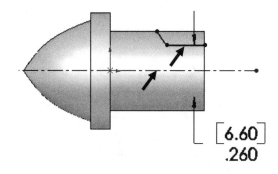

$\not\!{}^{}$ For Revolved features, the ∅ symbol is not displayed in the part. The ∅ symbol is displayed when inserted into the drawing.

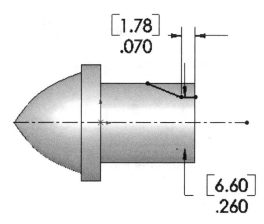

Insert the Revolved Cut Thin feature.

229) Click the **centerline**. Click **Revolved Cut** Cut from the Features toolbar.

230) Click **No** to the Warning Message, "Would you like the sketch to be automatically closed?"

231) Check the **Thin Feature** box. Enter **.150**in, [**3.81**] for Direction 1 Thickness. Click the **Reverse Direction arrow**.

232) Click **OK** ✅ from the Cut-Revolve
PropertyManager. Cut-Revolve-Thin1
is displayed in the FeatureManager.

233) Click **Save** 💾.

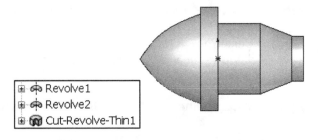

BULB Part-Dome Feature

A Dome feature creates spherical or elliptical shaped geometry. Use the Dome feature to create the Connector feature of the BULB. The Dome feature requires a face and a Height value.

Activity: BULB Part-Dome Feature

Insert the Dome feature.
234) Click the **back circular face** of Revolve1. Revolve1 is highlighted in the FeatureManager.

235) Click **Insert**, **Features**, **Dome** 🔵 Dome... from the Main menu.

236) Enter **.100**in, **[2.54]** for Distance.

237) Click **OK** ✅ from the Dome PropertyManager. Dome1 is displayed.

238) Click **Isometric view** 🔲.

239) Click **Save** 💾.

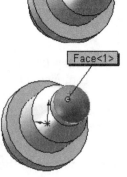

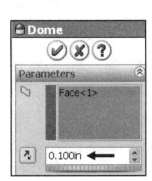

BULB Part-Circular Pattern Feature

The Pattern feature creates one or more instances of a feature or a group of features. The Circular Pattern feature places the instances around an axis of revolution.

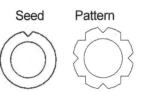

Seed   Pattern

The Circular Pattern feature requires a seed feature. The seed feature is the first feature in the pattern. The seed feature in this section is the V-shaped Extruded Cut feature.

Activity: BULB Part-Circular Pattern Feature

Create the Seed Cut.

240) Click the **front face** of the Base feature for the Sketch Plane. Revolve1 is highlighted in the FeatureManager.

241) Click **Sketch** Sketch from the Sketch toolbar.

242) Click the **outside circular edge**.

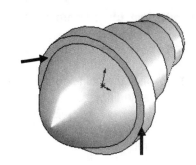

243) Click **Convert Entities** Convert from the Sketch toolbar.

244) Click **Front view** .

245) **Zoom in** $\mathbb{Q}$ on the top half of the BULB.

Sketch the Centerline.

246) Click **Centerline** Centerl... from the Sketch toolbar.

247) Sketch a **vertical centerline** coincident with the top and bottom circular circles and coincident with the Right Plane.

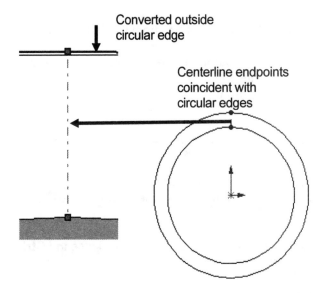

Converted outside circular edge

Centerline endpoints coincident with circular edges

Sketch a V-shaped line.
248) Click **Tools, Sketch Tools, Dynamic Mirror** from the Main menu.

249) Click the **centerline**.

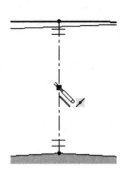

250) Click **Line** Line 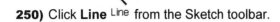 from the Sketch toolbar.

251) Click the **midpoint** of the centerline.

252) Click the coincident **outside circle edge to the left** of the centerline.

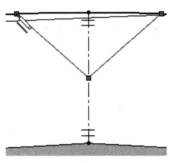

253) Click **Tools**, **Sketch Tools**, **Dynamic Mirror** from the Main menu.

Trim unwanted geometry.

254) Click **Trim Entities**  Trim from the Sketch toolbar.

255) Click **Power trim** from the Options box.

256) Click a **position** in the Graphics window and drag the mouse pointer until it intersects the **circle circumference**.

257) Click **OK** from the Trim PropertyManager.

Add a Perpendicular relation.
258) Click the **left** V shape line. Hold the **Ctrl** key down.

259) Click the **right** V shape line. Release the **Ctrl** key.

260) Click **Perpendicular** ⊥ from the Add Relations box.

261) Click **OK** from the Properties PropertyManager. The Sketch is fully defined.

Create an Extruded Cut feature.

262) Click **Extruded Cut** Cut from the Features toolbar.

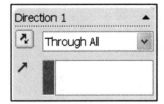

263) Select **Through All** for End Condition in Direction 1.

264) Click **OK** from the Cut-Extrude PropertyManager.

Fit the drawing to the Graphics window.

265) Press the **f** key. Click **Isometric view** . Click **Save** .

Reuse Geometry in the feature. The Extruded Cut feature utilized Centerline, Mirror Entity, and Geometric relations to create a sketch with no dimensions.

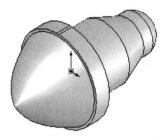

Cut-Extrude1 is the seed feature for the pattern. Create 4 copies of the seed feature. A copy of a feature is called an instance. Modify 4 instances to 8.

Insert the Circular Pattern feature.
266) Click **Cut-Extrude1** from the FeatureManager.

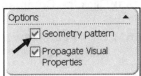

267) Click **Circular Pattern** Circular Pattern from the Features toolbar. The Circular Pattern PropertyManager is displayed.

268) Click inside the **Pattern Axis** box. Click **View**; check **Temporary Axes** from the main menu.

269) Click the **Temporary Axis**. Enter **4** in the Number of Instances spin box.

270) Check the **Equal spacing** box.

271) Check the **Geometry pattern** box.

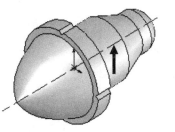

272) Click **OK** from the Circular Pattern PropertyManager.

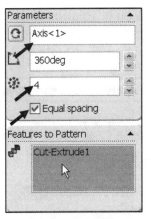

Edit the Circular Pattern feature.
273) Right-click **CirPattern1** from the FeatureManager.

274) Click **Edit Feature**. Enter **8** in the Number of Instances box.

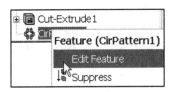

275) Click **OK** from the CirPattern1 PropertyManager.

276) Rename **Cut-Extrude1** to **Seed Cut**.

Hide the reference geometry.
277) Click **View**; uncheck **Temporary Axes** from the Main menu.

278) Click **Save** 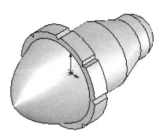.

 Rename the seed feature of a pattern to locate it quickly for future assembly.

Customizing Toolbars and Short Cut Keys

The default toolbars contain numerous icons that represent basic functions. Additional features and functions are available that are not displayed on the default toolbars.

You have utilized the z key for Zoom In/Out, the f key for Zoom to Fit, and Ctrl-C/Ctrl-V to Copy/Paste. Short Cut keys save time. Assign a key to execute a SolidWorks function. Create a Short Cut key for the Temporary Axis.

Activity: Customizing Toolbars and Short Cut Keys

Customize the toolbar.
279) Click **Tools**, **Customize** from the Main menu.

Place the Shape icon on the Features toolbar.
280) Click the **Commands** tab.

281) Click **Features** from the Categories box.

282) Drag the **Shape** icon into the Features toolbar.

Customize the Keyboard.
283) Click the **Keyboard** tab from the Customize dialog box.

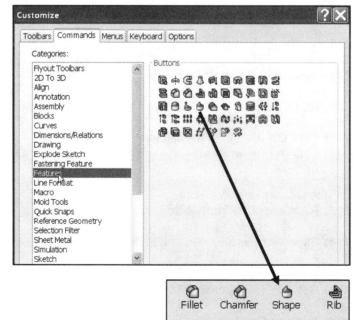

284) Select **View** for Categories. Select **Temporary Axes** for Commands.

285) Press the **Shift + R** keys. Click **OK**. Press the **Shift + R** keys to toggle the display of the Temporary Axes.

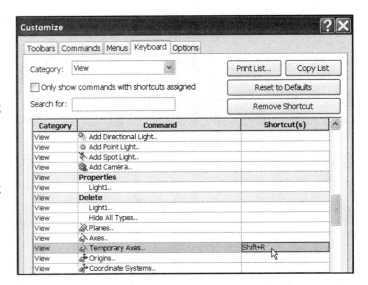

 Test the proposed Short Cut key, before you customize your keyboard. Refer to the default Keyboard Short Cut table in the Appendix.

Set up View Short Cut keys for Planes (P), Origins (O), Temporary Axis (R) and Hide All Types (H). You utilize these view commands often. Short Cut keys are displayed to the right of the command.

Additional information on Revolved Boss/Base, Spline, Circular Pattern, Dome, Line/Arc Sketching is located in SolidWorks Help Topics. Keywords: Revolved (features), Spline, Pattern (Circular), and Dome.

Review of the BULB Part.

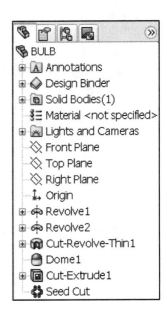

The Revolved Base feature utilized a sketched profile on the Right Plane and a centerline. The Revolved Boss feature utilized a Spline sketched profile. A Spline is a complex curve.

You created the Revolved Thin Cut feature at the base of the BULB to remove material. A centerline was inserted to add a diameter dimension. The Dome feature was inserted on the back face of the BULB. The Circular Pattern feature was created from an Extruded Cut. The Extruded Cut feature utilized existing geometry and required no dimensions.

Toolbars and keyboards were customized to save time. Always verify that a Short Cut key is not predefined in SolidWorks.

Project Summary

You are designing a FLASHLIGHT assembly. You created two parts in this project:

- LENS.
- BULB.

Both parts utilized the Revolved Base feature. The Revolved feature required a Sketch plane, Sketch Profile, Axis of revolution, and an Angle of rotation.

You created and edited the following features: Extruded Base, Extruded Boss, Extruded Cut, Revolved Base, Revolved Boss, Revolved Boss Thin, Revolved Thin Cut, Shell, Hole Wizard, Dome, and Circular Pattern.

You applied transparent optical properties to the LENS part and established the following Geometric relations: Equal, Coincident, Symmetric, Intersection, and Perpendicular.

The other parts for the FLASHLIGHT assembly are addressed in Project 3.

Project Terminology

Centerpoint Arc: An arc Sketch tool that requires a centerpoint, start point and end point.

Circular Pattern: A feature that creates a pattern of features or faces in a circular array about an axis.

Convert Entities: A sketch tool that projects one or more curves onto the current sketch plane. Select an edge, loop, face, curve, or external sketch contour, set of edges, or set of sketch curves.

Dome: A feature used to add a spherical or elliptical dome to a selected face.

Hole Wizard: The Hole Wizard feature is used to create specialized holes in a solid. The Hole Wizard creates simple, tapped, counterbore and countersunk holes using a step-by-step procedure.

Mirror Entities: A sketch tool that mirrors sketch geometry to the opposite side of a sketched centerline.

Offset Entities: A sketch tool utilized to create sketch curves offset by a specified distance. Select sketch entities, edges, loops, faces, curves, set of edges or a set of curves.

Revolved Boss/Base: A feature used to add material by revolutions. A Revolved feature requires a centerline, a sketch on a sketch plane and an angle of revolution. The sketch is revolved around the centerline.

Revolved Cut: A feature used to remove material by revolutions. A Revolved Cut requires a centerline, a sketch on a sketch plane and angle of revolution. The sketch is revolved around the centerline.

Shell: A feature used to remove faces of a part by a specified wall thickness.

Silhouette Edge: The imaginary edge of a cylinder or cylindrical face.

Spline: A complex sketch curve.

Thin option: The Thin option for the Revolved Boss and Revolved Cut utilizes an open sketch to add or remove material, respectively.

Questions

1. Identify and describe the function of the following features:

    *   Revolved Base.

    *   Revolved Boss.

    *   Revolved Cut.

    *   Revolved Cut Thin.

    *   Dome.

2. Describe a symmetric relation.

3. When is the Trim Entity Sketch tool used?

4. Explain the function of the Shell feature.

5. A Center point arc requires _____ points?

6. Describe the Hole Wizard feature.

7. What is a Spline?

8. Identify the required information for a Circular Pattern.

9. Name the Pull down menu that lists the Temporary Axis.

10. Describe the procedure to Show/Hide a Plane.

11. Describe the differences between Offset Entities and Convert Entities.

12. Identify the type of line required to utilize Mirror Entities.

13. Identify the geometric relation automatically created between Mirror Entities.

14. True of False. Select the arc center point to dimension an arc to its max condition.

15. True of False. The Transparency Optical Property is located in the Features toolbar.

16. Additional information of the Revolve Boss\Base and Revolve Cut features is located in _____ .

Exercises

Exercises 2.1a-2.1e:

Create the following parts. Utilize Geometric relations and Symmetry. Dimensions are not provided.

Exercise 2.1a: BREADBOX Part

Create the BREADBOX Part. Utilize the Shell feature to remove the Front face. The part is symmetric about the Right Plane.

Exercise 2.1b: RING Part

Create the RING Part. Utilize a Revolve Base feature.

Exercise 2.1c: DUMBBELL Part

Create the DUMBBELL Part. Utilize a Revolve Base feature.

Exercise 2.1d: SPINDLE Part

Utilize a Revolve Base feature. The holes are created with two Circular Pattern features. Utilize construction geometry and Geometric relations to center the seed for each pattern.

Exercise 2.1e: GAMEPIECE Part

Utilize Geometric relations and sketch tools to create the seed feature.

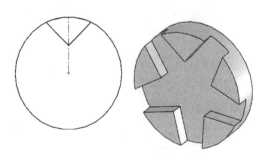

Exercise 2.2: Hole Wizard-Block Part

Create a Counter bore, Counter sink, Tapped, and Hole type
with the Hole Wizard feature on the top face. Utilize different
End Conditions.

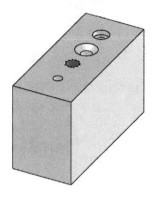

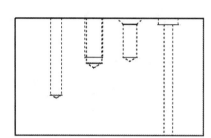

Exercise 2.3: D-Size Battery Part

Measure a D size battery to determine feature dimensions. Create the
D-Size Battery part.

Exercise 2.4: GLASS Parts

Create various GLASS Parts styles. Use
real objects to determine the overall size
and shape of the Base feature.

Project 3

Sweep, Loft, and Additional Features

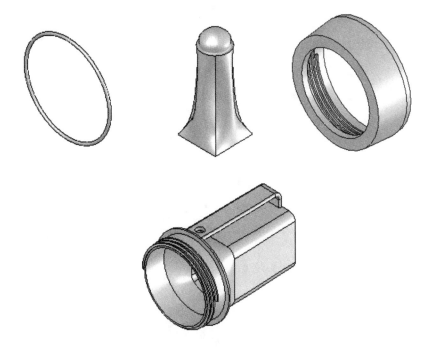

Below are the desired outcomes and usage competencies based on the completion of Project 3.

Project Desired Outcomes:	Usage Competencies:

• Create four FLASHLIGHT parts:
 	
   o O-RING.
   o SWITCH.
   o LENSCAP.
   o HOUSING.
	• Specific knowledge and understanding of the following Features: Extruded Base, Extruded Boss, Extruded Cut, Sweep Base, Sweep Boss, Loft Base, Loft Boss, Mirror, Draft, Shape, Rib, and Linear Pattern.

• Establish Geometric relations: Pierce, Tangent, Equal, Intersection, Coincident, and Midpoint.	• Ability to apply multiple Geometric relations to a model. • Skill to apply Design Intent to Sketches, Features, Parts, and Assemblies.

Notes:

Project 3-Sweep, Loft and Additional Features

Project Overview

Create four new parts for the FLASHLIGHT assembly:

- O-RING.
- SWITCH.
- LENSCAP.
- HOUSING.

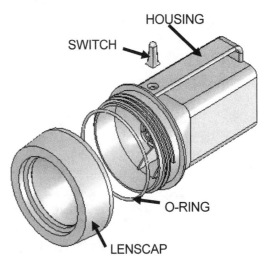

Project 3 introduces the Sweep and Loft features. The O-RING utilizes a Sweep Base feature. The SWITCH utilizes the Loft feature. The LENSCAP and HOUSING utilize the Sweep Boss and Loft Boss features.

A Sweep feature requires a minimum of two sketches: path and profile. Sketch the path (cross-section) and profile on different planes. The profile follows the path to create the following Sweep features:

- Sweep Base.
- Sweep Boss.

The Loft feature requires a minimum of two profiles sketched on different planes. The profiles are blended together to create the following Loft features:

- Loft Base.
- Loft Boss.

Utilize existing features to create the Rib, Linear Pattern, and Mirror features. Utilize existing faces to create the Draft and Shape features. The LENSCAP and HOUSING combines the Extruded Boss/Base, Extruded Cut, Revolved Thin Cut, Shell, and Circular Pattern with the Sweep and Loft feature.

After completing the activities in this project, you will be able to:

- Utilize the following Sketch tools: Point, Centerline, Convert Entities, Trim Entities, and Sketch Fillet.
- Establish the following Geometric relations: Pierce, Tangent, Equal, Intersection, Coincident, and Midpoint.

- Create the following features: Sweep Boss/Base, Loft Boss/Base, Mirror, Draft, Shape, Rib, and Linear Pattern.

- Review the Extruded Boss/Base, Extruded Cut, Revolve Cut Thin, Shell, and Circular Pattern features.

- Suppress and Un-suppress various features.

- Reuse geometry from sketches, features, and other parts to develop new geometry.

- Create four new parts for the FLASHLIGHT assembly:

   o O-RING.

   o SWITCH.

   o LENSCAP.

   o HOUSING.

O-RING Part-Sweep Base Feature

The O-RING part is positioned between the LENSCAP and the LENS. Create the O-RING with a Sweep Base feature. The Sweep-Base feature uses:

- A circular path sketched on the Front Plane.

- A small cross section profile sketched on the Right Plane.

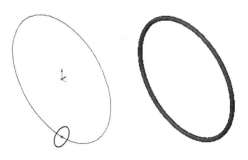

The Pierce geometric relation positions the center of the cross section profile on the sketched path.

Path & Profile   Sweep feature

Utilize the PART-IN-ANSI Template for inch units. Utilize the PART-MM-ISO Template for millimeter units. Millimeter dimensions are provided in brackets [x].

Activity: O-RING Part

Create the new part.

1) Click **File**, **New** □ from the Main menu. Click the **MY-TEMPLATES** tab.

2) Double-click **PART-IN-ANSI**, **[PART-MM-ISO]**.

3) Click **Save** 🖫 .

4) Select the **PROJECTS** folder.

5) Enter **O-RING** for File name.

6) Enter **O-RING FOR LENS** for Description. Click **Save**.

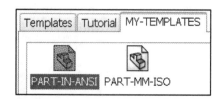

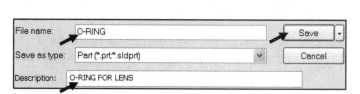

Create the Sweep path.
7) Click **Front Plane** from the FeatureManager for the Sketch plane.

8) Click **Sketch** Sketch .

9) Click **Circle** Circle from the Sketch toolbar.

10) Sketch a **circle** centered at the Origin 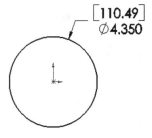.

Add a dimension.

11) Click **Smart Dimension** Smart Dimens... from the Sketch toolbar.

12) Click the **circumference** of the circle. Click a **position** off the profile.

13) Enter **4.350**in, [**110.49**].

Close the Sketch.

14) Click **Exit Sketch** Exit Sketch . Sketch1 is displayed in the FeatureManager.

15) Rename **Sketch1** to **Sketch-path**.

Create the Sweep profile.
16) Click **Isometric view** .

17) Click **Right Plane** from the FeatureManager.

18) Click **Sketch** Sketch .

19) Click **Circle** Circle from the Sketch toolbar.

20) Create a **small circle left** of the Sketch-path on the Right Plane.

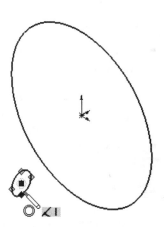

Add a Pierce relation.
21) Right-click **Select**.

22) Click the **small circle center** point.

23) Hold the **Ctrl** key down.

24) Click the **large circle** circumference. Release the **Ctrl** key.

25) Click **Pierce** from the Add Relations box. The center point of the small circle pierces the Sketch-path (large circle).

26) Click **OK** from the Properties PropertyManager.

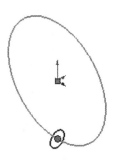

Add a dimension.

27) Click **Smart Dimension** Dimens... . Click the **circumference** of the small circle.

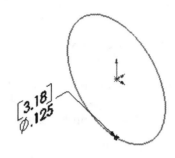

28) Click a **position** to the left of the profile.

29) Enter **.125**in, [**3.18**].

Close the Sketch.

30) Click **Exit Sketch** Sketch . Sketch2 is displayed in the FeatureManager.

31) Rename **Sketch2** to **Sketch-profile**.

The FeatureManager displays two sketches: Sketch-path and Sketch-profile. Create the Sketch-path before the Sketch-profile. The Sketch-profile requires a Pierce relation to the path.

 Improve visibility. Small profiles are difficult to dimension on large paths. Perform the following steps to create a detailed small profile:

- Create a large cross section profile that contains the required dimensions and relationships. The black profile is fully defined.

- Pierce the profile to the path. Add dimensions to reflect the true size.

- Rename the profile and path to quickly located sketches in the FeatureManager.

Insert the Sweep feature.

32) Click **Swept Boss/Base** Boss/B... from the Features toolbar. The Sweep PropertyManager is displayed. Sketch-profile is displayed in the Profile box.

33) **Expand** O-RING from the fly-out FeatureManager.

34) Click inside the **Path** box.

35) Click **Sketch-path** from the fly-out FeatureManager.

36) Click **OK** from the Sweep PropertyManager.

37) Rename **Sweep1** to **Base-Sweep**.

38) Click **Isometric view** .

39) Click **Save** .

Review of the O-RING Part

The O-RING part utilized a Sweep feature. The Sweep feature required a Sketched path and a Sketched profile. The path was a large circle sketched on the Front Plane. The profile was a small circle sketched on the Right Plane. The Pierce Geometric relation was utilized to attach the profile to the path.

The Sweep feature required a minimum of two sketches. You created a simple Sweep feature. Sweep features can be simple or complex.

Recognize the properties and understand the order of the sketches to create successful simple Sweep features. The following are the steps to create successful Sweeps:

- Create the path as a separate sketch. The path is open or closed. The path is a set curves contained in one sketch. The path can also be one curve or a set of model edges.

- Create each profile as a separate sketch. The profile is closed for a Sweep Boss/Base feature.

- Fully define each sketch. The sketch is displayed in black.

- Sketch the profile last before inserting the sweep feature.

- Position the start point of the path on the plane of the profile.

- Path, profile and solid geometry cannot intersect themselves.

Additional information on Sweep and Pierce are found in SolidWorks Help Topics. Keywords: Sweep, (overview, simple sweeps) and Pierce (relations).

SWITCH Part-Loft Base Feature

The SWITCH is a purchased part. The SWITCH is a complex assembly. Create the outside casing of the SWITCH as a simplified part. Create the SWITCH with the Loft Base feature.

The orientation of the SWITCH is based on the position in the assembly. The SWITCH is comprised of three cross section profiles. Sketch each profile on a different plane.

The first plane is the Top Plane. Create two reference planes parallel to the Top Plane.

Sketch one profile on each plane. The design intent of the sketch is to reduce the number of dimensions.

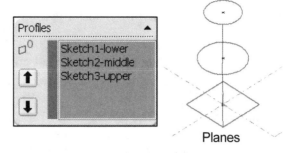

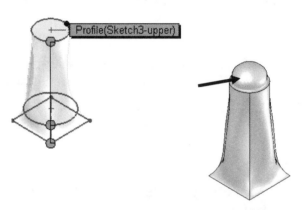

Planes

Utilize symmetry, construction geometry and Geometric Relations to control three sketches with one dimension.

Insert the Loft feature. Select the profiles to create the Loft feature.

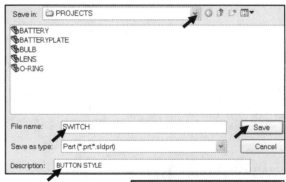

Insert the Shape feature to the top face of the Loft. Modify the dimensions to complete the SWITCH.

Activity: Switch Part-Loft Base Feature

Create a new part.

40) Click **File**, **New** ⬜ from the Main menu.

41) Click the **MY-TEMPLATES** tab.

42) Double-click **PART-IN-ANSI**, [**PART-MM-ISO**].

43) Click **Save** 💾.

44) Select the **PROJECTS** folder.

45) Enter **SWITCH** for File name.

46) Enter **BUTTON STYLE** for Description.

47) Click **Save**. The SWITCH FeatureManager is displayed.

Display the Top Plane.

48) Right-click **Top Plane** from the FeatureManager.

49) Click **Show**.

50) Click **Isometric view** .

Insert two Reference planes.

51) Hold the **Ctrl** key down. Click and drag the **Top Plane** upward. Release the **mouse button**. Release the **Ctrl** key.

52) Enter .**500**in, [**12.7**] for Offset Distance. Enter **2** for # of Planes to Create.

53) Click **OK** from the Plane PropertyManager.

54) Click **Front view** to display Plane1 and Plane2 offset from the Top Plane.

55) Click **Isometric view** .

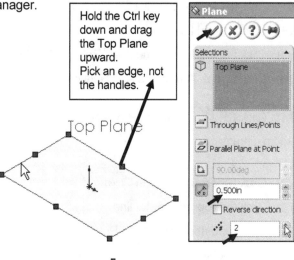

Hold the Ctrl key down and drag the Top Plane upward. Pick an edge, not the handles.

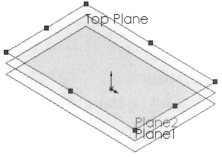

Insert Sketch1. Sketch1 is a square on the Top Plane.

56) Click **Top Plane** from the FeatureManager.

57) Click **Sketch** Sketch .

58) Click **Rectangle** Rectan... from the Sketch toolbar.

59) Sketch a **Rectangle** centered about the Origin as illustrated.

Create a diagonal centerline.

60) Click **Centerline** Centerl... from the Sketch toolbar.

61) Click the two **corner points** of the rectangle.

Add a Midpoint relation.

62) Right-click **Select**. Click the **Origin** .

63) Hold the **Ctrl** key down. Click the diagonal **centerline**.

64) Release the **Ctrl** key.

65) Click **Midpoint** from the Add Relations box.

66) Click **OK** from the Properties PropertyManager.

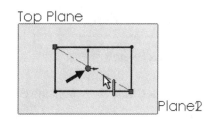

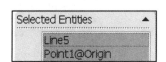

Selected Entities

Line5

Point1@Origin

Add an Equal relation.

67) Click the **left vertical** line.

68) Hold the **Ctrl** key down.

69) Click the **top horizontal line**. Release the **Ctrl** key.

70) Click **Equal =** from the Add Relations box.

71) Click **OK** from the Properties PropertyManager.

Add a dimension.

72) Click **Smart Dimension** Smart Dimens...

73) Click the **top horizontal** line.

74) Click a **position** above the Profile.

75) Enter **.500**in, [**12.7**].

Close the Sketch.

76) Click **Exit Sketch** Exit Sketch.

77) Rename **Sketch1** to **Sketch1-lower**.

78) Click **Save** 🖫.

Top Plane

Plane2

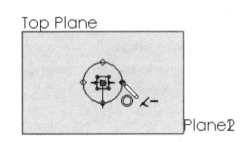

Insert Sketch2 on Plane1.

79) Click **Plane1** from the FeatureManager.

80) Click **Top view** 🗗.

81) Click **Sketch** Sketch.

82) Click **Circle** ⊕ Circle from the Sketch toolbar.

83) Create a **circle** centered at the Origin.

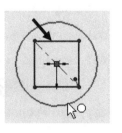

Top Plane

Plane2

Add a Tangent relation.

84) Right-click **Select**.

85) Click the **circumference** of the circle.

86) Hold the **Ctrl** key down.

87) Click the **top horizontal** Sketch1-lower line.

88) Release the **Ctrl** key.

89) Click **Tangent** ⟋ from the Add Relations box.

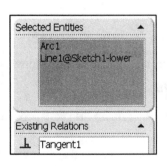

90) Click **OK** from the Properties PropertyManager.
Close the Sketch.

91) Click **Exit Sketch** .

92) Rename **Sketch2** to **Sketch2-middle**.

93) Click **Isometric view** 🔲 .

Insert Sketch3 on Plane2.
94) Click **Plane2** from the FeatureManager.

95) Click **Sketch** Sketch .

96) Click **Top view** ⊞ .

97) Click **Centerline** Centerl... from the Sketch toolbar.

98) Sketch a **centerline** coincident with the Origin and the upper right corner point.

99) Click **Point** Point from the Sketch toolbar.

100) Click the **midpoint** of the right diagonal centerline.

101) Click **Circle** Circle from the Sketch toolbar.

102) Create a **circle** centered at the Origin to the midpoint of the diagonal centerline as illustrated.

Close the Sketch.

103) Click **Exit Sketch** Sketch .

104) Rename **Sketch3** to **Sketch3-upper**.

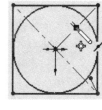

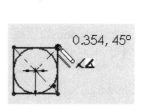

0.354, 45°

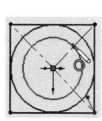

SWITCH
- 🅰 Annotations
- ◇ Design Binder
- ⋮≡ Material <not specified>
- 🔆 Lights and Cameras
- ◇ Front Plane
- ◇ Top Plane
- ◇ Right Plane
- ↳ Origin
- ◇ Plane1
- ◇ Plane2
- ℮ Sketch1-lower
- ℮ Sketch2-middle
- ℮ Sketch3-upper

Insert a Loft feature.

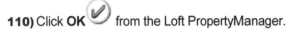

105) Click **Lofted Boss/Base** Boss/B...
from the Features toolbar.

106) Click **Isometric view** .

107) Click the **front corner** of Sketch1-
lower.

108) Click **Sketch2-middle**.

109) Click **Sketch3-upper**.

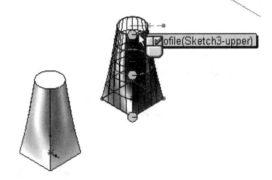

Click the front of
Sketch1-lower,
Sketch2-middle
and Sketch3-
upper.

110) Click **OK** from the Loft PropertyManager.

111) Rename **Loft1** to **Base Loft**.

Hide the planes.
112) Click **View**; uncheck **Planes** from the Main
menu.

Save the part.

113) Click **Save** .

The system displays a preview curve and preview loft as
you select the profiles. Use the Up button and Down button
in the Loft PropertyManager to rearrange the order of the
profiles.

Redefine incorrect selections efficiently. Right-click in
the Graphics window, click Clear Selections to remove
selected profiles. Select the correct profiles.

SWITCH Part-Shape Feature

Insert the Shape feature on the top face of the Loft Base feature. The Shape feature
deforms a surface. Control the surface deformation through the Pressure and Curve
Influence sliders. Preview the results. Adjust the sliders to obtain a similar shape display
in the illustrations.

Activity: SWITCH Part-Shape Feature

Insert the Shape feature.

114) Click the **top face** of the Base Loft feature.

115) Click **Insert**, **Features**, **Shape** 🔵 Shape... from the Main menu.

116) Click the **Controls** tab from the Shape Feature dialog box.

117) Drag the **Gains Pressure slider** to approximately 12. The Pressure slider deflates/inflates the shape of the surface.

118) Drag the **Advanced controls Resolution slider** to 8. The Resolution slider changes the number of points of the deformed face.

119) Click **OK** to display the Shape Feature.

Experiment with the Shape feature to display different results. The Characteristics sliders adjust the degree of bend and stretch in the surface.

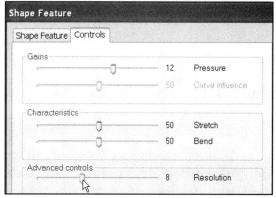

The top face of your Switch will vary depending on the Shape parameters.

The distance between the Loft planes contribute to the shape of the Loft feature. Modify the offset distance between the Top plane and Plane1.

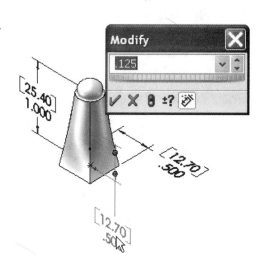

Modify the Loft Base feature.

120) Right-click **Annotations** from the FeatureManager.

121) Click **Show Feature Dimensions**.

122) Double-click on the Plane1 offset dimension, **.500**, [**12.700**].

123) Enter **.125**in, [**3.180**].

124) Click **Rebuild** 🔵.

125) Click the **Green Check mark** ✔.

126) Click **OK** ✅ from the Dimension PropertyManager

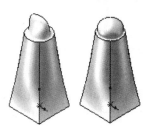

Hide Feature dimension.

127) Right-click **Annotations** in the FeatureManager.

128) Uncheck **Show Feature Dimensions**.

Display Feature Statistics.

129) Click **Tools, Feature Statistics** from the Main menu.

View the SWITCH feature statistics.

130) Click **Close** from the Feature Statistics dialog box.

131) Click **Save** 💾.

Feature Statistics			
Print...	Copy	Refresh	Close

SWITCH
Features 7, Solids 1, Surfaces 0

Feature Order	Time %	Time(s)
Shape Fea...	93.74	1.41
Base Loft	5.20	0.08
Sketch1-l...	1.07	0.02
Plane1	0.00	0.00
Plane2	0.00	0.00
Sketch2-...	0.00	0.00
Sketch3-u...	0.00	0.00

The Shape feature Control parameters produce various results. The Feature Statistics report displays the Rebuild time for the Shape feature and the other SWITCH features. As feature geometry becomes more complex, the rebuild time increases.

🔍 Additional information on Loft, Shape feature and Reference Planes are found in SolidWorks Help Topics. Keywords: Loft (simple), Shape (features) and Reference Geometry (Planes).

 Review of the SWITCH Part

The SWITCH utilized the Loft feature. The Loft feature required three planes. One profile was sketched on each plane. The three profiles were combined to create the Loft feature.

The Shape feature deformed geometry on the top face of the Loft. Through a series of sliding control parameters, the top faced deformed. The SWITCH utilized a simple Loft. Lofts become more complex with additional Guide Curves. Complex Lofts contain hundreds of profiles.

SWITCH
⊞ Annotations
⊞ Design Binder
⊞ Solid Bodies(1)
Material <not specified>
⊞ Lights and Cameras
Front Plane
Top Plane
Right Plane
Origin
Plane1
Plane2
⊞ Base Loft
Shape Feature1

Four Major Categories of Solid Features

The LENSCAP and HOUSING combine the four major categories of solid features:

- Extrude: Requires a profile.

- Revolve: Requires a profile and an axis of revolution.

- Sweep: Requires a profile and a path sketched on different planes.

- Loft: Requires two or more profiles sketched on different planes.

Identify the simple features of the LENSCAP and HOUSING. Extrude and Revolve are simple features. Only a single sketch profile is required. Sweep and Loft are more complex features. Two or more sketches are required.

Example: The O-RING was created as a Sweep. Could the O-RING utilize an Extruded feature? Answer: No. Extruding a circular profile produces a cylinder.

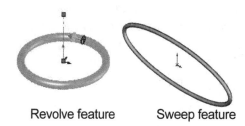

Can the O-RING utilize a Revolved feature? Answer: Yes. Revolving a circular profile about a centerline creates the O-RING.

Revolve feature   Sweep feature

A Sweep feature is required if the O-RING contained a non-circular path. Example: A Revolved feature does not work with an elliptical path or a more complex curve as in a paper clip.

Combine the four major features and additional features to create the LENSCAP and HOUSING.

LENSCAP Part

The LENSCAP part is a plastic part used to position the LENS to the HOUSING. The LENSCAP utilizes an Extruded Base, Extruded Cut, Extruded Thin Cut, Shell, Revolved Cut and Sweep features.

The design intent for the LENSCAP requires that a draft angle be incorporated into the Extruded Base and Revolved Cut feature. Create the Revolved Cut feature by referencing the Extrude Base feature geometry. If the draft angle changes, the Revolved Cut also changes.

Insert an Extruded Base feature with a circular profile on the Front Plane. Use the draft option in the Extrude PropertyManager. Enter 5° for draft angle.

Insert an Extruded Cut feature. The Extruded Cut feature should be equal to the diameter of the LENS Revolved Base feature.

Insert a Shell feature. Use the Shell feature and a constant wall thickness.

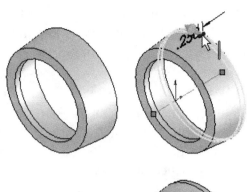

Insert a Revolved Cut feature on the back face. Sketch a single line on the Silhouette edge of the Extruded Base feature. Utilize the Thin Feature option in the Revolve PropertyManager.

Utilize a Sweep feature for the thread.

Insert a new reference plane for the start of the thread. Insert a Helical Curve for the path. Sketch a trapezoid for the profile.

LENSCAP Part-Extruded Base, Extruded Cut, and Shell Features

Create the new part, LENSCAP. Review the Extruded Base, Extruded Cut, and Shell features introduced in Project 4. The first feature is an Extruded Base feature. Select the Front Plane for the Sketch plane. Sketch a circle centered at the Origin for the profile. Utilize a draft angle of 5°.

Create an Extruded Cut feature on the front face of the Base feature. The diameter of the Extruded Cut equals the diameter of the Revolved Base feature of the LENS.

The Shell feature removes the front and back face from the LENSCAP part.

Activity: LENSCAP Part

Create a new part.

132) Click **File**, **New** ⬚ from the Main menu.

133) Click the **MY-TEMPLATES** tab.

134) Double-click **PART-IN-ANSI**, [**PART-MM-ISO**].

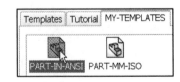

135) Click **Save** 💾.

136) Select the **PROJECTS** folder.

137) Enter **LENSCAP** for File name.

138) Enter **LENSCAP FOR 6V-FLASHLIGHT** for Description.

139) Click **Save**. The LENSCAP FeatureManager is displayed.

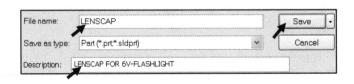

Create the Sketch for the Extruded Base.
140) Click **Front Plane** from the FeatureManager.

141) Click **Sketch** Sketch. Click **Circle** Circle from the Sketch toolbar.

142) Create a **circle** centered at the Origin .

Add a dimension.

143) Click **Smart Dimension** Smart Dimens....

144) Click the **circumference** of the circle.

145) Click a **position** of the profile.

146) Enter **4.900**in, [**124.46**].

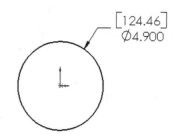

Insert an Extruded Base feature.

147) Click **Extruded Boss/Base** Extruded Boss/B... from the Features toolbar.

148) Click **Reverse Direction** .

149) Enter **1.725**in, [**43.82**] for Depth.

150) Click the **Draft On/Off** button.

151) Enter 5deg for Angle. Click the **Draft outward** box.

152) Click **OK** from the Extrude PropertyManager.

153) Rename **Extrude1** to **Base Extrude**.

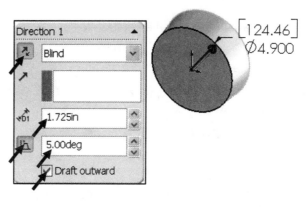

154) Click **Save** .

Create the Sketch for the Extruded Cut.
155) Click the **front face** for the Sketch plane.

156) Click **Sketch** Sketch. Click **Circle** Circle from the Sketch toolbar.

157) Create a **circle** centered at the Origin .

Add a dimension.

158) Click **Smart Dimension** Smart Dimens....

159) Click the **circumference** of the circle. Click a **position** of the profile.

160) Enter **3.875**in, [**98.43**].

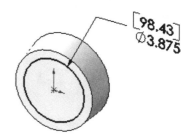

Insert an Extruded Cut feature.

161) Click **Extruded Cut** Cut from the Features toolbar. Blind is the default End Condition.

162) Enter **.275**in, [**6.99**] for Depth.

163) Click the **Draft On/Off** button.

164) Enter **5**deg for Draft Angle.

165) Click **OK** ✓ from the Cut-Extrude PropertyManager.

166) Rename **Cut-Extrude1** to **Front-Cut**.

167) Click **Save** 💾.

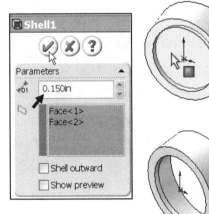

Insert the Shell feature.

168) Click **Shell** Shell from the Features toolbar. The Shell1 PropertyManager is displayed.

169) Click the **front face** of the Front-Cut.

170) Press the **left arrow** approximately 8 times to view the back face.

171) Click the **back face** of the Base Extrude.

172) Enter **.150**in, [**3.81**] for Thickness.

173) Click **OK** ✓ from the Shell1 PropertyManager. Shell1 is displayed in the FeatureManager.

174) Click **Isometric view** .

Display the inside of the Shell.

175) Click **Right view** .

176) Click **Hidden Lines Visible** .

177) Click **Save** 💾.

Note: Use the inside gap created by the Shell feature to seat the O-RING in the assembly.

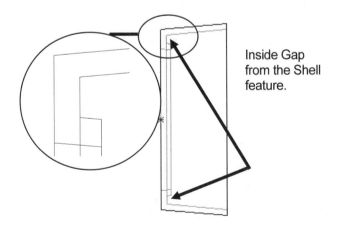

Inside Gap from the Shell feature.

LENSCAP Part-Revolved Thin Cut Feature

The Revolved Thin Cut feature removes material by rotating a sketched profile around a centerline.

The Right Plane is the Sketch plane. The design intent requires that the Revolved Cut maintains the same draft angle as the Extruded Base feature.

Utilize the Convert Entities Sketch tool to create the profile. Small thin cuts are utilized in plastic parts. Utilize the Revolved Thin Cut feature for cylindrical geometry in the next activity.

Sweep Cut Example

Utilize a Sweep Cut for non-cylindrical geometry. The semi-circular Sweep Cut profile is explored in the project exercises.

Activity: LENSCAP Part-Revolved Cut Thin Feature

Create the Sketch.
178) Click **Right Plane** from the FeatureManager.

179) Click **Sketch** Sketch .

Sketch the Centerline.

180) Click **Centerline** Centerl... from the Sketch toolbar.

181) Sketch a **horizontal centerline** through the Origin.

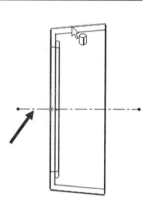

Create the profile.
182) Right-click **Select**.

183) Click the **top silhouette outside** edge.

184) Click **Convert Entities** Convert from the Sketch toolbar.

185) Click and drag the **left endpoint 2/3** towards the right endpoint.

186) Release the **mouse button**.

Add a dimension.

Smart
187) Click **Smart Dimension** Dimens... from the Sketch toolbar.

188) Click the **line**. The aligned dimension arrows are parallel to the profile line.

189) Drag the **text upward** and to the left.

190) Enter **.250**in, **[6.35]**.

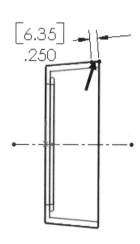

Insert a Revolved Cut feature.

191) Click **Revolved Cut** Cut from the Features toolbar. Do not close the Sketch. The warning message states; "The sketch is currently open."

192) Click **No**. The Cut-Revolve PropertyManager is displayed.

193) Click **Reverse Direction** in the Thin Feature box.

194) Enter .050in, [**1.27**] for Direction 1 Thickness.

195) Click **OK** from the Cut-Revolve PropertyManager.

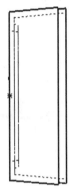

Display the Revolve-Thin Cut.
196) **Rotate** the part to view the back face.

197) Click **Isometric view** .

198) Click **Shaded With Edges** .

199) Rename **Cut-Revolve-Thin1** to **BackCut**.

200) Click **Save** .

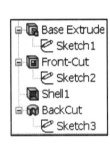

LENSCAP Part-Thread, Sweep Feature, and Helix/Spiral Curve

Utilize the Sweep feature to create the required threads. The thread requires a spiral path. The path is called the ThreadPath. The thread requires a Sketched profile. This cross section profile is called the ThreadSection.

The plastic thread on the LENSCAP requires a smooth lead in. The thread is not flush with the back face. Use an offset Plane to start the thread.

There are numerous steps required to create a thread:

- Create a new Plane for the start of the thread.

- Create the thread path. Utilize Convert Entities and Insert, Curve Helix/Spiral.

- Create a large thread cross section profile for improve visibility.

- Insert the Sweep feature.

- Reduce the size of the thread cross section.

Activity: LENSCAP Part-Thread Path Feature

Create the offset plane.

201) **Rotate** 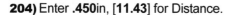 and **Zoom to Area** on the back face of the LENSCAP.

202) Click the **narrow back face** of the Base Extrude feature.

203) Click **Insert**, **Reference Geometry**, **Plane** from the Main menu. The Plane PropertyManager is displayed.

204) Enter **.450**in, **[11.43]** for Distance.

205) Click the **Reverse direction** box.

206) Click **OK** from the Plane PropertyManager.

207) Rename **Plane1** to **ThreadPlane**.

Display the Isometric view with Hidden Lines Removed.

208) Click **Isometric view** .

209) Click **Hidden Lines Removed** .

210) Click **Save** .

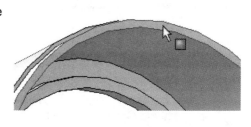

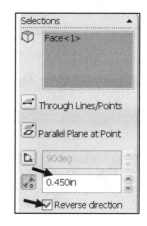

Utilize Convent Entities Sketch tool to extract the back circular edge of the LENSCAP to the ThreadPlane.

Create the Thread path.
211) Click **ThreadPlane** from the FeatureManager.

212) Click **Sketch** Sketch.

213) Click the **back inside circular edge** of the Shell as illustrated.

214) Click **Convert Entities** Convert from the Sketch toolbar.

215) Click **Top view** . The circular edge is displayed on the ThreadPlane.

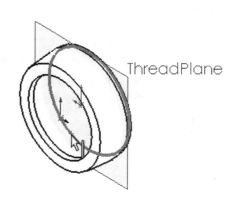

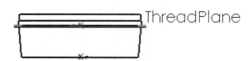

Insert the Helix/Spiral curve path.

216) Click **Insert**, **Curve**, **Helix/Spiral** ⧎ Helix/Spiral...
from the Main menu. The Helix/Spiral
PropertyManager is displayed.

217) Enter .**250**in, [**6.35**] for Pitch.

218) Check the **Reverse direction** box.

219) Enter **2.5** for Revolutions.

220) Enter **0** for Starting angle. The Helix start point and
end point are Coincident with the Top Plane.

221) Check the **Clockwise** box.

222) Click the **Taper Helix** box.

223) Enter **5**deg for Angle.

224) Uncheck the **Taper outward** box.

225) Click **OK** ✅ from the Helix/Spiral
PropertyManager.

226) Rename
Helix/Spiral1 to
ThreadPath.

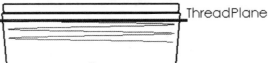

ThreadPlane

227) Click **Save** 💾.

The Helix tapers with the inside wall of the
LENSCAP. Position the Helix within the wall
thickness to prevent errors in the Sweep.

Sketch the profile on the Top Plane. Position the
profile to the Top right of the LENSCAP in order
to pierce to the ThreadPath in the correct location.

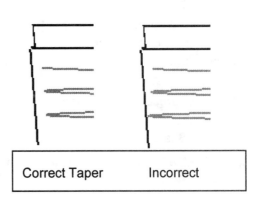

Correct Taper   Incorrect

Hide the ThreadPlane.
228) Right-click **ThreadPlane** from the FeatureManager.

229) Click **Hide**.

Select the Plane for the Thread.
230) Click **Top Plane** from the FeatureManager.

Sketch to the Top right ➡

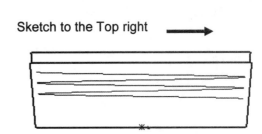

Sketch the profile.

231) Click **Sketch** Sketch.

232) Click **Top view** 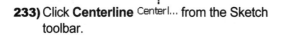.

233) Click **Centerline** Centerl... from the Sketch toolbar.

234) Create a short **vertical centerline** off to the upper top of the ThreadPath feature.

235) Create a second **centerline** horizontal from the Midpoint to the left of the vertical line.

236) Create the third centerline coincident with the left horizontal endpoint. Drag the **centerline upward** until it is approximately the same size as the right vertical line.

237) Create the fourth **centerline** coincident with the left horizontal endpoint. Drag the **centerline** downward until it is approximately the same size as the left vertical line.

Add an Equal relation.
238) Right-click **Select**.

239) Click the **right vertical** line.

240) Hold the **Ctrl** key down. Click the **two left vertical lines**.

241) Release the **Ctrl** key. Click **Equal** = from the Add Relations box.

242) Click **OK** ✔ from the Properties PropertyManager.

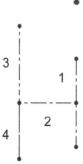

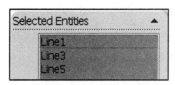

💡 Utilize centerlines and construction geometry with Geometric relations to maintain relationships with minimal dimensions.

💡 Check View, Sketch Relations from the Main menu to display the sketch relation symbols in the Graphics window.

Add a dimension.

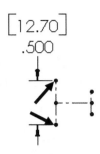

243) Click **Smart Dimension**  from the Sketch toolbar.

244) Click the two **left vertical endpoints**.

245) Click a **position** to the left.

246) Enter **.500**in, [**12.7**].

Sketch the profile. The profile is a trapezoid.

247) Click **Line** Line from the Sketch toolbar.

248) Click the **endpoints** of the vertical centerlines to create the trapezoid.

249) Double-click the **first point** to close and end the line.

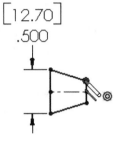

Add an Equal relation.
250) Right-click **Select**. Click the **left vertical line**. Hold the **Ctrl** key down.

251) Click the **top** and **bottom lines** of the trapezoid.

252) Release the **Ctrl** key.

253) Click **Equal = ** from the Add Relations box.

254) Click **OK** from the Properties PropertyManager.

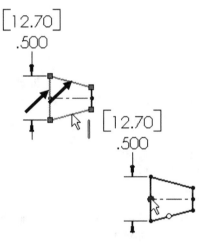

Note: Move the sketch profile above the LENSCAP if required. Window-select the profile and dimension. Utilize Move/Copy Move or Copy from the Sketch toolbar. Click and drag the sketch to a position above the top right corner of the LENSCAP.

Select Edge on the left side

Add a Pierce relation.
255) Click the **left midpoint** of the trapezoid. Hold the **Ctrl** key down. Click the **starting left back edge** of the ThreadPath.

256) Release the **Ctrl** key.

257) Click **Pierce** from the Add Relations box.

258) Click **OK** from the Properties PropertyManager.

Display the sketch in an Isometric view.

259) Click **Isometric view** .

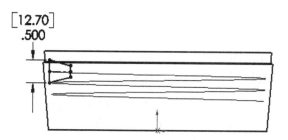

Modify the dimension.

260) Double click the **.500** dimension text.

261) Enter **.125**in, **[3.18]**.

Close the Sketch.

262) Click **Exit Sketch** .

263) Rename **Sketch5** to **ThreadSection**.

264) Click **Save** 💾.

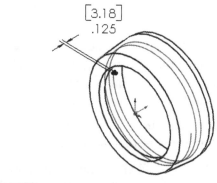

Insert a Sweep feature.

265) Click **Swept Boss/Base** Swept Boss/B... from the Features toolbar. If required, click **ThreadSection** for Profile.

266) Click inside the **Path** box.

267) Click **ThreadPath** from the fly-out FeatureManager.

268) Click **OK** ✅ from the Sweep PropertyManager. Sweep1 is displayed in the FeatureManager.

269) Rename **Sweep1** to **Thread**.

270) Click **Shaded With Edges** 🔲.

271) Click **Save** 💾.

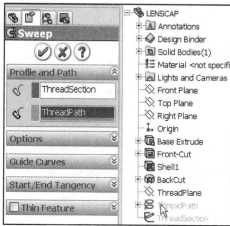

💡 Sweep geometry cannot intersect itself. If the ThreadSection geometry intersects itself, the cross section is too large. Reduce the cross section size and recreate the Sweep feature.

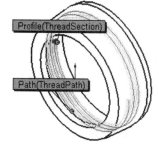

The Thread feature is composed of the following: ThreadSection and ThreadPath.

The ThreadPath contains the circular Sketch and the Helical curve.

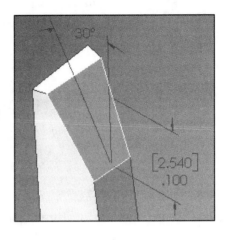

Most threads require a beveled edge or smooth edge for the thread part start point. A 30° Chamfer feature can be utilized on the starting edge of the trapezoid face. This action is left as an exercise.

 Create continuous Sweep features in a single step. Pierce the cross section profile at the start of the sweep path for a continuous Sweep feature.

Un-suppress the Pattern feature to resolve both the Pattern feature and the seed feature at the same time.

The LENSCAP is complete. Review the LENSCAP before moving onto the last part of the FLASHLIGHT.

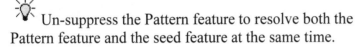 Review of the LENSCAP Part.

The LENSCAP utilized the Extruded Base feature with the Draft Angle option. The Extruded Cut feature created an opening for the LENS. You utilized the Shell feature with constant wall thickness to remove the front and back faces.

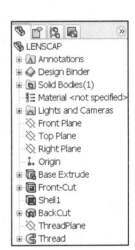

The Revolved Cut Thin feature created the back cut with a single line. The line utilized Convert Entities to maintain the same Draft Angle as the Extruded Base feature.

You utilized a Sweep with a Helical Curve and Thread profile to create the Thread.

HOUSING Part

The HOUSING is a plastic part utilized to contain the BATTERY and to support the LENS. The HOUSING utilizes an Extruded Base, Extruded Boss, Extruded Cut, Loft, Draft, Sweep, Rib, Mirror, and Linear Pattern features.

Insert an Extruded Base feature centered at the Origin.

Insert a Loft Boss feature. The first profile is the converted circular edge of the Extruded Base. The second profile is a sketched on the BatteryLoftPlane.

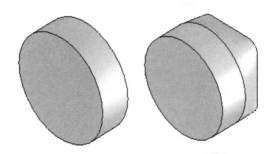

Insert an Extruded Boss feature. The sketch is a converted edge from the Loft Boss. The depth is determined from the height of the BATTERY.

Insert a Shell feature to create a thin walled part.

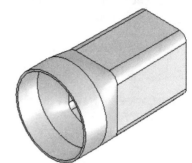

Insert the second Extruded Boss feature. Create a solid circular ring on the back circular face of the Extruded Base feature. Insert the Draft feature to add a draft angle to the circular face of the HOUSING. The design intent for the Extruded Base feature requires you to maintain the same LENSCAP draft angle.

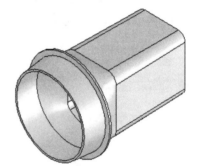

Insert a Sweep feature for the Thread. Insert a Sweep feature for the Handle. Reuse the Thread profile from the LENSCAP part. Insert an Extruded Cut feature to create the hole for the SWITCH.

Insert the Rib feature on the back face of the HOUSING. Insert a Linear Pattern feature to create a row of Ribs.

Insert a Rib feature along the bottom of the HOUSING. Utilize the Mirror feature to create a second Rib.

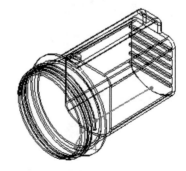

Reuse geometry between parts. The LENSCAP thread is the same as the HOUSING thread. Copy the ThreadSection from the LENSCAP to the HOUSING.

Reuse geometry between features. The Linear Pattern and Mirror Pattern utilized existing features.

Reuse geometry between sketches. The Convert Entities Sketch tool, symmetry, and Geometric relations are utilized in the HOUSING features.

Activity: HOUSING Part-Extruded Base Feature

Create the new part.

272) Click **File, New** from the Main menu. Click the **MY-TEMPLATES** tab.

273) Double-click **PART-IN-ANSI**, [**PART-MM-ISO**].

274) Click **Save**. Select the **PROJECTS** folder.

275) Enter **HOUSING** for File name. Enter **HOUSING FOR 6VOLT FLASHLIGHT** for Description. Click **Save**.

Create the Sketch.
276) Click **Front Plane** from the FeatureManager.

277) Click **Sketch** Sketch. Click **Circle** Circle from the Sketch toolbar.

278) Create a **circle** centered at the Origin.

Add a dimension.

279) Click **Smart Dimension** Smart Dimens... from the Sketch toolbar.

280) Click the **circumference**.

281) Enter **4.375**in, [**111.13**].

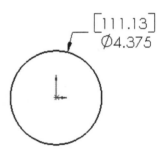

Insert an Extruded Base feature.

282) Click **Extruded Boss/Base** Extruded Boss/B... from the Features toolbar.

283) Enter **1.300**in, [**33.02**] for Depth. Accept the default settings.

284) Click **OK** from the Extrude PropertyManager.

285) Rename **Extrude1** to **Base Extrude**.

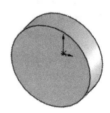

286) Click **Save**.

HOUSING Part-Loft Boss Feature

The Loft Boss feature is composed of two profiles. The first sketch is named Sketch-Circle. The second sketch is named Sketch-Square.

Create the first profile from the back face of the Extruded feature. Utilize the Convert Entities sketch tool to extract the circular geometry to the back face.

Create the second profile on an Offset Plane. The FLASHLIGHT components must remain aligned to a common centerline. Insert dimensions that reference the Origin and build symmetry into the sketch. Utilize the Mirror Entities Sketch tool.

Activity: HOUSING Part-Loft Boss Feature

Create the first profile.
287) Click the **back face** of the Base Extrude feature.

288) Click **Sketch** Sketch.

289) Click **Convert Entities** Convert from the Sketch toolbar to extract the face to the Sketch plane.

Close the Sketch.

290) Click **Exit Sketch** Exit Sketch.

291) Rename **Sketch2** to **SketchCircle**.

Create an offset plane.
292) Click the **back face** of the Base Extrude feature.

293) Click **Insert**, **Reference Geometry**, **Plane** from the Main menu. The Plane PropertyManager is displayed.

294) Enter **1.300**in, **[33.02]** for Distance.

295) Click **Top view** to verify the Plane position.

296) Click **OK** from the Plane PropertyManager.

297) Rename **Plane1** to **BatteryLoftPlane**.

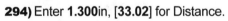
BatteryLoftPlane

298) Click **Rebuild**.

299) Click **Save**.

HOUSING
- Annotations
- Design Binder
- Solid Bodies(1)
- Material <not specified>
- Lights and Cameras
- Front Plane
- Top Plane
- Right Plane
- Origin
- Base Extrude
- SketchCircle

Create the second profile.

300) Click **BatteryLoftPlane** from the FeatureManager.

301) Click **Sketch** Sketch.

302) Click **Back view** .

303) Click the **circumference** of the circle.

304) Click **Convert Entities** Convert from the Sketch toolbar.

305) Click **Centerline** Centerl... from the Sketch toolbar.

306) Sketch a **vertical centerline** coincident to the Origin to the top edge of the circle.

307) Click **Line** Line from the Sketch toolbar.

308) Sketch a **horizontal line** to the right side of the centerline.

309) Sketch a **vertical line** down to the circumference.

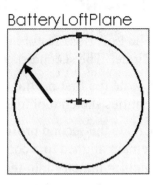

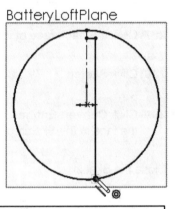

310) Click **Sketch Fillet** Fillet from the Sketch toolbar.

311) Click the **horizontal line**.

312) Click the **vertical line**.

313) Enter **.100**in, [**2.54**] for Radius.

314) Click **OK** from the Sketch Fillet PropertyManager.

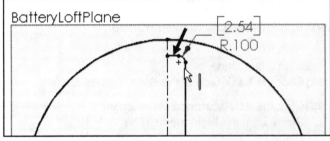

Mirror the profile.

315) Click **Mirror Entities** Mirror from the Sketch toolbar.

316) Click the **horizontal line**, **fillet**, and **vertical line**. The selected sketch entities are displayed in the Entities to mirror box.

317) Click inside the **Mirror about** box.

318) Click the **centerline**. Line1 is displayed in the Mirror about box.

319) Click **OK** ✅ from the Mirror PropertyManager.

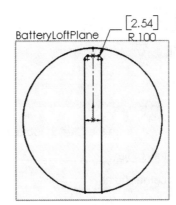

Trim unwanted geometry.

320) Click **Trim Entities** Trim from the Sketch toolbar.

321) Click **Power trim** 🔧 from the Option box.

322) Click a **position** to the far right of the circle in the Graphics window.

323) Drag the **mouse pointer** to intersect the circle. The geometry is removed,

324) Perform the same **actions** on the left side of the circle to remove the geometry.

325) Click **OK** ✅ from the Trim PropertyManager.

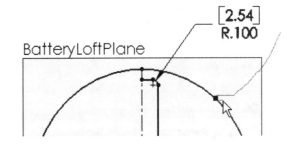

Add dimensions.

326) Click **Smart Dimension** Smart Dimens... from the Sketch toolbar.

Create the horizontal dimension.
327) Click the **left vertical** line.

328) Click the **right vertical** line.

329) Click a **position** above the profile.

330) Enter **3.100**in, [**78.74**].

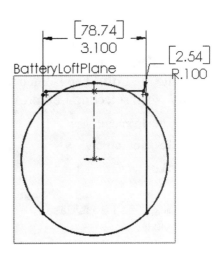

Create the vertical dimension.

331) Click the **Origin** ↳.

332) Click the **top horizontal** line.

333) Click a **position** to the right of the profile.

334) Enter **1.600**in, [**40.64**].

Modify the fillet dimension.
335) Double-click the **R.100** fillet dimension.

336) Enter **.500**in, [**12.7**].

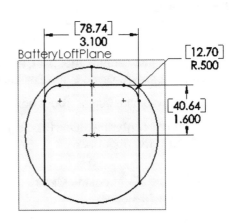

Remove all sharp edges.

337) Click **Sketch Fillet** Fillet from the Sketch toolbar.

338) Enter **.500**in, [**12.7**] for Radius.

339) Click the **lower left** corner point.

340) Click the **lower right** corner point.

341) Click **OK** from the Sketch Fillet PropertyManager.

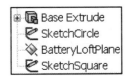

Close the Sketch.

342) Click **Exit Sketch** Sketch .

343) Rename **Sketch3** to **SketchSquare**.

344) Click **Save** 💾.

The Loft feature is composed of the SketchSquare and the SketchCircle. Select two individual profiles to create the Loft. The Isometric view provides clarity when selecting Loft profiles.

Display the Isometric view.
345) Click **Isometric view** 🔲 .

Insert a Loft feature.

346) Click **Lofted Boss/Base** Boss/B... from the Features toolbar.

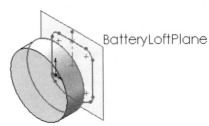

BatteryLoftPlane

347) Click the **top right corner** of the SketchSquare.

348) Click the **upper right side** of the Sketch Circle.

349) Click **OK** ✅ from the Loft PropertyManager.

350) Rename **Loft1** to **Boss-Loft1**.

351) Click **Save** 💾.

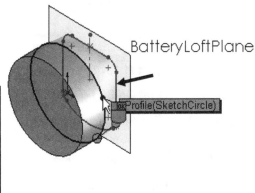

💡 Organize the FeatureManager to locate Loft profiles and planes. Insert the Loft reference planes directly before the Loft feature. Rename the planes, profiles, and guide curves with clear descriptive names.

HOUSING Part-First Extruded Boss Feature

Create the first Extruded Boss feature from the square face of the Loft. How do you estimate the depth of the Extruded Boss feature? Answer: The Extruded Base feature of the BATTERY is 4.1in, [104.14].

Ribs are required to support the BATTERY. Design for Rib construction. Ribs add strength to the HOUSING and support the BATTERY. Use a 4.4in, [111.76] depth as the first estimate. Adjust the estimated depth dimension later if required in the FLASHLIGHT assembly.

The Extruded Boss feature is symmetric about the Right Plane. Utilize Convert Entities to extract the back face of the Boss-Loft. No sketch dimensions are required.

Activity: HOUSING Part-First Extruded Boss Feature

Select the Sketch Plane.

352) Click **Back view** 🔲.

353) Click the **back face** of Boss-Loft1.

Insert the Sketch.

354) Click **Sketch** Sketch.

355) Click **Convert Entities** Convert from the Sketch toolbar.

BatteryLoftPlane

Insert an Extruded Boss feature.

Extruded

356) Click **Extruded Boss/Base** Boss/B... from the Features toolbar.

357) Enter **4.400**in, **[111.76]** for Depth.

358) Check the **Draft On/Off** button.

359) Enter **1**deg for Draft Angle.

360) Click **OK** ✅ from the Extrude PropertyManager.

361) Click **Right view** ⬚. Rename **Extrude2** to **Boss-Battery**.

362) Click **Save** 💾.

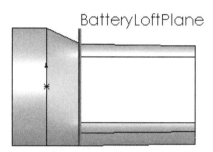

BatteryLoftPlane

HOUSING Part-Shell Feature

The Shell feature removes material. Use the Shell feature to remove the front face of the HOUSING. In the injection-molded process, the body wall thickness remains constant.

Activity: HOUSING Part-Shell Feature

Insert the Shell feature.

363) Click **Isometric view** 🔲.

364) Click **Shell** Shell from the Features toolbar. The Shell1 PropertyManager is displayed.

365) Click the **front face** of the Extruded feature.

366) Enter **.100**in, **[2.54]** for Thickness.

367) Click **OK** ✅ from the Shell1 PropertyManager.

368) Click **Save** 💾.

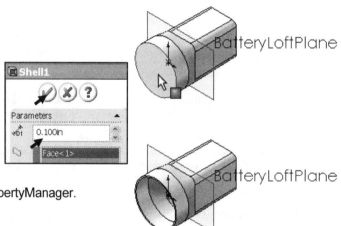

BatteryLoftPlane

BatteryLoftPlane

💡 The Shell feature position in the FeatureManager determines the geometry of additional features. Features created before the Shell contained the wall thickness specified in the Thickness option. Position features of different thickness such as the Rib feature and Thread Sweep feature after the Shell. Features inserted after the Shell remain solid.

HOUSING Part-Second Extruded Boss Feature

The second Extruded Boss feature creates a solid circular ring on the back circular face of the Extruded Base feature. The solid ring is a cosmetic stop for the LENSCAP and provides rigidity at the transition of the HOUSING. Design for change. The Extruded Boss feature updates if the Shell thickness changes.

Utilize the Front Plane for the sketch. Select the inside circular edge of the Shell. Utilize Convert Entities to obtain the inside circle. Utilize the Circle Sketch tool to create the outside circle. Extrude the feature towards the front face.

Activity: HOUSING Part-Second Extruded Boss Feature

Select the Sketch Plane.
369) Click **Front Plane** from the FeatureManager.

Create the Sketch.
370) Click **Sketch** Sketch.

371) Click the **front inside circular edge** of Shell1.

372) Click **Convert Entities** Convert from the Sketch toolbar.

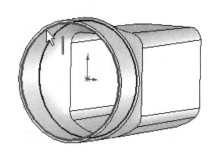

Create the outside circle.
373) Click **Front view** .

374) Click **Circle** Circle from the Sketch toolbar.

375) Create a **circle** centered at the Origin.

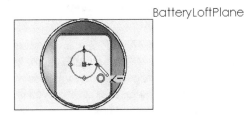
BatteryLoftPlane

Add a dimension.
376) Click **Smart Dimension** Smart Dimens....

377) Click the **circumference** of the circle.

378) Enter **5.125**in, [**130.18**].

$$[130.18]$$
$$\varnothing 5.125$$
BatteryLoftPlane

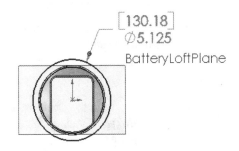

Insert an Extruded Boss feature.
379) Click **Extruded Boss/Base** Extruded Boss/B... from the Features toolbar.

380) Enter **.100**in, [**2.54**] for Depth.

381) Click **OK** from the Extrude PropertyManager.

382) Click **Isometric view** . Rename **Extrude3** to **Boss-Stop**.

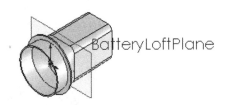
BatteryLoftPlane

383) Click **Save** .

HOUSING Part-Draft Feature

The Draft feature tapers selected model faces by a specified angle by utilizing a Neutral Plane or Parting Line. The Neutral Plane option utilizes a plane or face to determine the pull direction when creating a mold.

The Parting Line option drafts surfaces around a parting line of a mold. Utilize the Parting Line option for non-planar surfaces. Apply the Draft feature to solid and surface models.

A 5° draft is required to insure proper thread mating between the LENSCAP and the HOUSING. The LENSCAP Extruded Base feature has a 5° draft angle.

The outside face of the Extruded Base feature HOUSING requires a 5° draft angle. The inside HOUSING wall does not require a draft angle. The Extruded Base feature has a 5° draft angle. Use the Draft feature to create a draft angle. The front circular face is the Neutral Plane. The outside cylindrical surface is the face to draft.

You created the Extruded Boss/Base and Extrude Cut features with the draft angle option. The Draft feature differs from the Extruded feature, draft angle option. The Draft feature allows you to select multiple faces to taper.

Activity: HOUSING Part-Draft Feature

Insert the Draft feature.

384) Click the thin **front circular face** of the Base Extrude feature.

385) Click **Draft** Draft from the Features toolbar. The Draft PropertyManager is displayed. The front circular face is displayed in the Neutral Plane text box.

386) Click inside the **Faces to Draft** box.

387) Click the **outside circular** face of Base Extrude as illustrated.

388) Enter **5**deg for Draft Angle.

389) Click **OK** from the Draft PropertyManager. Draft1 is displayed in the FeatureManager.

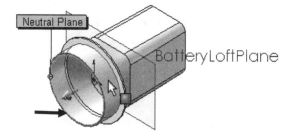

Display the draft angle and the
straight interior.

390) Click **Right view**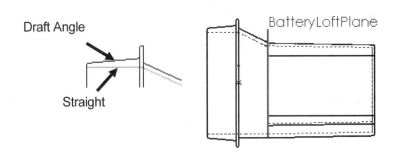

391) Click **Hidden Lines
    Visible** .

392) Click **Save** .

Order of feature creation is important. Apply threads after the Draft feature for
plastic parts to maintain a constant thread thickness.

HOUSING Part-Thread with Sweep Feature

The HOUSING requires a thread. Create the threads for the HOUSING on the outside of
the Draft feature. Create the thread with the Sweep feature. The thread requires two
sketches: ThreadPath and ThreadSection. The LENSCAP and HOUSING Thread utilize
the same technique. Create a ThreadPlane. Utilize Convert Entities to create a circular
sketch referencing the HOUSING Base Extrude feature. Insert a Helix/Spiral curve to
create the path.

Reuse geometry between parts. The ThreadSection is copied from the LENSCAP and is
inserted into the HOUSING Top Plane.

Activity: HOUSING Part-Thread with Sweep Feature

Insert the ThreadPlane.
393) Click **Shaded With Edges** .

394) Click **Isometric view** .

395) Click the **thin front circular face**,
    Base Extrude.

396) Click **Insert**, **Reference
    Geometry**, **Plane** from the Main
    menu. The Plane
    PropertyManager is displayed.

397) Click the **Reverse direction** box.

398) Enter **.125**in, **[3.18]** for Distance.

399) Click **OK** from the Plane
    PropertyManager.

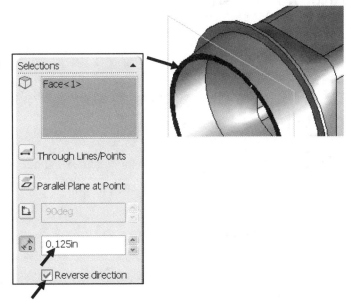

400) Click **Save** 💾.

401) Rename **Plane2** to **ThreadPlane**.

Insert the ThreadPath.

402) Click **Sketch** Sketch.

403) Select the **front outside circular edge** of the Base Extrude.

404) Click **Convert Entities** Convert. The circular edge is displayed on the ThreadPlane.

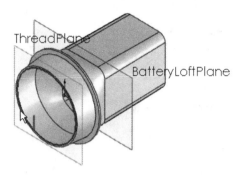

Insert the Helix/Spiral curve.
405) Click **Insert**, **Curve**, **Helix/Spiral** from the Main menu.

406) Enter .**250**in, [6.35] for Pitch.

407) Click the **Reverse direction** box.

408) Enter **2.5** for Revolution.

409) Enter **180**deg in the Start angle spin box. The Helix start point and end point are Coincident with the Top Plane.

410) Click the **Taper Helix** box.

411) Enter **5**deg for Angle.

412) Click the **Taper outward** box.

413) Click **OK** ✓ from the Helix/Spiral PropertyManager.

414) Rename **Helix/Spiral1** to **ThreadPath**.

415) Click **Isometric view** 🧊.

416) Click **Save** 💾.

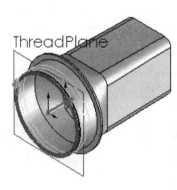

Copy the LENSCAP ThreadSection.
417) Open the LENSCAP part.

418) Expand the Thread feature from the FeatureManager.

419) Click **ThreadSection** from the FeatureManager.

420) Click **Edit**, **Copy** from the Main menu.

421) Close the LENSCAP.

Open the HOUSING.
422) Return to the Housing.

Paste the LENSCAP ThreadSection.
423) Click **Top Plane** from the HOUSING FeatureManager.

424) Click **Edit**, **Paste** from the Main menu. The ThreadSection is displayed on the Top Plane. The new Sketch7 name is added to the bottom of the FeatureManager.

425) Rename **Sketch7** to **ThreadSection**.

426) Click **Save** 💾.

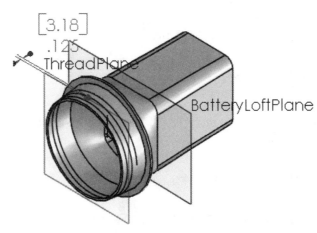

Add a Pierce relation.
427) Right-click **ThreadSection** from the FeatureManager.

428) Click **Edit Sketch**.

429) Click **ThreadSection** from the HOUSING FeatureManager.

430) Zoom to Area 🔍 on the Midpoint of the ThreadSection.

431) Click the **Midpoint** of the ThreadSection.

432) Click **Isometric view** 🔲.

433) Hold the **Ctrl** key down.

434) Click the **right back edge** of the ThreadPath.

435) Release the **Ctrl** key.

436) Click **Pierce** from the Add Relations box.

437) Click **OK** ✅ from the Properties PropertyManager.

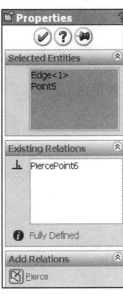

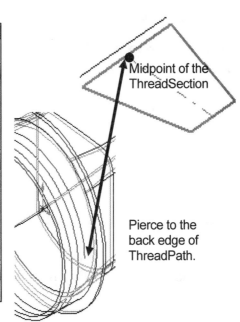

Midpoint of the ThreadSection

Pierce to the back edge of ThreadPath.

Caution: Do not click the front edge of the
ThreadPath. The Thread is then created out of
the HOUSING.

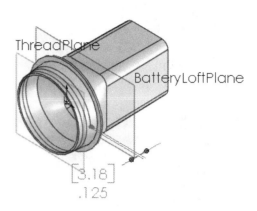

Close the Sketch.

Exit

438) Click **Exit Sketch** Sketch . ThreadSection is fully
defined.

Insert the Sweep feature.

Swept

439) Click **Swept** Boss/B... from the Feature toolbar. The
Swept PropertyManager is displayed.

440) Expand HOUSING from the fly-out
FeatureManager.

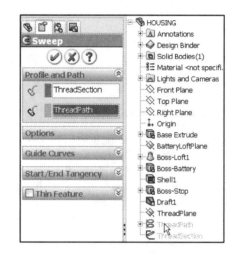

441) Click inside the **Profile** box.

442) Click **ThreadSection** from the fly-out
FeatureManager.

443) Click inside the **Path** box.

444) Click **ThreadPath** from the fly-out FeatureManager.

445) Click **OK** ✔ from the Sweep PropertyManager.

446) Rename **Sweep1** to **Thread**.

447) Click **Save** 🖫 .

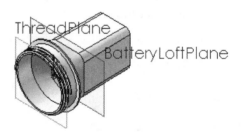

💡 Creating a ThreadPlane provides flexibility to the design. The ThreadPlane allows
for a smoother lead. Utilize the ThreadPlane offset dimension to adjust the start of the
thread.

HOUSING Part-Handle with Sweep Feature

Create the handle with the Sweep feature. The Sweep feature consists of a sketched path
and cross section profile. Sketch the path on the Right Plane. The sketch uses edges
from existing features. Sketch the profile on the back circular face of the Boss-Stop
feature.

Activity: HOUSING Part-Handle with Sweep Feature

Create the Sweep path sketch.

448) Click **Right Plane** from the FeatureManager.

449) Click **Sketch**  Sketch .

450) Click **Right view** ⊡ .

451) Click **Hidden Lines Removed** ⬚ .

452) Click **Line** Line from the Sketch toolbar.

453) Sketch a **horizontal line** below the top of the Boss Stop. Add a horizontal relation if needed.

454) Sketch a **vertical line** to the right top corner of the Housing. Add a vertical relation if needed.

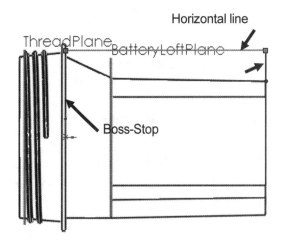

Horizontal line

ThreadPlane BatteryLoftPlane

Boss-Stop

Insert a 2D Fillet.

455) Click **Sketch Fillet** Sketch Fillet from the Sketch toolbar.

456) Click the **upper right corner** of the sketch lines.

457) Enter **.500**in, [**12.7**] for Radius.

458) Click **OK** ✅ from the Sketch Fillet PropertyManager.

Add a Coincident relation.

459) Click the **left end point** of the horizontal line.

460) Hold the **Ctrl** key down.

461) Click the **right vertical edge** of the Boss Stop.

462) Release the **Ctrl** key.

12.70
R.500

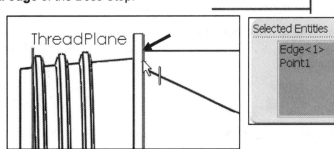

ThreadPlane

Selected Entities

Edge<1>
Point1

463) Click **Coincident** ⟨ from the Add Relations box.

464) Click **OK** ✅ from the
Properties PropertyManager.

Add an Intersection relation.
465) Click the **bottom end point** of
the vertical line. Hold the **Ctrl**
key down.

466) Click the **right vertical edge** of
the Housing.

467) Click the **horizontal edge** of
the Housing.

468) Release the **Ctrl** key. Click
Intersection ✗ from the Add
Relations box.

469) Click **OK** ✅ from the
Properties PropertyManager.

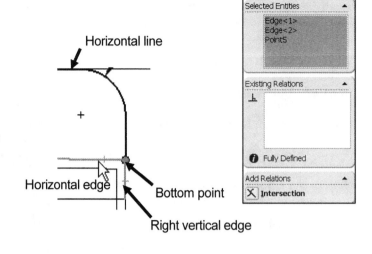

Add a dimension.

470) Click **Smart Dimension** Smart Dimens... .

471) Click the **Origin**. Click the
horizontal line.

472) Click a **position** to the right.

473) Enter **2.500**in, [**63.5**].

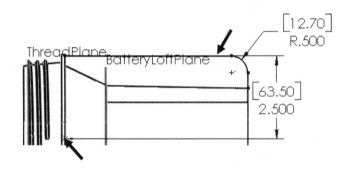

Close the Sketch.

474) Click **Exit Sketch** Exit Sketch .

475) Rename **Sketch8** to **HandlePath**.

476) Click **Save** 💾 .

Create the Sweep Profile.
477) Click **Back view** 🔲 .

478) Click the **back circular face** of the Boss-Stop
feature.

479) Click **Sketch** Sketch .

480) Click **Centerline** Centerl... from the Sketch toolbar.

481) Sketch a **vertical centerline** collinear with the
Right Plane, coincident to the Origin.

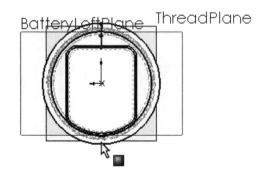

482) **Zoom in** 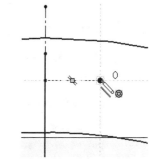 on the top of the Boss-Stop.

483) Sketch a **horizontal centerline**. The left end point of the centerline is coincident with the vertical centerline on the Boss-Stop feature. Do not select existing feature geometry.

484) Click **Line** Line from the Sketch toolbar.

485) Sketch a **line** above the horizontal centerline.

486) Click **Tangent Arc** Tangent Arc from the Sketch toolbar.

487) Sketch a **90° arc**.

488) Click **Tangent Arc** Tangent Arc to exit.

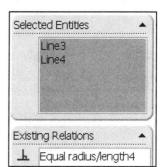

Add an Equal relation.
489) Click the **horizontal centerline**.

490) Hold the **Ctrl** key down.

491) Click the **horizontal line**.

492) Release the **Ctrl** key.

493) Click **Equal** = from the Add Relations box.

494) Click **OK** from the Properties PropertyManager.

Add a Horizontal relation.
495) Click the **right endpoint** of the tangent arc.

496) Hold the **Ctrl** key down.

497) Click the **arc center point**.

498) Click the left **end point** of the centerline.

499) Release the **Ctrl** key.

500) Click **Horizontal** ▬ from the Add Relations box.

501) Click **OK** from the Properties PropertyManager.

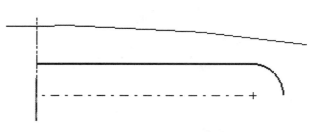

Mirror about the horizontal centerline.

502) Click **Mirror Entities** Mirror from the Sketch toolbar.

503) Click the **horizontal** line.

504) Click the **90° arc**.

505) Click inside the **Mirror about** box.

506) Click the **horizontal centerline**. The selected sketch entities are displayed in the Entities to mirror box.

507) Click **OK**  from the Mirror PropertyManager.

Mirror about the vertical centerline.

508) Click **Mirror Entities** Mirror from the Sketch toolbar.

509) Window-Select the **two horizontal lines**, the **horizontal centerline** and the **90° arc**. The selected sketch entities are displayed in the Entities to mirror box.

510) Click inside the **Mirror about** box.

511) Click the **vertical** centerline.

512) Click **OK** from the Mirror PropertyManager.

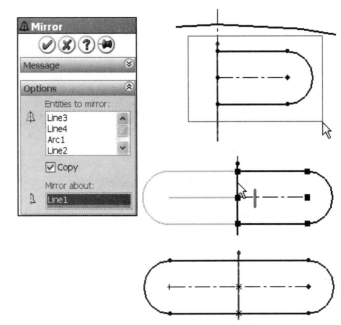

Add dimensions.

513) Click **Smart Dimension** Dimens... from the Sketch toolbar.

514) Enter **1.000**in, **[25.4]** between the arc center points.

515) Enter **.100**in, **[2.54]** for Radius.

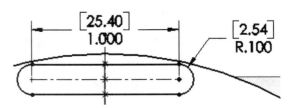

Add a Pierce relation.
516) Right-click **Select**.

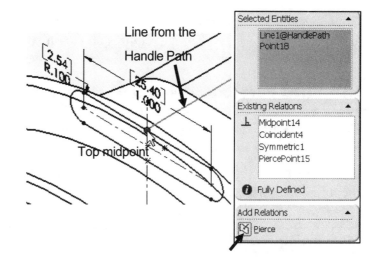

517) Click the **top midpoint** of the Sketch profile.

518) Click **Isometric view** .

519) Hold the **Ctrl** key down.

520) Click the **line** from the HandlePath.

521) Release the **Ctrl** key.

522) Click **Pierce** from the Add Relations box.

523) Click **OK** from the Properties PropertyManager.

Close the Sketch.

524) Click **Exit Sketch** .

525) Rename **Sketch9** to **HandleProfile**.

526) Hide ThreadPlane. **Hide** BatterlyLoftPlane.

Insert the Sweep feature.

527) Click **Swept Boss/Base** Boss/B... from the Features toolbar. The Sweep PropertyManager is displayed.

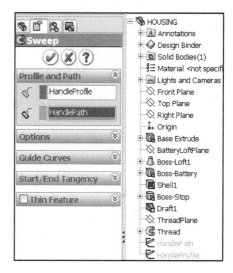

528) Click **HandleProfile** from the fly-out FeatureManager. HandleProfile is displayed in the Profile box.

529) Click inside the **Path** box.

530) Click **HandlePath** from the fly-out FeatureManager. HandlePath is displayed in the Path box.

531) Click **OK** from the Sweep PropertyManager. Sweep2 is displayed in the FeatureManager.

Fit the profile to the Graphics window.
532) Press the **f** key.

533) Click **Shaded With Edges**.

534) Rename **Sweep2** to **Handle**.

535) Click **Save**.

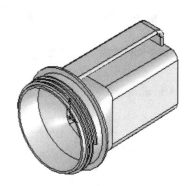

How does the Sweep2 feature interact with the other parts in the FLASHLIGHT assembly? Answer: The Handle requires an Extruded Cut to insert the SWITCH.

HOUSING Part-Extruded Cut Feature with UpToSurface

Create an Extruded Cut in the Handle for the SWITCH. Utilize the top face of the Handle for the Sketch plane. Create a circular sketch centered on the Handle.

Utilize the UpToSurface End Condition. Select the inside surface of the HOUSING for the reference surface.

Activity: HOUSING Part-Extruded Cut Feature with UpToSurface End Condition

---

Select the Sketch plane.
536) Click the **top face** of the Handle.

Insert the Sketch.

537) Click **Sketch** Sketch .

538) Click **Top view** .

539) Click **Circle** Circle from the Sketch toolbar.

540) Sketch a **circle** on the Handle near the front as illustrated.

Add a Vertical relation.
541) Right-click **Select**.

542) Click the **Origin**.

543) Hold the **Ctrl** key down.

544) Click the **center point** of the circle.

545) Release the **Ctrl** key.

546) Click **Vertical** I from the Add Relations box.

547) Click **OK** from the Properties PropertyManager.

Add dimensions.

548) Click **Smart Dimension** Dimens... from the Sketch toolbar.

549) Enter .510in, [**12.95**] for diameter.

550) Enter .450in, [**11.43**] for the distance from the Origin.

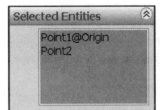
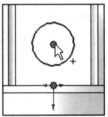

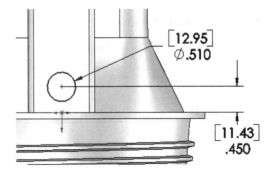

Insert an Extruded Cut feature.

551) Rotate the model to view the inside Shell1.

552) Click **Extruded Cut** Cut from the Features toolbar. The Cut-Extrude PropertyManager is displayed.

553) Select **Up To Surface** for End Condition in Direction 1.

554) Click the **top inside face** of the Shell1. Face<1> is displayed in the Face/Plane box.

555) Click **OK** from the Cut-Extrude PropertyManager.

556) Rename **Cut-Extrude1** to **SwitchHole**.

557) Click **Isometric view** .

558) Click **Save** .

HOUSING Part-First Rib and Linear Pattern Feature

The Rib feature adds material between contours of existing geometry. Use ribs to add structural integrity to a part.

A rib requires:

- A Sketch.
- Thickness.
- Extrusion direction.

The first rib profile is sketched on the Top Plane. A 1° draft angle is required for manufacturing. Determine the rib thickness by the manufacturing process and the material.

Note: Rule of thumb states that the rib thickness is ½ the part wall thickness. The rib thickness dimension is .100in, [2.54] for illustration purposes.

The HOUSING requires multiple ribs to support the BATTERY. A Linear Pattern creates multiple instances of a feature along a straight line. Create the Linear Pattern feature in two directions along the same vertical edge of the HOUSING.

Activity: HOUSING Part-First Rib and Linear Pattern Feature

Display all hidden lines.

559) Click **Hidden Lines Visible** ⬚.

Select the Sketch.
560) Click **Top Plane** from the FeatureManager.

561) Click **Sketch** Sketch.

562) Click **Top view** ⬚.

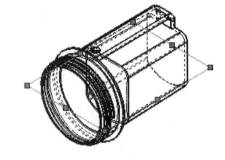

563) Click **Line** Line from the Sketch toolbar.

564) Sketch a **horizontal line**. The endpoints are located on either side of the Handle as illustrated.

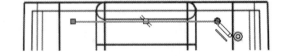

Add a dimension.

565) Click **Smart Dimension** Dimens... from the Sketch toolbar.

566) Click the **inner back edge**.

567) Click the **horizontal** line.

568) Click a **position** to the right of the profile.

569) Enter **.175**in, [**4.45**].

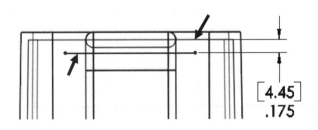

Insert a Rib feature.

570) Click **Rib** Rib  from the Features toolbar.

571) Click the **Both Sides** button.

572) Enter **.100**in, [**2.54**] for Rib Thickness.

573) Click the **Parallel to Sketch** button. The Rib direction arrow points to the back. Flip the material side if required. Select the Flip material side box if the direction arrow does not point towards the back.

574) Click the **Draft On/Off** button.

575) Enter **1**deg for Draft Angle.

576) Click **Front view** .

577) Click the **back inside face** of the HOUSING for the Body.

578) Click **OK** from the Rib PropertyManager. Rib1 is displayed in the FeatureManager.

579) Click **Isometric view** .

580) Click **Save** .

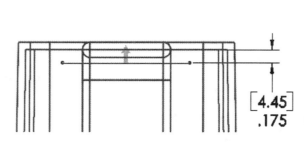

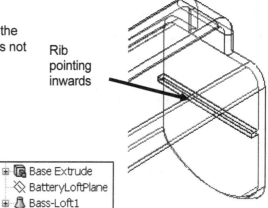

Rib pointing inwards

Base Extrude
BatteryLoftPlane
Bass-Loft1
Boss-Battery
Shell1
Boss-Stop
Draft1
ThreadPlane
Thread
Handle
SwitchHole
Rib1

Existing geometry defines the Rib boundaries. The Rib does not penetrate through the wall.

Insert the Linear Pattern feature.

581) **Zoom to Area** on Rib1.

582) Click **Rib1** from the FeatureManager.

583) Click **Linear Pattern** Pattern from the Features toolbar. The Linear Pattern PropertyManager is displayed. Rib1 is displayed in the Features to Pattern box.

584) Click inside the **Direction 1 Pattern Direction** box.

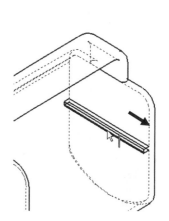

585) Click the **hidden upper back vertical edge** of Shell1. The direction arrow points upward. Click the Reverse direction button if required.

586) Enter **.500**in, [**12.7**] for Spacing.

587) Enter **3** for Number of Instances.

588) Click inside the **Direction 2 Pattern Direction** box.

589) Click the **hidden lower back vertical edge** of Shell1. The direction arrow points downward. Click the Reverse direction button if required.

590) Enter **.500**in, [**12.7**] for Spacing.

591) Enter **3** for Number of Instances.

592) Click the **Pattern seed only** box.

593) Drag the Linear Pattern **Scroll bar** downward to display the Options box.

594) Check the **Geometry Pattern** box.

595) Click **OK**  from the Linear Pattern PropertyManager. LPattern1 is displayed.

596) Click **Isometric view** .

597) Click **Save** .

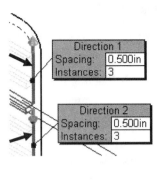

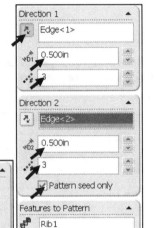

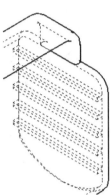

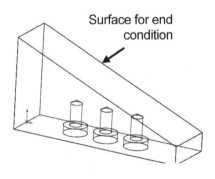

Surface for end condition

Utilize the Geometry pattern option to efficiently create and rebuild patterns. Know when to check the Geometry pattern.

Check the Geometry pattern box when you require an exact copy of the seed feature. Each instance is an exact copy of the faces and edges of the original feature. End conditions are not calculated. This option saves rebuild time.

Uncheck the Geometry pattern box when you require the end condition to vary. Each instance will have a different end condition. Each instance is offset from the selected surface by the same amount.

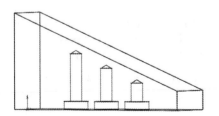

Suppress Patterns when not required. Patterns contain repetitive geometry that takes time to rebuild. Pattern features also clutter the part during the model creation process. Suppress patterns as you continue to create more complex features in the part. Unsuppress a feature to restore the display and load into memory for future calculations. Hide features to improve clarity. Show feature to display hidden features.

Rib sketches are not required to be fully defined. The Linear Rib option blends sketched geometry into existing contours of the model.

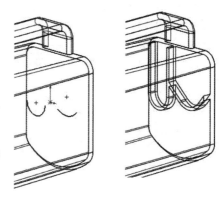

Example: Create an offset reference plane from the inside back face of the HOUSING.

Sketch two under defined arcs. Insert a Rib feature with the Linear option. The Rib extends to the Shell walls.

HOUSING Part-Second Rib Feature

The second Rib feature supports and centers the BATTERY. The Rib is sketched on a reference plane created through a point on the Handle and parallel with the Right Plane. The Rib sketch references the Origin and existing geometry in the HOUSING. Utilize an Intersection and Coincident relation to define the sketch.

Activity: HOUSING Part-Second Rib Feature

Insert the Plane.

598) Click **Wireframe** ⬚.

599) **Zoom to Area** 🔍 on the back right side of the Handle.

600) Click **Insert**, **Reference Geometry**, **Plane** from the Main menu. The Plane PropertyManager is displayed.

601) Click **Parallel Plane at Point**. The Point-Plane option requires a point and a plane.

602) Click **Right Plane** from the fly-out FeatureManager.

603) Click the **vertex** (point) at the back right of the handle as illustrated. The selected sketch entities are displayed in the Selections box.

604) Click **OK** ✓ from the Plane PropertyManager.

605) Rename **Plane1** to **LongRibPlane**.

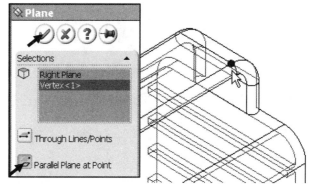

Fit to the Graphics window.

606) Press the **f** key.

607) Click **Save** 💾 .

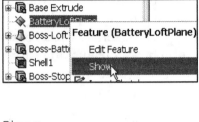

Create the second Rib.
608) **Show** the BatteryLoftPlane.

609) Click **LongRibPlane** from the
FeatureManager. This is you Sketch plane.

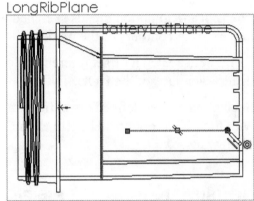

Insert the Sketch.

610) Click **Sketch** Sketch .

611) Click **Right view** 🗖 .

612) Click **Line** Line from the Sketch toolbar.

613) Sketch a **horizontal line**. Do not select the
edges of the Shell1 feature.

Add a Coincident relation.
614) Right-click **Select**. Click the **left end point** of
the horizontal sketch line.

615) Hold the **Ctrl** key
down.

616) Click
BatteryLoftPlane
from the fly-out
FeatureManager.

617) Release the **Ctrl** key.

618) Click **Coincident** ⟋
from the Add
Relations box.

619) Click **OK** ✅ from the Properties
PropertyManager.

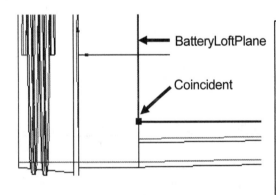

Add a dimension.

620) Click **Smart Dimension** Smart Dimens... .

621) Click the **horizontal line**.

622) Click the **Origin**. Click a **position** for the
vertical linear dimension.

623) Enter **1.300**in, **[33.02]**.

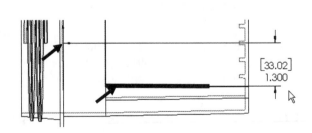

💡 When the sketch and reference geometry become complex, create dimensions by selecting Reference Planes and the Origin in the FeatureManager.

💡 Dimension the rib from the Origin, not from an edge or surface for design flexibility. The Origin remains constant. Modify edges and surfaces with the Fillet feature.

Sketch an arc.

624) Zoom to Area 🔍 on the horizontal Sketch line.

625) Click **Tangent Arc** 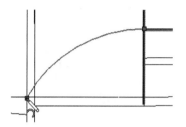 from the Sketch toolbar.

626) Click the **left end** of the horizontal line.

627) Click the **intersection** of the Shell1 and Boss Stop features.

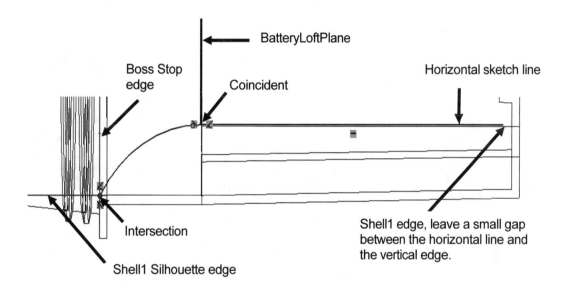

BatteryLoftPlane

Boss Stop edge

Coincident

Horizontal sketch line

Shell1 edge, leave a small gap between the horizontal line and the vertical edge.

Intersection

Shell1 Silhouette edge

Add an Intersection relation.

628) Right-click **Select**.

629) Click the **end point** of the arc.

630) Hold the **Ctrl** key down.

631) Click the **Shell1 Silhouette Edge** of the lower horizontal inside wall.

632) Click the left **vertical Boss-Stop edge**. Release the **Ctrl** key.

633) Click **Intersection** ✕ from the Add Relations box.

634) Click **OK** ✅ from the Properties PropertyManager.

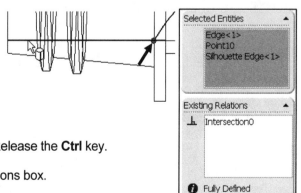

Insert the Rib feature.

635) Click **Rib** Rib from the Features toolbar.

636) Click the **Both Sides** button.

637) Enter **.075**in, **[1.91]** for Rib Thickness.

638) Click the **Draft On/Off** button.

639) Enter **1**deg for Angle.

640) Click the **Draft outward** box.

641) Click the **Flip material side** check box if required. The direction arrow points towards the bottom.

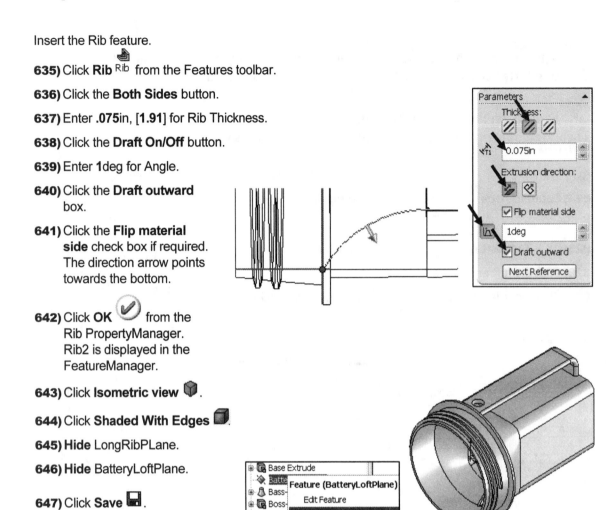

642) Click **OK** from the Rib PropertyManager. Rib2 is displayed in the FeatureManager.

643) Click **Isometric view**.

644) Click **Shaded With Edges**.

645) Hide LongRibPLane.

646) Hide BatteryLoftPlane.

647) Click **Save**.

HOUSING Part-Mirror Feature

An additional rib is required to support the BATTERY. Reuse features with the Mirror feature to create a rib symmetric about the Right Plane.

The Mirror feature requires:

- Mirror Face or Plane reference.

- Features or Faces to Mirror.

Utilize the Mirror feature. Select the Right Plane for the Mirror Plane. Select Rib2 from the fly-out FeatureManager to mirror.

Activity: HOUSING Part-Mirror Feature

Insert the Mirror feature.

648) Click **Mirror** Mirror from the Features toolbar. The Mirror PropertyManager is displayed.

649) Click inside the **Mirror Face/Plane** box.

650) Click **Right Plane** from the fly-out FeatureManager.

651) If required, click **Rib2** from the fly-out FeatureManager. Rib2 is displayed in the Features to Mirror box.

652) Click **OK** ✅ from the Mirror PropertyManager. Mirror1 is displayed.

653) Click **Trimetric view** . Click **Save** .

Close all parts.
654) Click **Window**, **Close All** from the Main menu.

The parts for the FLASHLIGHT are complete! Review the HOUSING before moving on to the FLASHLIGHT assembly.

 Review of the HOUSING Part.

The HOUSING utilized the Extruded Base feature with the draft angle option. The Loft feature was created to blend the circular face of the LENS with the rectangular face of the BATTERY.

The Shell feature removed material with a constant wall thickness. The Draft feature utilized the front face as the Neutral plane.

You created a Thread similar to the LENSCAP Thread. The Thread profile was copied from the LENSCAP and inserted into the Top Plane of the HOUSING. The Extruded Cut feature was utilized to create a hole for the SWITCH. The Rib features were utilized in a Linear Pattern and Mirror feature.

Each feature has additional options that are applied to create different geometry. The Offset From Surface End Condition created an Extruded Cut on the curved surface of the HOUSING and LENSCAP. The Reverse offset and Translate surface options produced a cut depth constant throughout the curved surface.

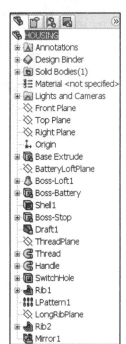

Project Summary

You created four parts for the FLASHLIGHT assembly: O-RING, SWITCH, LENSCAP, and HOUSING. The FLASHLIGHT parts contain over a 100 features, reference planes, sketches, and components. You organized the features in each part.

The O-RING part utilized a Sweep Base feature. The SWITCH part utilized a Loft Base feature. The simple Sweep feature requires two sketches: a path and a profile. A complex Sweep feature requires multiple sketches and Guide Curves. The Loft feature requires two or more sketches created on different planes.

The LENSCAP and HOUSING part utilized a variety of features. You applied design intent to reuse geometry through Geometric relationships, symmetry, and patterns. Review the project exercises before moving on to Project 4.

Project Terminology

Circular Pattern: A feature used to create instances of a seed feature rotated about an axis of revolution. You utilized a Circular Pattern to create Extruded Cuts around the LENSCAP.

Draft: A feature used to add a specified draft angle to a face. You utilized a Draft feature with the Neutral Plane option.

Extruded Thin Cut: A feature used to remove material by extruding an open profile.

Helix/Spiral Curve: A Helix is a curve with pitch. The Helix is created about an axis. You utilized a Helix Curve to create a thread for the LENSCAP.

Linear Pattern: A feature used to create instances of a seed feature in a rectangular array, along one or two edges. The Linear Pattern was utilized to create multiple instances of the HOUSING Rib1 feature.

Loft: A feature used to blend two or more profiles on separate Planes. A Loft Boss adds material. A Loft Cut removes material. The HOUSING part utilized a Loft Boss feature to transition a circular profile of the LENSCAP to a square profile of the BATTERY.

Mirror: The feature used to create a symmetric feature about a Mirror Plane. The Mirror feature created a second Rib, symmetric about the Right Plane.

Revolved Cut Thin: A feature used to remove material by rotating a sketched profile around a centerline.

Rib: A feature used to add material between contours of existing geometry. Use Ribs to add structural integrity to a part.

Shape: A feature used to deform a surface created by expanding, constraining, and tightening a selected surface. A deformed surface is flexible, much like a membrane.

Suppressed: A feature or component not loaded into memory. A feature is suppressed or unsuppressed. A component is suppressed or resolved. Suppress features and components to improve model rebuild time.

Sweep: A Sweep Boss/Base feature adds material. A Sweep Cut removes material. A Sweep requires a profile sketch and a path sketch. A Sweep feature moves a profile along a path. The Sweep Boss tool is located on the Features toolbar. The Sweep Cut tool is located in the Insert menu.

Questions

1. Identify the function of the following features:

   - Sweep.

   - Revolved Cut Thin.

   - Loft.

   - Rib.

   - Circular Pattern.

   - Linear Pattern.

2. Describe a Suppressed feature.

3. Why would you suppress a feature?

4. The Rib features require a sketch, thickness and a _____ direction.

5. What is a Pierce relation?

6. Describe how to create a thread using the Sweep feature. Provide an example.

7. Explain how to create a Linear Pattern. Provide an example.

8. Describe the Shape feature.

9. Identify two advantages of utilizing Convert Entities in a sketch to obtain the profile.

10. How is symmetry built into a sketch? Provide an example.

11. How is symmetry built into a feature? Provide an example.

12. Define a Guide Curve. Identify the features that utilize Guide Curves.

13. Describe a Draft feature.

14. Identify the differences between a Draft feature and the Draft Angle option in the Extruded Boss/Base feature.

15. Describe the differences between a Circular Pattern and a Linear Pattern.

16. Identify the advantages of the Convert Entities tool.

17. True or False. A Loft feature can only be inserted as the first feature in a part. Explain your answer.

18. A Sweep feature adds and removes material. Identify the location on the Main Pull down menu that contains the Sweep Cut feature. Hint: SolidWorks Help Topics.

19. Review the Features toolbar. Identify the name of each feature.

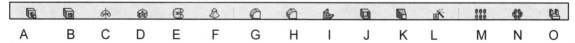

A   B   C   D   E   F   G   H   I   J   K   L   M   N   O

Exercises

Exercise 3.1: QUATTRO-SEAL-O-RING Part

- Create the QUATTRO-SEAL-O-RING part as a single Sweep feature.

- Create a 100mm diameter Circle on the Front Plane for the path, Sketch1.

- Create the symmetric cross section on the Top Plane for the profile, Sketch2.

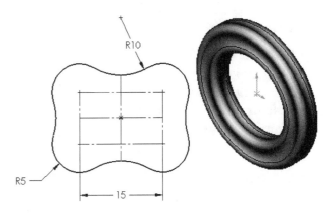

Exercise 3.2: HOOK Part

- Create the HOOK part. Utilize a Sweep Base feature.

- Create the profile, Sketch1 on the Front Plane. Create the path, Sketch2 on the Top Plane.

- Create the bottom Thread as a Sweep Cut feature.

- Create Plane1, offset .020,[.51mm] from the Top Plane.

- Create the Helix Curve for the path. Pitch 0.050 in, Revolution 4.0, Starting Angle 0.0 deg. Sketch a circle ∅.020,[.51mm] on the Right Plane for the Thread profile.

- Chamfer the bottom face.

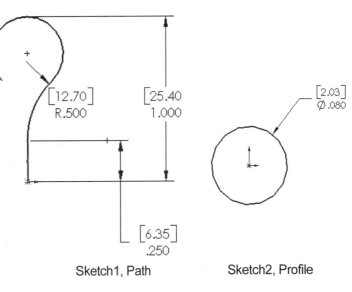

Sketch1, Path   Sketch2, Profile

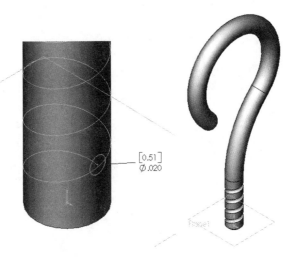

Exercise 3.3a: OFFSET-LOFT Part

- Create the OFFSET-LOFT part as a single Loft Base Feature.

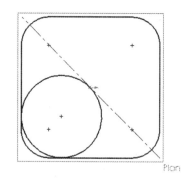

- Sketch a square on the Top Plane. Sketch a Circle on Plane1. Utilize Geometric Relations in the sketch. No dimensions are provided.

Exercise 3.3b: WEIGHT Part

- Create the WEIGHT part as a single Loft Base Feature.

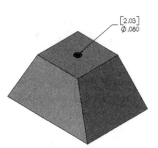

- The Top Plane and Plane1 are 0.5, [12.7mm] apart. Sketch a rectangle 1.000, [25.40mm] x .750, [19.05] on the Top Plane.

- Sketch a square .500, [12.70mm] on Plane1. Add a centered ∅.080, [2.03mm] Thru Hole.

Exercise 3.3c: SWEEP-CUT CASE Part

- Utilize a Sweep Cut to remove material from the CASE. The profile for the Sweep Cut is a semi-circle.

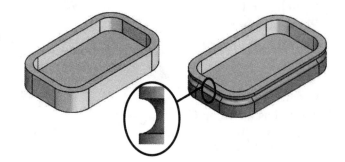

Exercise 3.4c: MUG Part

- Create the handle on the MUG.

- Utilize a Revolved Base feature.

- Utilize Tools, Sketch Entities, Text option to insert the sketch text.

Exercise 3.5: Triangular Shaped Bottle Part

A plastic BOTTLE is created from a variety of SolidWorks features.

- Create the shoulder of the BOTTLE with the Loft Base feature.

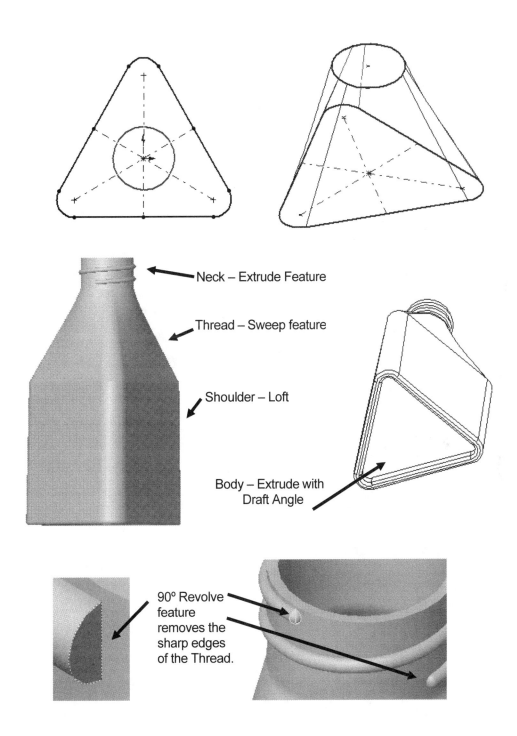

Neck – Extrude Feature

Thread – Sweep feature

Shoulder – Loft

Body – Extrude with Draft Angle

90° Revolve feature removes the sharp edges of the Thread.

Notes:

Notes:

Project 4

Assembly Modeling

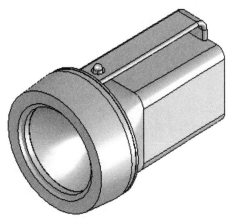

Below are the desired outcomes and usage competencies based on the completion of Project 4.

Project Desired Outcomes:	Usage Competencies:

• Create four assemblies in this project:
 	
   o LENSANDBULB assembly.
 	
   o CAPANDLENS assembly.
 	
   o BATTERYANDPLATE assembly.
 	
   o FLASHLIGHT assembly.
	• Develop an understanding of Assembly modeling techniques.
	
	• Combine the LENSANDBULB assembly, CAPANDLENS assembly, BATTERYANDPLATE assembly, HOUSING part, and SWITCH part to create the FLASHLIGHT assembly.
	
	• Ability to use the following Assembly tools: Insert Component, Hide/Show, Change Suppression, Mate, Move Component, Rotate Component, Exploded View, and Interference Detection.

• Create an Inch and Metric Assembly Template.
 	
   o ASM-IN-ANSI.
 	
   o ASM-MM-ISO.
	• Ability to apply Document Properties and to create Custom Assembly Templates.

Notes:

Project 4-Assembly Modeling

Project Overview

Create four assemblies in this project:

1. LENSANDBULB assembly.

2. CAPANDLENS assembly.

3. BATTERYANDPLATE assembly.

4. FLASHLIGHT assembly.

Create an inch and metric Assembly Template.

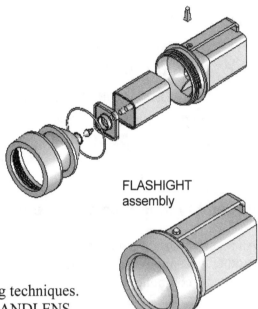

FLASHIGHT assembly

*   ASM-IN-ANSI.

*   ASM-MM-ISO.

Develop an understanding of assembly modeling techniques. Combine the LENSANDBULB assembly, CAPANDLENS assembly, BATTERYANDPLATE assembly, HOUSING part, and SWITCH part to create the FLASHLIGHT assembly.

Review Mate types. Create the following Mate relationships:

*   Coincident.

*   Concentric.

*   Distance.

Utilize the following Assembly tools from the Assembly toolbar: Insert Component, Hide/Show, Change Suppression, Mate, Move Component, Rotate Component, Exploded View, and Interference Detection.

After completing the activities in this project, you will be able to:

*   Create two Assembly Templates: ASM-IN-ANSI and ASM-MM-ISO.

*   Apply the following Standard Mates: Coincident, Concentric, and Distance.

*   Utilize the following Assembly tools: Insert Component, Hide/Show Component, Mate, Move Component, Rotate Component, Interference Detection, and Suppress/Resolve.

- Export a .STL file of the HOUSING part.

- Develop an eDrawing for the FLASHLIGHT assembly.

- Create an Exploded view of the FLASHLIGHT assembly.

- Animate a Collapse view and an Exploded view.

- Organize assemblies into sub-assemblies.

- Create four Assemblies:

    o LENSANDBULB.

    o BATTERYANDPLATE.

    o CAPANDLENS.

    o FLASHLIGHT.

Assembly Modeling Overview

An assembly is a document that contains two or more parts. An assembly inserted into another assembly is called a sub-assembly. A part or assembly inserted into an assembly is called a component.

Establishing the correct component relationship in an assembly requires forethought on component interaction. Mates are geometric relationships that align and fit components in an assembly. Mates remove degrees of freedom from a component.

In dynamics, motion of an object is described in linear and rotational terms. Components possess linear motion along the x, y, and z-axes and rotational motion around the x, y, and z-axes.

In an assembly, each component has 6 degrees of freedom: 3 translational (linear) and 3 rotational. Mates remove degrees of freedom. All components are rigid bodies.

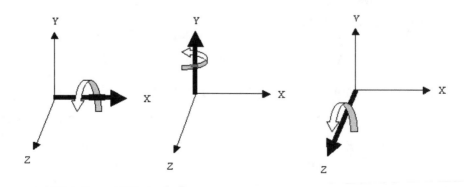

The components do not flex or deform. Components are assembled with Standard Mate types. The Standard Mate types are Coincident, Parallel, Perpendicular, Tangent, Concentric, Distance and Angle. The mate types are displayed in the Mate PropertyManager, but only the mates that are applicable to the current selections are available.

The Advanced Mate types are Symmetric, Cam, Width, Gear, Rack Pinion, and Limit.

Mates require geometry from two different components.

Selected geometry includes Planar Faces, Cylindrical faces, Linear edges, Circular/Arc edges, Vertices, Axes, Temporary axes, Planes, Points, and Origins.

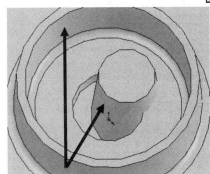

Mates reflect the physical behavior of a component in an assembly. Example: Utilize a Concentric Mate between the BATTERY Extruded Boss (Terminal) cylindrical face and the BATTERYPLATE Extruded Boss (Holder) face.

The FLASHLIGHT assembly consists of the following components:

FLASHLIGHT Components:	
BATTERY	BATTERYPLATE
LENS	BULB
O-RING	SWITCH
LENSCAP	HOUSING

How do you organize these components into the FLASHLIGHT assembly? Answer: Create an assembly component layout diagram to determine which components to group into a sub-assembly.

FLASHLIGHT Assembly

Plan the sub-assembly component layout diagram.

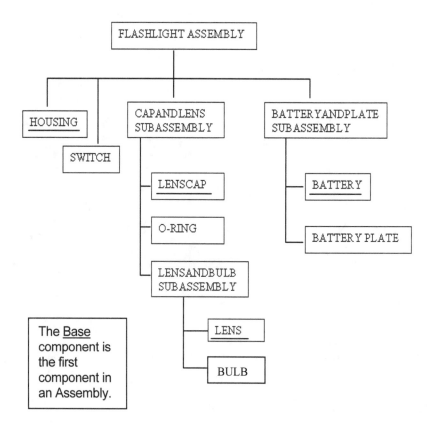

Assembly Layout Structure

The FLASHLIGHT assembly steps are as follows:

• Create the LENSANDBULB sub-assembly from the LENS and BULB component. The LENS is the Base component.

• Create the BATTERYANDPLATE sub-assembly from the BATTERY and BATTERYPLATE component.

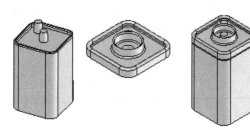

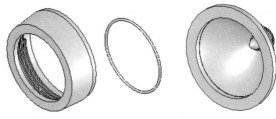

- Create the CAPANDLENS sub-
  assembly from the LENSCAP,
  O-RING and LENSANDBULB sub-
  assembly. The LENSCAP is the Base
  component.

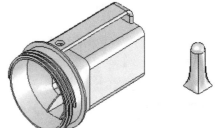

- Create the FLASHLIGHT assembly. The
  HOUSING is the Base component. Insert the
  SWITCH, CAPANDLENS and
  BATTERYANDPLATE component.

- Modify the dimensions to complete the FLASHLIGHT
  assembly.

Assembly Techniques

Assembly modeling requires time and practice. Below are
helpful hints and techniques to address the Bottom up design
modeling approach.

- Create an assembly layout structure. The layout structure will organize the sub-
  assemblies and components and save time.

- Insert sub-assemblies and components as lightweight components. Lightweight
  components save on file size, rebuild time, and overall complexity.

- Set Lightweight components in the Tools, Options command.

- Use the Zoom and Rotate commands to select the correct geometry in the Mate
  process. Zoom to select the correct face, edge, plane, etc.

- Improve display. Apply various colors to features and components.

- Mate with Reference planes when addressing complex geometry. Example: The
  O-RING does not contain a flat surface or edge.

- Activate the Temporary Axes and Planes from the Main menu.

- Select Reference planes from the fly-out FeatureManager. Expand the component in
  the FeatureManager to view the planes.

Example: Select the Right Plane of the LENS and the Right Plane of the BULB to be
collinear. Do not select the Right Plane of the HOUSING if you want to create a
reference between the LENS and the BULB.

Remove display complexity. Hide components and features. Suppress components and features when not required.

- Use the Move Component and Rotate Component commands before mating. Position the component in the correct orientation.

- Remove unwanted entries. Use Right-click Clear Selections or Right-click Delete from the Assembly Mate Selections text box.

- Verify the position of the mated components. Use Top, Front, Right, and Section views.

- Use caution when you view the color blue in an assembly. Blue indicates that a part is being edited in the context of the assembly.

- Avoid unwanted references. Verify your geometry selections with the PropertyManager.

Assembly Template

An Assembly Document Template is the foundation of the assembly. The FLASHLIGHT assembly and its sub-assemblies require the Assembly Document Template. Utilize the default Assembly Template. Modify the Dimensioning Standard and Units. Create an Assembly Document Template using inch units, ASM-IN-ANSI. Create an Assembly Document Template using millimeter units, ASM-MM-ISO. Save the Templates in the MY-TEMPLATES folder.

Activity: Assembly Templates-ANSI

Create an Assembly Template.

1)   Click **File, New** ⬜ from the Main menu. Double-click
     Assembly from the Templates tab. The Insert Component
     PropertyManager is displayed.

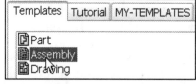

2)   Click **Cancel** ⊗ from the Insert Component
     PropertyManager.

Set the Assembly Document Template options.
3)   Click **Tools, Options, Document Properties** tab from the Main menu.

Create an ANSI assembly template.
4)   Select **ANSI** for Dimensioning standard.

5)   Click **Units**. Select **IPS, (inch, pound, second)** for Unit system.

6)   Enter **3** in the Length units Decimal box.

7)   Enter **0** for Angular units Decimal box.

8)   Click **OK**.

Save the assembly template.

9)   Click **File**, **Save As** from the Main menu.

10)   Select the **Assembly Template (*asmdot)** from the Save As type box.

11)   Select the **SOLIDWORKS-MODELS 2007/MY-TEMPLATES** folder.

12)   Enter **ASM-IN-ANSI** in the File name box. Click **Save**.

File name:	ASM-IN-ANSI		Save
Save as type:	Assembly Templates (*.asmdot)	⌄	Cancel

Activity: Assembly Templates-ISO

Create an ISO assembly template.

13)   Click **File**, **New** ⬜ from the Main menu. Double-click **Assembly** from the Templates tab.

14)   Click **Cancel** ⊗ from the Insert Component PropertyManager.

Set the Assembly Document Template options.

15)   Click **Tools**, **Options**, **Document Properties** tab from the Main menu.

16)   Select **ISO** from the Dimensioning standard box.

17)   Click **Units**. Select **MMGS, (millimeter, gram, second)** for Unit system.

18)   Enter **2** in the Length units Decimal box. Enter **0** in the Angular units Decimal box. Click **OK**.

Save the assembly template.

19)   Click **File**, **Save As** from the Main menu.

20)   Select the **Assembly Template (*asmdot)** from the Save As type box.

21)   Select the **SOLIDWORKS-MODELS 2007/MY-TEMPLATES** folder.

22)   Enter **ASM-MM-ISO** in the File name box.

23)   Click **Save**.

LENSANDBULB Sub-assembly

Create the LENSANDBULB sub-assembly. The LENS is the Base component. LENSANDBULB sub-assembly mates the BULB component to the LENS component. The Right Plane of the LENS and the Right Plane of the BULB are Coincident.

The Top Plane of the LENS and the Top Plane of the BULB are Coincident. The inside Counterbore face of the LENS and the back face of the BULB utilize a Distance mate. The LENS name is added to the LENSANDBULB assembly FeatureManager with the symbol (f). The symbol (f) represents a fixed component. A fixed component cannot move and is locked to the assembly Origin.

The Fixed component state can be removed to create a component that is free to move or rotate. To remove the fixed state, Right-click on the component name in the FeatureManager. Click Float. The component is free to move and rotate.

Suppress the Lens Shield feature to view all surfaces during the mate process. Utilize Open Part to open the LENS from inside the LENSANDBULB assembly.

Change Suppre...

Utilize Change Suppression State Suppre... from the Assembly toolbar or Suppress ↓�ⓑ Suppress from the assembly FeatureManager to Suppress a component. Utilize the Set to Resolved 🐚 Set to Resolved option to restore the component. The Mates of a Suppressed component are also Suppressed.

🐚 Suppress
🐚 Lightweight
🐚 Resolve

Activity: LENSANDBULB Sub-assembly

Close all documents.

24) Click **Windows**, **Close All** from the Main menu.

Create the LENSANDBULB sub-assembly.

25) Click **File**, **New** ⬜ from the Main menu. Click the **MY-TEMPLATES** tab.

26) Double-click **ASM-IN-ANSI, [ASM-MM-ISO]**.

Insert the LENS.

27) Click **View**; check **Origins** from the Main menu,

28) Click **Browse** from the Insert Component PropertyManager. Select **Part** for Files of type.

29) Double-click **LENS** from the PROJECTS folder. Click the **Origin** ↳ of the Assembly. The mouse pointer displays the Insert Component fixed at the Origin icon 🐚 .

30) Click **Save** 💾. Select the **PROJECTS** folder. Enter **LENSANDBULB** for File name. Click **Save**.

Insert the BULB.

Insert

31) Click **Insert Components** Compo... from the Assembly toolbar. Click **Browse**. Double-click **BULB** from the PROJECTS folder.

32) Click a **position** in front of the LENS as illustrated.

33) Click **Shaded With Edges** 🔲 .

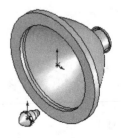

Fit to the Graphics window.

34) Press the **f** key.

Save the LENSANDBULB.

35) Click **Save** 💾.

Suppress the LensShield feature.
36) **Expand** LENS from the FeatureManager.

37) Right-click **LensShield** from the FeatureManager.

38) Click **Feature Properties**.

39) Check the **Suppressed** box.

40) Click **OK** from the Feature Properties dialog box.

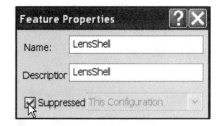

Insert a Coincident Mate.

41) Click **Mate** Mate from the Assembly toolbar. The Mate PropertyManager is displayed.

42) **Expand** the fly-out FeatureManager.

43) Click **Right Plane** of the LENS from the fly-out FeatureManager.

44) **Expand** BULB from the fly-out FeatureManager.

45) Click **Right Plane** of the BULB from the fly-out FeatureManager. Coincident is selected by default.

46) Click **OK** ✔.

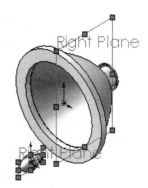

Insert the second Coincident Mate.
47) Click **Top Plane** of the LENS from the fly-out FeatureManager.

48) Click **Top Plane** of the BULB from the fly-out FeatureManager. Coincident is selected by default.

49) Click **OK** ✔.

Select face geometry efficiently. Position the mouse pointer in the middle of the face. Do not position the mouse pointer near the edge of the face. Zoom in on geometry. Utilize the Face Selection Filter for narrow faces.

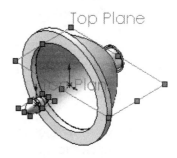

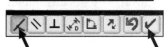

Insert a Coincident Mate.

50) **Zoom in** and **Rotate** ⟳ on the Counterbore.

51) Select the **Counterbore face** of the LENS.

52) Click the **bottom flat face** of the BULB. Coincident ∠ is selected by default.

53) Click **OK** ✔.

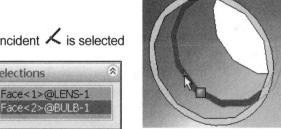

Close the Mate PropertyManager.

54) Click **OK** ⊘ from the Mate PropertyManager. The LENSANDBULB is fully defined.

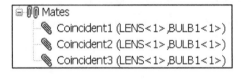

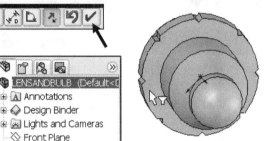

Display the Mate types.
55) **Expand** the Mates folder from the FeatureManager. View the created mates.

56) Click **Right view** ⬚.

Save the LENSANDBULB.
57) Click **Isometric view** ⬛.

58) Click **Save** 💾.

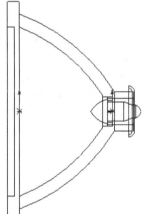

💡 If the wrong face or edge is selected, click the face or edge again to remove it from the Mate Selections text box. Right-click Clear Selections to remove all geometry from the Mate Selections text box. To delete a Mate from the FeatureManager, right-click on the Mate, click Delete.

BATTERYANDPLATE Sub-assembly

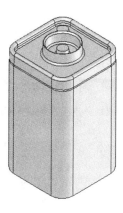

Create the BATTERYANDPLATE sub-assembly. Utilize two Coincident Mates and one Concentric Mate to assemble the BATTERYPLATE component to the BATTERY component.

Note: Utilize the Selection Filter required. Select planes from the FeatureManager when the Selection Filters are activated.

Activity: BATTERYANDPLATE Sub-assembly

Create the BATTERYANDPLATE sub-assembly.

59) Click **File, New** from the Main menu.

60) Click the **MY-TEMPLATES** tab.

61) Double-click **ASM-IN-ANSI**. The Insert Component PropertyManager is displayed.

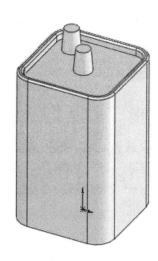

Insert the BATTERY part.

62) Click **View**; check **Origins** from the Main menu.

63) Click **Browse** from the Insert Component PropertyManager.

64) Double-click **BATTERY** from the PROJECTS folder.

Place the BATTERY.

65) Click the **Origin** of the Assembly.

Save the BATTERYANDPLATE sub-assembly.

66) Click **Save**.

67) Select the **PROJECTS** folder.

68) Enter **BATTERYANDPLATE** for File name.

69) Enter **BATTERY AND PLATE FOR 6-VOLT FLASHLIGHT** for Description.

70) Click **Save**. The BATTERYANDPLATE FeatureManager is displayed. The BATTERY is fixed to the Origin.

Insert the BATTERYPLATE part.

Insert

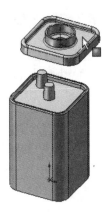

71) Click **Insert Components** Compo... from the Assembly toolbar.

72) Click **Browse**.

73) Double-click **BATTERYPLATE** from the PROJECTS folder.

74) Click a **position** above the BATTERY as illustrated.

Insert a Coincident Mate.

75) Press the **Up Arrow** key, approximately 6 times to display the narrow outside bottom face of the BATTERYPLATE.

76) Click **Mate** Mate from the Assembly toolbar.

77) Click the **narrow outside bottom face** of the BATTERYPLATE.

78) Press the **Down Arrow** key, approximately 8 times to display the top face of the BATTERY.

79) **Zoom In** . on the top face.

80) Click the **top narrow flat face** of the BATTERY Base Extrude feature.

Coincident is selected by default.

81) Click **OK** .

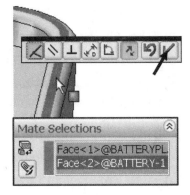
Mate Selections
Face<1>@BATTERYPL
Face<2>@BATTERY-1

Insert a Coincident Mate.

82) Click **Right Plane** of the BATTERY from the FeatureManager.

83) Click **Right Plane** of the BATTERYPLATE from the FeatureManager. Coincident is selected by default.

84) Click **OK** .

Mate Selections
Right Plane@BATTEF
Right Plane@BATTEF

Insert a Concentric Mate.

85) Click the **cylindrical face** Terminal feature of the BATTERY.

86) Click the **cylindrical face** Holder feature of the BATTERYPLATE. Concentric is selected by default.

87) Click **OK** .

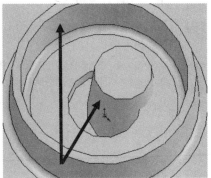
Mate Selections
Face<3>@BATTERY
Face<4>@BATTERY

88) Click **OK** ✅ from the Mate PropertyManager.

Save the BATTERYANDPLATE.

89) Click **Isometric view** 🔲.

90) Click **Save** 💾.

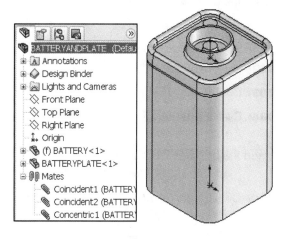

CAPANDLENS Sub-assembly

Create the CAPANDLENS sub-assembly. Utilize two Coincident Mates and one Distance Mate to assemble the O-RING to the LENSCAP. Utilize three Coincident Mates to assemble the LENSANDBULB sub-assembly to the LENSCAP component.

Caution: Select the correct reference. Expand the LENSCAP and O-RING. Click the Right Plane within the LENSCAP. Click the Right Plane within the O-RING.

Activity: CAPANDLENS Sub-assembly

Create the CAPANDLENS sub-assembly.

91) Click **File, New** 🗋 from the Main menu.

92) Click the **MY-TEMPLATES** tab. Double-click **ASM-IN-ANSI**.

Insert the LENSCAP sub-assembly.

93) Click **View**; check **Origin** from the Main menu.

94) Click **Browse** from the Insert Component PropertyManager.

95) Double-click **LENSCAP** from the PROJECTS folder.

96) Click the **Origin** ⌶ of the Assembly. The LENSCAP is fixed to the Origin.

Save the CAPANDLENS assembly.

97) Click **Save** 💾. Select the **PROJECTS** folder.

98) Enter **CAPANDLENS** for File name.

99) Enter **LENSCAP AND LENS** for Description.

100) Click **Save**.

Insert the O-RING part.

101) Click **Insert Components** Compo... from the Assembly toolbar.

102) Click **Browse**.

103) Double-click **O-RING** from the PROJECTS folder.

104) Click a **position** behind the LENSCAP as illustrated.

Insert the LENSANDBULB assembly.

105) Click **Insert Components** Compo... from the Assembly toolbar.

106) Click **Browse**. Select **Assembly** for Files of type.

107) Double-click **LENSANDBULB** from the PROJECTS folder.

108) Click a **position** behind the O-RING.

109) Click **Isometric view** .

Move and Hide Components.
110) Click and drag the **O-RING** and **LENSANDBULB** to position equally spaced in the Graphics window.

111) Right-click **LENSANDBULB** from the FeatureManager.

112) Click **Hide** Hide .

Insert three Mates between the LENSCAP and O-RING.

113) Click **Mate** Mate from the Assembly toolbar. The Mate PropertyManager is displayed.

Insert a Coincident Mate.
114) Click **Right Plane** of the LENSCAP from the fly-out FeatureManager.

115) Click **Right Plane** of the O-RING from the fly-out FeatureManager. Coincident is selected by default.

116) Click **OK** ✔.

Insert a second Coincident Mate.
117) Click **Top Plane** of the LENSCAP from the fly-out FeatureManager.

118) Click **Top Plane** of the O-RING from the fly-out FeatureManager. Coincident is selected by default.

119) Click **OK** ✔.

Insert a Distance Mate.

120) Click the Shell1 **back inside face** of the LENSCAP as illustrated.

121) Click **Front Plane** of the O-RING from the fly-out FeatureManager.

122) Click **Distance** .

123) Enter **.125/2**in, **[3.175/2mm]**.

124) Click **OK** ✔.

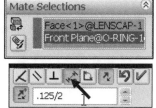

125) Click **OK** ✅ from the Mate PropertyManager.

126) Click **Isometric view** .

127) Click **Save** .

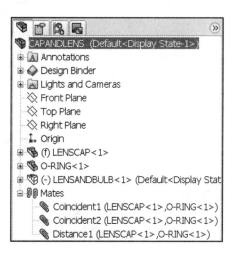

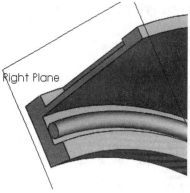

How is the Distance Mate, .0625, [1.588] calculated? Answer:

O-RING Radius (.1250in/2) = .0625in.

O-RING Radius [3.175mm/2] = [1.5875].

🔆 Utilize a Section View to locate internal geometry for mating and verify position of components.

🔆 Build flexibility into the Mate. The Distance Mate option offers additional flexibility over the Coincident Mate option. A Distance Mate value can be modified in a future design.

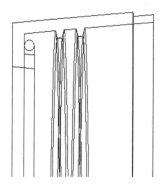

Show the LENSANDBULB.
128) Right-click **LENSANDBULB** from the FeatureManager.

129) Click **Show**  Show.

Fit the Model to the Graphics window.
130) Press the **f** key.

131) Click **Mate** Mate from the Assembly toolbar.

Insert a Coincident Mate.
132) Click **Right Plane** of the LENSCAP from the FeatureManager.

133) Click **Right Plane** of the LENSANDBULB from the FeatureManager. Coincident is selected by default.

134) Click **OK** ✔.

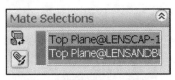

Insert a Coincident Mate.
135) Click **Top Plane** of the LENSCAP from the FeatureManager.

136) Click **Top Plane** of the LENSANDBULB from the FeatureManager. Coincident is selected by default.

137) Click **OK** ✔.

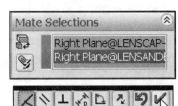

Insert a Coincident Mate.
138) Click the flat inside **narrow back face** of the LENSCAP.

139) Click the **front flat face** of the LENSANDBULB. Coincident ⊾ is selected by default.

140) Click **OK** ✔.

141) Click **OK** ⊘ from the Mate PropertyManager.

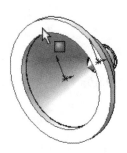

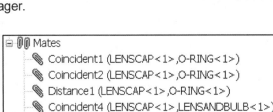

Mates
- Coincident1 (LENSCAP<1>,O-RING<1>)
- Coincident2 (LENSCAP<1>,O-RING<1>)
- Distance1 (LENSCAP<1>,O-RING<1>)
- Coincident4 (LENSCAP<1>,LENSANDBULB<1>)
- Coincident5 (LENSCAP<1>,LENSANDBULB<1>)
- Coincident6 (LENSCAP<1>,LENSANDBULB<1>)
- Coincident7 (LENSCAP<1>,LENSANDBULB<1>)

Confirm the location of the O-RING.

142) Click **Right Plane** of the CAPANDLENS from the FeatureManager.

143) Click **Section view** 🔲. The Section View PropertyManager is displayed.

144) Click **Isometric view** 🔲.

145) Check the **Section 2** box.

146) Click **Top Plane** from the FeatureManager.

147) Click **OK** ✅ from the Section View PropertyManager.

Save the CAPANDLENS sub-assembly.

148) Click **Section view** 🔲.

149) Click **Save** 💾.

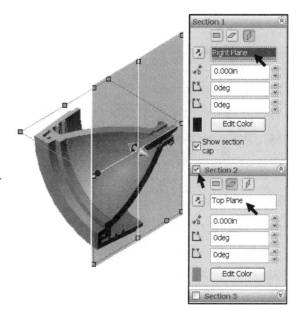

The LENSANDBULB, BATTERYANDPLATE, and CAPANDLENS sub-assemblies are complete. The components in each assembly are fully defined. No minus (-) sign or red error flags exist in the FeatureManager. Insert the sub-assemblies into the final FLASHLIGHT assembly.

FLASHLIGHT Assembly

Create the FLASHLIGHT assembly. The HOUSING is the Base component. The FLASHLIGHT assembly mates the HOUSING to the SWITCH component. The FLASHLIGHT assembly mates the CAPANDLENS and BATTERYANDPLATE.

Activity: FLASHLIGHT Assembly

Create the FLASHLIGHT assembly.

150) Click **File**, **New** 🗋 from the Main menu.

151) Click the **MY-TEMPLATES** tab.

152) Double-click **ASM-IN-ANSI**.

Insert the HOUSING and SWITCH.

153) Click **View**; check **Origin** from the Main menu.

154) Click **Browse** from the Insert Component PropertyManager.

155) Select **Parts** for Files of type. Double-click **HOUSING** from the PROJECTS folder.

156) Click the **Origin** ⌐ of the Assembly.

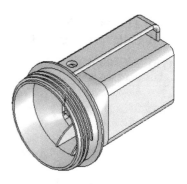

157) Click **Insert Components** Compo... from the Assembly toolbar.

158) Click **Browse**.

159) Double-click **SWITCH** from the PROJECTS folder.

160) Click a **position** in front of the HOUSING as illustrated.

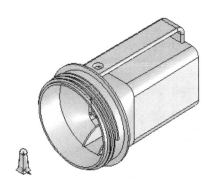

Save the FLASHLIGHT assembly.

161) Click **Save** 💾.

162) Select the **PROJECTS** folder.

163) Enter **FLASHLIGHT** for File name.

164) Enter **FLASHLIGHT ASSEMBLY** for Description.

165) Click **Save**.

Insert a Coincident Mate.

166) Click **Mate** Mate from the Assembly toolbar.

167) Click **Right Plane** of the HOUSING from the fly-out FeatureManager.

168) Click **Right Plane** of the SWITCH from the fly-out FeatureManager. Coincident is selected by default.

169) Click **OK** ✔.

Insert a Coincident Mate.

170) Click **View**; check **Temporary Axes** from the Main menu.

171) Click the **Temporary axis** inside the Switch Hole of the HOUSING as illustrated.

172) Click **Front Plane** of the SWITCH from the FeatureManager. Coincident is selected by default.

173) Click **OK** ✔.

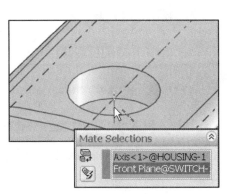

Insert a Distance Mate.

174) Click the **top face** of the Handle.

175) Click the **Vertex (point)** on the Loft top face of the SWITCH.

176) Click **Distance** ↙ᴰ.

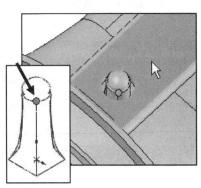

177) Enter **.100in**, **[2.54]**. Check Flip Direction if required.

178) Click **OK** ✔.

179) Click **OK** ✅ from the Mate PropertyManager.

Insert the CAPANDLENS assembly.
180) Click **View**; uncheck **Temporary Axes** from the Main menu.

181) Click **Insert Components** Compo... from the Assembly toolbar.

182) Click **Browse**.

183) Select **Assembly** for Files of type.

184) Double-click **CAPANDLENS** from the PROJECTS folder.

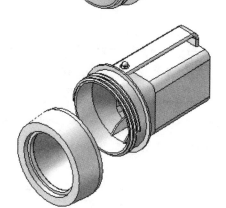

Place the Assembly.
185) Click a **position** in front of the HOUSING.

186) Click **View**; uncheck **Origins** from the Main menu.

Insert Mates between the HOUSING component and the CAPANDLENS sub-assembly.

187) Click **Mate** Mate from the Assembly toolbar.

Insert a Coincident Mate.
188) Click **Right Plane** of the HOUSING from the fly-out FeatureManager.

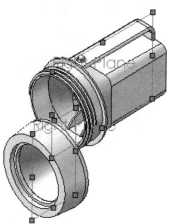

189) Click **Right Plane** of the CAPANDLENS from the fly-out FeatureManager. Coincident is selected by default.

190) Click **OK** ✔.

Insert a Coincident Mate.
191) Click **Top Plane** of the HOUSING from the fly-out FeatureManager.

192) Click **Top Plane** of the CAPANDLENS from the fly-out FeatureManager. Coincident is selected by default.

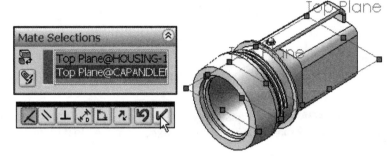

193) Click **OK** ✔.

Insert a Coincident Mate.
194) Click the **front face of the Boss-Stop** on the HOUSING as illustrated.

Rotate the view.
195) Press the **Left Arrow Key** to view the back face.

196) Click the **back face** of the CAPANDLENS as illustrated. The two selected faces are displayed in the Mate Selections box. Coincident is selected by default.

197) Click **OK** ✔.

198) Click **OK** ⊘ from the Mate PropertyManager.

Save the FLASHLIGHT assembly.
199) Click **Isometric view** ▣.

200) Click **Save** 🖫.

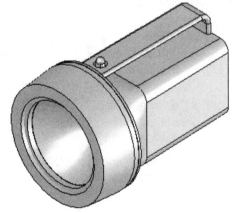

Insert the BATTERYANDPLATE sub-assembly.

Insert

201) Click **Insert Components** Compo... from the Assembly toolbar.

202) Click **Browse**.

203) Select **Assembly** for Files of type.

204) Double-click **BATTERYANDPLATE** from the PROJECTS folder.

205) Click a **position** to the left of the HOUSING.

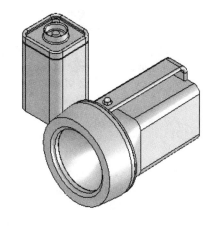

Rotate the part.
206) Click **BATTERYANDPLATE** from the FeatureManager.

Rotate

207) Click **Rotate Component** Compo... from the Assembly toolbar. The Rotate Component PropertyManager is displayed.

208) Rotate the **BATTERYANDPLATE** until it is approximately parallel with the HOUSING.

209) Click **OK** from the Rotate Component PropertyManager.

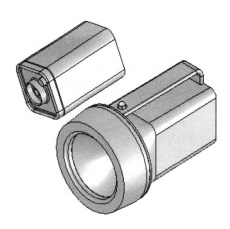

Insert a Coincident Mate.

210) Click **Mate** Mate from the Assembly toolbar.

211) Click **Right Plane** of the HOUSING from the fly-out FeatureManager.

212) Click **Front Plane** of the BATTERYANDPLATE from the fly-out FeatureManager. The selected Planes are displayed in the Mate Selections box. Coincident is selected by default.

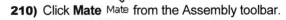

213) Click **OK** ✔.

214) Move the **BATTERYANDYPLATE** in front of the HOUSING as illustrated.

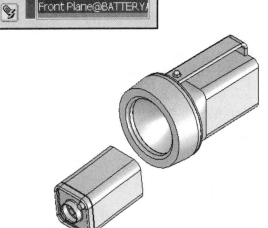

Insert a Coincident Mate.

215) Click **Top Plane** of the HOUSING from the FeatureManager.

216) Click **Right Plane** of the BATTERYANDPLATE from the FeatureManager. Coincident is selected by default.

217) Click **OK** ✔.

218) Click **OK** 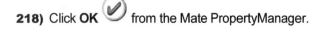 from the Mate PropertyManager.

Display the Section view.

219) Click **Right Plane** from the FLASHLIGHT Assembly FeatureManager.

220) Click **Section view** 🗐. The Section View PropertyManager is displayed.

221) Click **OK** ✅ from the Section View PropertyManager.

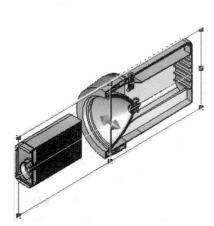

Move the BATTERYANDPLATE in front of the HOUSING.

222) Click and drag the **BATTERYANDPLATE** in front of the HOUSING.

Insert a Coincident Mate.

223) Click **Mate** Mate from the Assembly toolbar.

224) Click the **back center Rib1 face** of the HOUSING.

225) Click the **bottom face** of the BATTERYANDPLATE. Coincident is selected by default.

226) Click **OK** ✔.

227) Click **Isometric view** ⬛.

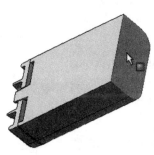

228) Click **OK** ✅ from the Mate PropertyManager.

Display the Full view.

229) Click **Section view** 🗐.

Save the FLASHLIGHT.

230) Click **Save** 💾.

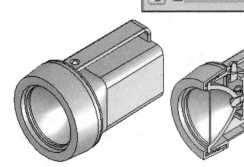

231) Click **Yes** to update all components.

Additional information on Assembly, Move Component, Rotate Component, and Mates is available in SolidWorks Help Topics.

Review of the FLASHLIGHT Assembly.

The FLASHLIGHT assembly consisted of the CAPANDLENS sub-assembly, BATTERYANDPLATE sub-assembly, HOUSING part, and SWITCH part. The CAPANDLENS sub-assembly contained the BULBANDLENS sub-assembly, the O-RING, and the LENSCAP part.

Through the Assembly Layout illustration you simplified the number of components into a series of smaller assemblies. You also enhanced your modeling techniques and skills.

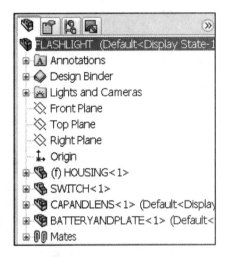

You still have a few more areas to address. One of the biggest design issues in assembly modeling is interference. Let's investigate the FLASHLIGHT assembly.

Addressing Interference Issues

There is an interference issue between the FLASHLIGHT components. Address the design issue. Adjust Rib2 on the HOUSING. Test with the Interference Check command. The FLASHLIGHT assembly is illustrated in inches.

Activity: FLASHLIGH Assembly-Interference Issues

Check for interference.

Interfer...

232) Click **Interference Detection** Detection from the Assembly toolbar.

233) Delete **FLASHLIGHT.SLDASM** from the Selected Components box.

234) Click **BATTERYANDPLATE** from the FeatureManager.

235) Click **HOUSING** from the FeatureManager.

236) Click **Calculate**. The interference is displayed in red in the Graphics window.

237) Click each **Interference** in the Results box to view
the interference in red with Rib2 of the HOUSING.

238) Click **OK** from the Interference Detection
PropertyManager.

Modify the Rib2 dimension.
239) Expand HOUSING from the FeatureManager.

240) Double-click the **Rib2** feature.

241) Click **Hidden Lines Removed** ⬜.

242) Double click **1.300**, [**33.02**].

243) Enter **1.350in**, [**34.29**].

244) Click **Rebuild** 🔴.

Recheck for Interference.

245) Click **Interference Detection** Detection from the
Assembly toolbar.   The Interference Detection PropertyManager is
displayed.

246) Delete **FLASHLIGHT.SLDASM** from the Selected Components
box.

247) Click **BATTERYANDPLATE** from the FeatureManager.

248) Click **HOUSING** from the FeatureManager.

249) Click the **Calculate** button. No Interference is displayed in the
Results box. The FLASHLIGHT design is complete.

250) Click **OK** from the Interference Detection PropertyManager.

Save the FLASHLIGHT.
251) Click **Shaded With Edges** ⬜.

252) Click **Save** 💾.

253) Click **YES** to the question, "Rebuild the assembly and update the components".

Exploded View

The Exploded View illustrates how to assemble the components in an assembly. Create an Exploded View with seven steps in the FLASHLIGHT assembly. Click and drag components in the Graphics window. The Manipulator icon ⋏ indicates the direction to explode. Select an alternate component edge for the Explode direction.

Drag the component in the Graphics window or enter an exact value in the Explode distance box. In this activity, manipulate the top-level components in the assembly. In the project exercises, create exploded views for each sub-assembly and utilize the Re-use sub-assembly explode 🗗 option in the top level assembly.

Access the Explode view option as follows:

- Right-click the configuration name in the ConfigurationManager.

- Select the Exploded View tool from the Assembly toolbar.

- Select Insert, Exploded View from the Main menu.

The Assembly Exploder utilizes a PropertyManager.

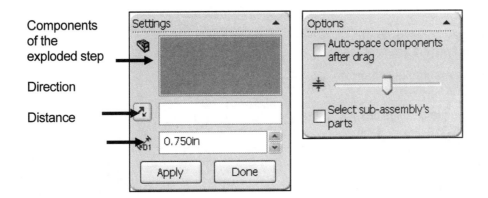

Components
of the
exploded step

Direction

Distance

Activity: FLASHLIGHT Assembly-Exploded View

Insert an Exploded view.

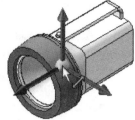

254) Click **Exploded View** View from the Assembly toolbar. The Explode PropertyManager is displayed.

Create Explode Step1.

255) Check **Select sub-assembly's parts** in the Options box.

256) Click **CAPANDLENS** from the Graphics window.

257) Click and drag the **blue manipulator handle** to the left.

258) Release the **mouse** button.

259) Click **Done** from the Settings box. Explode Step1 is created.

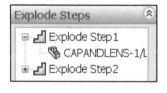

Fit the Model to the Graphics window.
260) Press the **f** key.

Create Explode Step2.
261) Click **SWITCH** from the FeatureManager.

262) Drag the **green manipulator handle** upward.

263) Click **Done** from the Settings box. Explode Step2 is created.

Create Explode Step3.
264) Click **LensCover of LENS** in the Graphics window.

265) Drag the blue **manipulator handle** to the left.

266) Click **Done** from the Settings box.

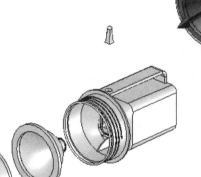

Create Explode Step4.
267) Click **O-RING** from the FeatureManager.

268) Drag the blue **manipulator handle** to the front of the LensCover of LENS.

269) Click **Done** from the Settings box.

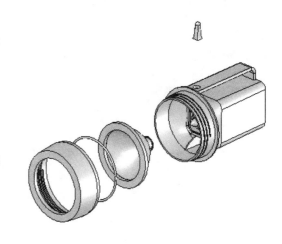

Create Explode Step5.
270) Click **BULB** from the FeatureManager.

271) Drag the blue **manipulator handle** to the back of the LensCover.

272) Click **Done**.

Create Explode Step6.
273) Click **HOUSING** from the FeatureManager.

274) Drag the **blue manipulator handle** backwards to expose the BATTERYANDPLATE.

275) Click **Done** from the Settings box.

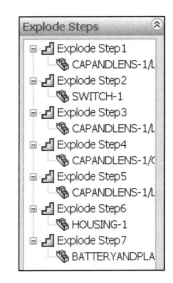

Create Explode Step7
276) Click **BATTERYPLATE** from the FeatureManager.

277) Drag the blue **manipulator handle** forward.

278) Click **Done** from the Settings box.

279) Click **OK** ✅ for the Explode PropertyManager.

Fit the Model to the Graphics window.
280) Press the **f** key.

Remove the Exploded State.
281) **Right-click** in the Graphics window.

282) Click **Collapse** from the Pop-up menu.

283) Click **Isometric view** 🔲.

284) Click **Save** 💾.

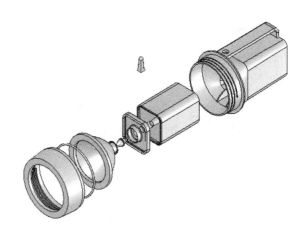

Export Files and eDrawings

You receive a call from the sales department. They inform you that the customer increased the initial order by 200,000 units. However, the customer requires a prototype to verify the design in six days. What do you do? Answer: Contact a Rapid Prototype supplier. You export three SolidWorks files:

- HOUSING.

- LENSCAP.

- BATTERYPLATE.

Use the Stereo Lithography (STL) format. Email the three files to a Rapid Prototype supplier. Example: Paperless Parts Inc. (www.paperlessparts.com). A Stereolithography (SLA) supplier provides physical models from 3D drawings. 2D drawings are not required. Export the HOUSING. SolidWorks eDrawings provides a facility for you to animate, view and create compressed documents to send to colleagues, customers and vendors. Publish an eDrawing of the FLASHLIGHT assembly.

Activity: Export Files and eDrawings

Open and Export the HOUSING.
285) Right-click on **HOUSING** in the FLASHLIGHT Graphics window.

286) Click **Open Part**.

287) Click **File**, **Save As**. A warning message states that, "HOUSING.SLDPRT is being referenced by other open documents.

288) Click **OK**.

289) Select **STL (*.stl)** from the Save as type box.

290) Drag the **dialog box** to the left to view the Graphics window.

291) Click **Options** in the lower right corner of the Save dialog box. The Export Options dialog box is displayed.

292) Check **Binary** from the Output as box.

293) Click **Course** for Resolution.

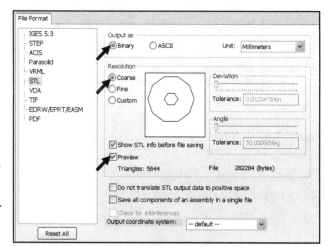

Display the STL triangular faceted model.
294) Click **Preview**.

295) Drag the **dialog box** to the left to view the Graphics window.

Create the binary STL file.
296) Click **OK** from the Export Option dialog box.

297) Click **Save** from the Save As dialog box. A status report is provided.

298) Click **Yes**.

Publish an eDrawing and email the document to a colleague.

Create the eDrawing and animation.
299) Click **Tools**, **Add-ins**, **eDrawings 2007** from the Main menu.

300) Click **OK** from the Add-Ins box. Note: The eDrawings toolbar contains two icons.

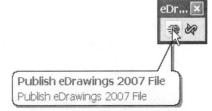

View the eDrawing animation.
301) Click **eDrawing** .

302) Click **Play** .

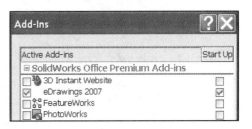

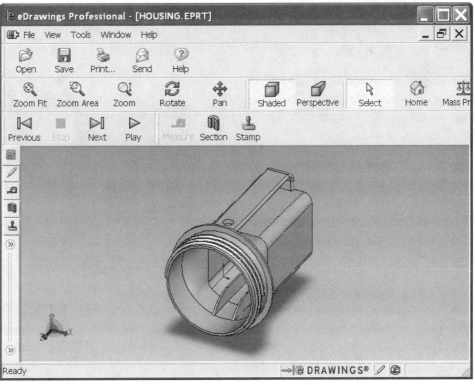

SolidWorks 2007: The Basics

Stop the animation.

303) Click **Stop** Stop .

Save the eDrawing.

304) Click **Save** Save from the eDrawing Main menu.

305) Select the **PROJECTS** folder.

306) Enter **FLASHLIGHT** for File name. Click **Save**.

307) Click **Close** ✖ from the eDrawing screen.

It is time to go home. The telephone rings. The customer is ready to place the order. Tomorrow you will receive the purchase order.

The customer also discusses a new purchase order that requires a major design change to the handle. You work with your industrial designer and discuss the two options. The first option utilizes Guide Curves on a Sweep feature.

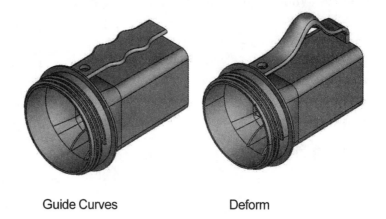

Guide Curves   Deform

The second option utilizes the Deform feature. These features are explored in a discussion on the multimedia CD contained in the text.

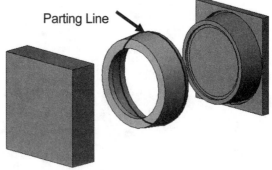

Parting Line

You contact your mold maker and send an eDrawing of the LENSCAP.

The mold maker recommends placing the parting line at the edge of the Revolved Cut surface and reversing the Draft Angle direction. The mold maker also recommends a snap fit versus a thread to reduce cost. The Core-Cavity mold tooling is explored in the project exercises.

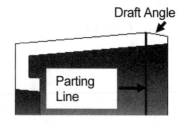

Draft Angle

Parting Line

PAGE 4 - 32

Additional information on Interference Detection, eDrawings, STL files (stereolithography), Guide Curves, Deform and Mold Tools are available in SolidWorks Help Topics.

Project Summary

The FLASHLIGHT contains over 100 features, Reference planes, sketches, and components. You organized the features in each part. You developed an assembly layout structure to organize your components.

The O-RING utilized a Sweep Base feature. The SWITCH utilized a Loft Base feature. The simple Sweep feature requires two sketches: a path and a profile. A complex Sweep requires multiple sketches and Guide Curves. The Loft feature requires two or more sketches created on different planes.

The LENSCAP and HOUSING utilized a variety of features. You applied design intent to reuse geometry through Geometric Relationships, symmetry and patterns.

The assembly required an Assembly Template. You utilized the ASM-IN-ANSI Template to create the LENSANDBULB, CAPANDLENS, BATTERYANDPLATE and FLASHLIGHT assemblies.

You created an STL file of the Housing and an eDrawing of the FLASHLIGHT assembly to communicate with your vendor, mold maker and customer. Review the project exercises before moving on to Project 5.

Project Terminology

Assembly Component Layout Diagram: A diagram used to plan the top-level assembly organization. Organize parts into smaller subassemblies. Create a flow chart or manual sketch to classify components.

Assembly Techniques: Methods utilized to create efficient and accurate assemblies.

Mates: A Mate is a geometric relationship between components in an assembly.

Component: A part or assembly inserted into a new assembly.

eDrawings: A compressed document used to animate and view SolidWorks documents.

Interference Detection: A tool used to determine the amount of interference between components in an assembly.

Stereo Lithography (STL) format: STL format is the type of file format requested by Rapid Prototype manufacturers.

Questions

1. True or False. A Part Template is the foundation for an assembly document. Explain you answer.

2. Describe the difference between the Distance Mate option and the Coincident Mate option. Provide an example.

3. Describe an assembly or sub-assembly. Are they the same?

4. Describe five proven assembly modeling techniques. Can you add a few more?

5. Explain how to determine an interference between components in an assembly. Provide an example.

6. Describe the Deform feature.

7. Describe Mates. Why are Mates important in assembling components?

8. In an assembly, each component has_____# degrees of freedom. Name them.

9. True or False. A fixed component cannot move and is locked to the Origin.

10. Describe a Section view.

11. What are Suppressed features and components? Provide an example.

12. Identify the type a faces utilized for a Concentric Mate.

13. List the standard Mate types. Where would you locate additional information on a Tangent Mate?

14. True or False. Only Planes are utilized for Mate References. Explain your answer.

15. True or False. Only faces are utilized for Mate References. Explain your answer.

16. Define the steps required to create an Exploded view.

17. Identify the Assembly Tools in the Assembly Toolbar below:

A	B	C	D
E	F	G	H

A   B   C   D   E   F   G   H

Exercises

Exercise 4.1: LINK-AND-HOOK Assembly

Create a HOOK-WEIGHT sub-assembly.

The HOOK and WEIGHT parts were developed in Project 3 Exercises.

Model a FLAT-BAR part.

Insert the HOOK-WEIGHT sub-assembly into the LINK-AND-HOOK assembly.

Insert two SHAFT-COLLAR (Exercise 1.4) and AXLE (Exercise 1.3) into the final assembly.

Note: There is more than one mating technique for this exercise. Incorporate symmetry into the assembly. Divide large assemblies into smaller sub-assemblies.

Utilize the Design Library, Add Folder. Browse and select the Folder that contains all your parts.

Drag the parts directly into the assembly.

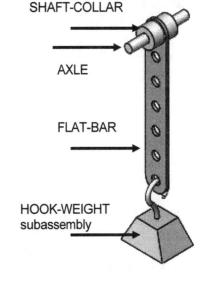

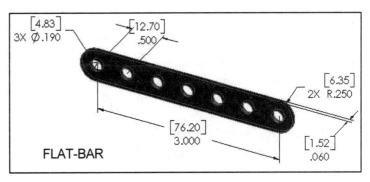

Exercise 4.2: D-CELL-HOLDER Assembly

Create a D-CELL-HOLDER assembly to
contain 4 D-CELL parts.

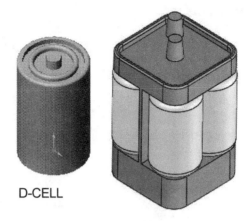

D-CELL

Exercise 4.3: FLASHLIGHT DESIGN CHANGES

Review the HOUSING. The mold for the HOUSING
requires that all sharp edges are removed.

Add Fillet features throughout the FeatureManager to
remove the sharp edges from the inside and outside of
the HOUSING.

The HOUSING LongRibs are too thick. The current
Ribs cause problems in the mold. Divide the current
Rib thickness by 2.

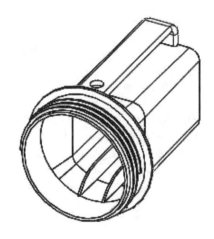

The HOUSING Handle is too short. A large human
hand cannot comfortably hold the Handle. Redesign
the Sweep path of the Handle.

Exercise 4.4: Exploded View

Create an Exploded View of the CAPANDLENS sub-assembly. Animate the Collapse.

Time = 0 seconds   Time = 1 seconds   Time = 2 seconds

Project 5

Fundamentals of Drawing

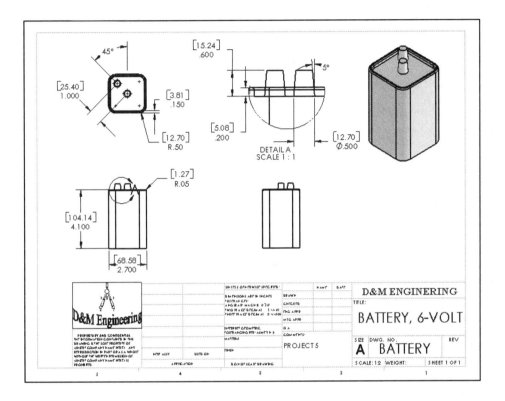

Below are the desired outcomes and usage competencies based on the completion of Project 5.

Project Desired Outcomes:	**Usage Competencies:**
• Custom Drawing and Sheet Template.	• Ability to define Dimensioning standard, Units, and Precision. Create: Title block information, and a Company logo.
• Three drawings: BATTERY, FLASHLIGHT, and O-RING-DESIGN-TABLE.	• Skill to create the following drawing views: Standard, Detail, Section, and Exploded. Proficiency to insert, and modify dimensions, BOM, Balloon text, and Annotations.
• O-RING Design Table.	• Capability to create three configurations in a design table: Small, Medium, and Large.

Notes:

Notes:

Project 5-Fundamentals of Drawing

Project Overview

Create three drawings in this project:

- BATTERY.

- FLASHLIGHT.

- O-RING-DESIGN-TABLE.

The BATTERY part drawing contains the Front, Top, Right, Detail, and Isometric views. Orient the views to fit the drawing sheet. Incorporate the BATTERY part dimensions into the drawing.

The FLASHLIGHT assembly drawing contains an Exploded view, a Bill of Materials, and balloon text. The Balloon items correspond to the Item Number in the BOM. The numeric Part number is a user-defined property in each part.

Insert a Design Table for the O-RING part. A Design Table is an Excel spreadsheet that contains parameters. Define the Sketch-path and Sketch-profile diameters of the Sweep feature.

	A	B	C	D	E
1	Design Table for: O-RING-DESIGN-TABLE				
2	Millimeters	D1@Sketch-path	D1@Sketch-profile		
3	Default	110.49	3.175		
4	Small	100	3		
5	Medium	150	4		
6	Large	200	10		

Create three configurations:

- Small.

- Medium.

- Large.

The O-RING-DESIGN-TABLE drawing contains three configurations of the O-RING. Utilize the drawing view properties to control each part configuration.

The three drawings utilize a custom Drawing Template and Sheet Format. The Drawing Template defines the dimensioning standard, units, and precision. The Sheet Format contains the Title block information and a Company logo.

There are two major design modes used to develop a drawing: Edit Sheet Format and Edit Sheet. Work between the two drawing modes in this project. The Edit Sheet Format mode provides the ability to:

- Change the Title block size and text headings.

- Incorporate a Company logo.

- Add drawing, design, or company text.

The Edit Sheet mode provides the ability to:

- Add or modify views.

- Add or modify dimensions.

- Add or modify text.

After completing the activities in this project, you will be able to:

- Utilize the Drawing and Annotation toolbar for the following features: Model View, Projected View, Detail View, Note, Model Items, and Balloon.

- Create two Drawing Templates: A-IN-ANSI and A-MM-ISO.

- Insert, move, and edit part and drawing dimensions.

- Develop a Design Table for the O-RING part and insert the correct configuration into a drawing.

- Insert an Exploded view with a Bill of Materials.

- Apply the Edit Sheet and Edit Sheet Format modes.

New Drawing and the Drawing Template

The foundation of a new SolidWorks drawing is the Drawing Template. Drawing size, drawing standards, company information, manufacturing, and or assembly requirements, units and other properties are defined in the Drawing Template.

The Sheet Format is incorporated into the Drawing Template. The Sheet Format contains the border, title block information, revision block information, company name, and or logo information, Custom Properties and SolidWorks Properties.

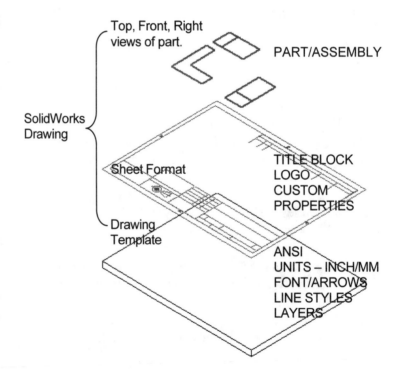

Top, Front, Right views of part.

PART/ASSEMBLY

SolidWorks Drawing

Sheet Format

TITLE BLOCK
LOGO
CUSTOM
PROPERTIES

Drawing Template

ANSI
UNITS – INCH/MM
FONT/ARROWS
LINE STYLES
LAYERS

Custom Properties and SolidWorks Properties are shared values between documents.

Views from the part or assembly are inserted into the SolidWorks Drawing. Views are inserted in Third or First Angle projection. Notes and dimensions for millimeter drawings are provided in brackets [x] for this project.

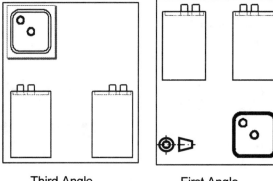

Utilize an A-size Drawing Template with Sheet Format for the BATTERY drawing and FLASHLIGHT assembly drawing. A copy of the default Drawing Template illustrated in this activity is contained in the

Third Angle   First Angle

SOLIDWORKS-MODELS 2007\MY-TEMPLATES folder on the book's Multimedia CD. The default Drawing Templates contain predefined Title block Notes linked to Custom Properties and SolidWorks Properties.

For printers supporting millimeter paper sizes, utilize the Printer, Properties and Scale to Fit option.

Activity: New Drawing and the Drawing Template

Close all parts and drawings.
1)   Click **Windows**, **Close All** from the Main menu.

Create a new drawing.
2)   Click **File**, **New** ☐ from the Main menu.

3)   Double-click **Drawing** from the Templates tab.

4)   Select **A-Landscape**. Click **OK**.

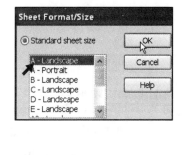

The A-Landscape paper is displayed in the Graphics window. The sheet border defines the drawing size, 11" × 8.5" and (279.4mm × 215.9mm).

The Drawings toolbar is displayed in the CommandManager. Draw1 is the default drawing name. Sheet1 is the default first sheet name.

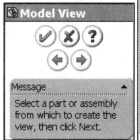

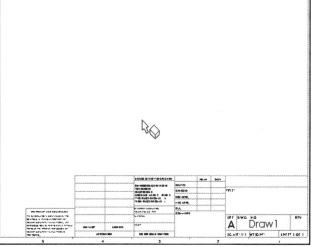

The Control Area alternates between Drawings, Sketch, and Annotations toolbars. The Model View PropertyManager is selected by default.

A New Drawing invokes the Model View PropertyManager if the Start Command When Creating New Drawing option is checked.

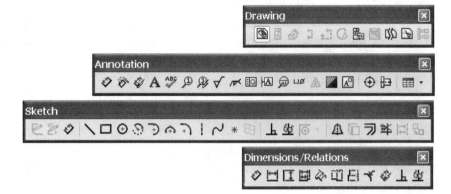

Note: Right-click in the gray area and check the Drawing, Annotation, Sketch, and Dimension/Relations toolbar. Drag individual toolbars to the borders of the Graphics window. Utilize the CommandManager or individual toolbars in this Project.

Set Sheet Properties and Document Properties for the Drawing Template. Sheet Properties control the Sheet Size, Sheet Scale and Type of Projection. Document Properties control the display of dimensions, annotations and symbols in the drawing.

Exit model view.

5)   Click **Cancel** ⊗ from the Model View PropertyManager if required. The Draw1 FeatureManager is displayed to the left of the Graphics window.

Set Sheet Properties.

6)   Right-click in the **Graphics window.**

7)   Click **Properties**. The Sheet Properties are displayed.

8)   Select Sheet Scale **1:1**.

9)   Select **Third Angle** for Type of projection.

10)   Click **OK**.

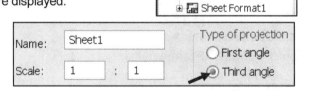

Set Document Properties.

11)   Click **Tools**, **Options**, **Document Properties** tab from the Main menu.

12)   Select **ANSI**, **[ISO]** for Dimensioning standard.

13)   Click **Units**.

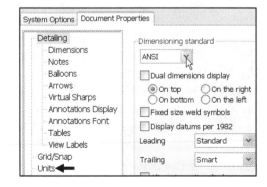

14) Select **IPS**, [**MMGS**] for Unit system.

15) Enter **3**, [**2**] for Length units Decimal places.

16) Enter **0** for Angular units Decimal places.

17) Click **OK**.

Detailing options provide the ability to address: dimensioning standards, text style, center marks, extension lines, arrow styles, tolerance, and precision.

There are numerous text styles and sizes available in SolidWorks.

Save the Drawing.

18) Click **Save** 💾 .

19) Select the **MY-TEMPLATES** folder. Accept the defaults.

20) Click **Save**. The Draw1 FeatureManager is displayed.

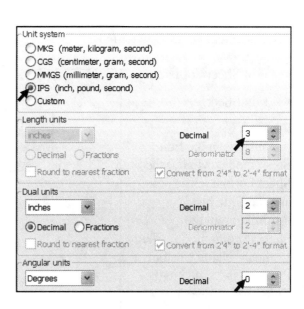

Title Block

The Title block contains text fields linked to System Properties and Custom Properties. System Properties are determined from the SolidWorks documents. Custom Property values are assigned to named variables. Save time. Utilize System Properties and define Custom Properties in your Sheet Formats.

System Properties and Custom Properties for Title Block:			
System Properties Linked to fields in default Sheet Formats:	**Custom Properties of drawings linked to fields in default Sheet Formats:**		**Custom Properties of parts and assemblies linked to fields in default Sheet Formats:**
SW-File Name (in DWG. NO. field):	CompanyName:	EngineeringApproval:	Description (in TITLE field):
SW-Sheet Scale:	CheckedBy:	EngAppDate:	Weight:
SW-Current Sheet:	CheckedDate:	ManufacturingApproval:	Material:
SW-Total Sheets:	DrawnBy:	MfgAppDate:	Finish:
	DrawnDate:	QAApproval:	Revision:
	EngineeringApproval:	QAAppDate:	

The document contains two modes:

- Edit Sheet Format.

- Edit Sheet.

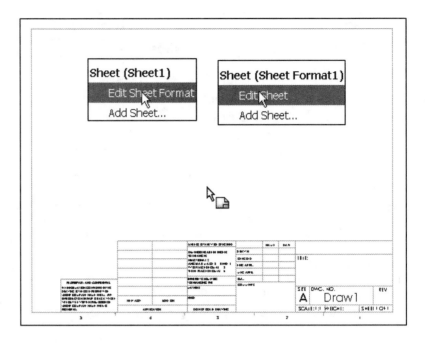

Insert views and dimensions in the Edit Sheet mode. Modify the Sheet Format text, lines, and the Title block information in the Edit Sheet Format mode. The CompanyName Custom Property is located in the Title block above the TITLE box. There is no value defined for CompanyName. A small text box indicates an empty field. Define a value for the Custom Property CompanyName. Example: D&M ENGINEERING. The Tolerance block is located in the Title block.

The Tolerance block provides information to the manufacturer on the minimum and maximum variation for each dimension on the drawing.

If a specific tolerance or note is provided on the drawing, the specific tolerance or note will override the information in the Tolerance block. General tolerance values are based on the design requirements and the manufacturing process. Modify the Tolerance block in the Sheet Format for ASME Y14.5 machined parts. Delete unnecessary text. The FRACTIONAL text refers to inches. The BEND text refers to sheet metal parts.

Activity: Title Block

Invoke the Edit Sheet Format Mode.
21) Right-click **Edit Sheet Format** from the Pop-up menu in the Graphics window. The Title block lines are displayed in blue.

22) Click **Zoom to Area** 🔍 on the Sheet Format Title block.

23) Deactivate **Zoom to Area** 🔍.

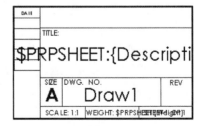

Define COMPANYNAME Custom Property.
24) Click a **position** above the TITLE box.

25) Right-click **Properties**. The Note text is $PRP:"COMPANYNAME".

26) Click **Propertylink**.

27) Click the **File Properties** button from the Link to Property dialog box.

28) Click the **Custom** tab from the Summary Information dialog box.

29) Select **CompanyName** from the Property Name box.

30) Click inside the **Value / Text Expression** box. Enter: **D&M ENGINEERING**.

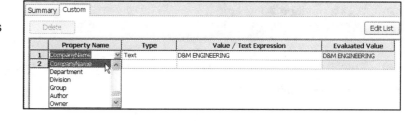

31) Click inside the **Evaluated Value** box. The CompanyName is displayed.

32) Click **OK** from the Summary Information dialog box.

33) Click **OK** from the Link to Property dialog box.

Modify the font size.

34) Uncheck the **Use document's font** box.

35) Click the **Font** button.

Select a new Font size.

36) Click **Bold**.

37) Click **Points**.

38) Select **18**. Click **OK**.

39) Click **OK**. The text is displayed in the Title block.

40) Click **OK** from the Note PropertyManager.

Modify the Tolerance Note in the text box.

41) Double-click the text **INTERPRET GEOMETRIC TOLERANCING PER:**

42) Enter **ASME Y14.5** as illustrated.

43) Click **OK** from the Note PropertyManager.

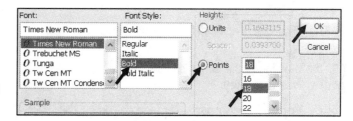

Click outside the Note text box to end the Note, or Click OK from the Note PropertyManager.

Position the mouse pointer over the Linked Note to display the Custom Property value. Tolerance values are different for inch and millimeter templates. Enter the Tolerance values for the inch template. Enter the Tolerance values for the millimeter template.

Modify the Tolerance Note with Properties.

44) Right-click the **Tolerance block** text.

45) Click **Properties**.

46) Delete the text **FRACTIONAL <MOD-PM>**.

47) Delete the text **BEND <MOD-PM>**.

48) Click a **position** at the end of the ANGULAR line.

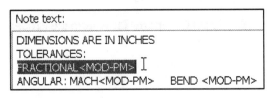

49) Enter **0**.

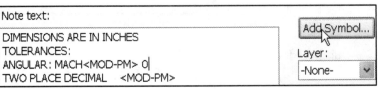

50) Click **Add Symbol**.

51) Select **Degree** from the Modifying Symbols library.

52) Click **OK**.

53) Enter **30′** for minutes of a degree.

54) Enter TWO PLACE DECIMAL **+/- .01**.

55) Enter THREE PLACE DECIMAL **+/- .005**.

56) Click **OK**.

57) Click **OK** ✓ from the Notes PropertyManager.

Fit the drawing to the Graphics window.

58) Press the **f** key.

Note: For millimeter parts, replace the word INCHES with MILLIMETERS. Utilize ONE PLACE DECIMAL +/- 0.5 and TWO PLACE DECIMAL +/- 0.15. Delete the THREE PLACE DECIMAL entry. ASME Y14.5 displays a leading 0 for millimeter values and no leading 0 for inch values for dimensions and tolerances < 1.

Various symbols are available through the Add Symbol button in the Properties dialog box. The Add Symbol 😊 icon is also accessible through the Note PropertyManager. The ± symbol is located in the Modify Symbols list. The ± symbol is displayed as <MOD-PM>. The degree symbol ° is displayed as <MOD-DEG>. Select icon symbols or enter values from the keyboard.

Interpretation of tolerances is as follows for dimensions:

- The angular dimension 110° is machined between 109.5° and 110.5°.

- The dimension 2.04 is machined between 2.03 and 2.05.

Additional Custom Properties and Notes are added later in this project.

Company Logo and Save Sheet Format

The Company logo is a picture file inserted as an OLE object into the Sheet Format. A Company logo is normally located in the Title block. Insert the logo file into the custom Sheet Format.

Example: The logo file Compass.jpg is located in the SOLIDWORKS-MODELS 2007\MY-SHEETFORMATS folder in the book's Multimedia CD. You can utilize any picture file, scanned image, or bitmap. Copy the MY-SHEETFORMATS folder from the Multimedia CD to the SOLIDWORKS-MODELS 2007 folder. Utilize the Save Sheet Format option to save your Custom Sheet Format. Utilize the Save As option to save the Drawing Template.

Activity: Company Logo and Save Sheet Format

Insert a Company Logo.

59) Copy the folder **MY-SHEETFORMATS** from the Multimedia CD to the My Documents\ SOLIDWORKS-MODELS 2007 folder.

60) Click **Insert, Object** from the Main toolbar.

61) Click **Create from File**.

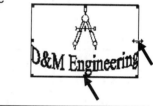

62) Click **Browse**.

63) Select **MY-SHEETFORMATS\Compass.jpg**.

64) Click **OK**.

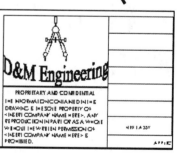

65) Drag the picture handles to size the **picture** to the left side of the Title block.

Return to the Edit Sheet mode.
66) Right-click in the **Graphics window**.

67) Click **Edit Sheet**. The Title block is displayed in black.

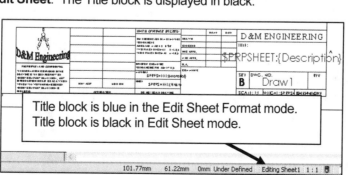

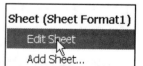

Title block is blue in the Edit Sheet Format mode.
Title block is black in Edit Sheet mode.

Fit the Sheet Format to the Graphics window.
68) Press the **f** key.

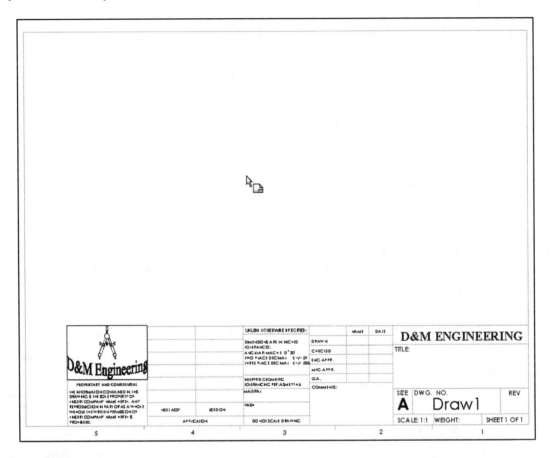

Save the Sheet Format as a Custom Sheet Format. Combine the Sheet Format with the Drawing Template to create a Custom Drawing Template. Use the Custom Sheet Format and Drawing Template to create drawings in this project.

Save the Sheet Format.
69) Click **File**, **Save Sheet Format** from the Main menu.

70) Select the **PROJECTS** folder.

71) Enter **MY-A-FORMAT** for File name. Note: .slddrt file extension.

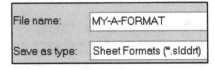

72) Click **Save**.

The Sheet Format1 icon is displayed in the Feature Manager.

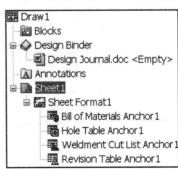

Save the Drawing Template.
73) Click **File**, **Save As** from the Main menu.

74) Select the **MY-TEMPLATES** folder.

75) Select **Drawing Templates (*.drwdot)** for Save as type.

76)   Enter **A-IN-ANSI**, **[A-MM-ISO]** for File name.

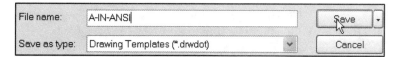

77)   Click **Save**.

Close all documents.

78)   Click **Window**, **Close All** from the Main menu.

Verify the template.

79)   Click **File**, **New** from the Main menu.

80)   Click the **MY-TEMPLATES** tab.

81)   Double-click the **A-IN-ANSI**, **[A-MM-ISO]** Drawing Template. The Drawing Template is displayed with the Sheet Format.

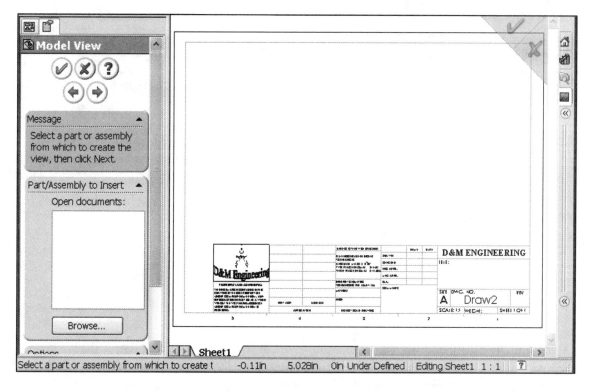

The Draw2-Sheet1 drawing is displayed in the Graphics window. The Model View PropertyManager is selected by default. The Draw# - Sheet1 is a sequential number created in the current SolidWorks session.

Utilize the A-IN-ANSI, [A- MM-ISO] Drawing Template for the BATTERY drawing.

Utilize descriptive filenames for the Drawing Template that contains the size, dimension standard, and units.

Note: File Locations is a System Option. The option is active only for the current session of SolidWorks in some network environments.

Combine custom Drawing Templates and Sheet Formats to match your company's drawing standards. Save the empty Drawing Template and Sheet Format separately to reuse information.

Additional details on Drawing Templates, Sheet Format and Custom Properties are available in SolidWorks Help Topics. Keywords: Documents (templates, properties), Sheet Formats (new, new drawings, note text), Properties (drawing sheets) and Customize Drawing Sheet Formats.

Empty Drawing Template / Custom Sheet Format / Custom Drawing Template

ANSI

A Custom Properties

B Custom Properties

ISO

MACHINE PARTS

PLASTIC PARTS

SHEET METAL PARTS

 Review Drawing Templates

A custom Drawing Template was created from the default Drawing Template. Sheet Properties and Document Properties controlled the sheet size, scale, units, and dimension display. The Sheet Format contained a Title block and Custom Property information. A Company Logo was inserted and you modified the Title block. The Save Sheet Format option was utilized to save the MY-A-FORMAT.slddrt Sheet Format.

The File, Save As option was utilized to save the A-IN-ANSI, [A-MM-ISO].drwdot Drawing Template. The Sheet Format was saved in the MY-SHEETFORMATS folder. The Drawing Template was saved in the MY-TEMPLATES folder.

BATTERY Drawing

A drawing contains part views, geometric dimensioning and tolerances, notes, and other related design information. When a part is modified, the drawing automatically updates. When a driving dimension in the drawing is modified, the part is automatically updated.

Create the BATTERY drawing from the BATTERY part. Utilize the Model View feature in the Drawings toolbar. The Front view is the first view inserted into the drawing. The Top view and Right view are Projected views. Insert dimensions into the drawing with the Insert Model Items feature.

Activity: BATTERY Drawing

Create a new drawing.

82) Click **Browse** from the Model View PropertyManager.

83) Double-click **BATTERY** part from the PROJECTS folder.

Insert the Front, Top, and Right view.

84) Click **Multiple views** from the Number of Views box.

85) Click ***Top** and ***Right** view from the Orientation box. Note: *Front is activated by default.

86) Click **OK** from the Model View PropertyManager. Three views are displayed.

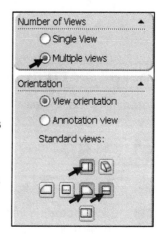

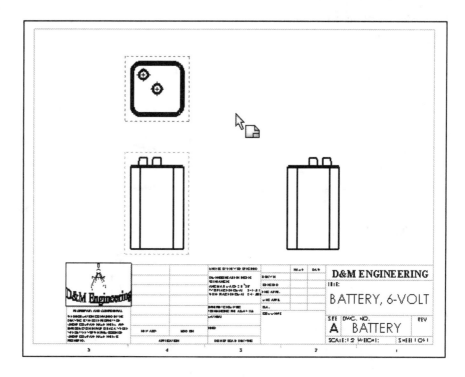

Note: A part cannot be inserted into a drawing when the Edit Sheet Format mode is selected. You are required to be in the Edit Sheet mode.

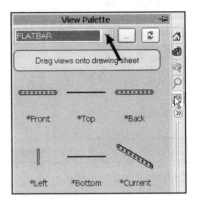

Move parent and child views independently by dragging their view boundary. Hold the Shift key down and select multiple views to move as a group.

The View Palette is new for 2007. Click the View Palette icon in the Task Pane. Click the drop down arrow to view an open part or click the Browse button to locate a part. Click and Drag the desired view/views into the active drawing sheet.

Activity: BATTERY Drawing-Insert a View

Insert an Isometric view.

Model
View

87) Click **Model View** from the Drawings toolbar.

88) Click **Next** from the Model View PropertyManager.

89) Click ***Isometric** from the Orientation box. The Isometric view is placed on the mouse pointer.

90) Click a **position** in the upper right corner of the Graphics window on Sheet1.

91) Click **OK** from the Drawing View4 PropertyManager.

View the Sheet Scale.

92) Right-click a **position** inside the Graphics window, Sheet1 boundary.

93) Click **Properties**. The Sheet Scale is 1:2.

94) Click **OK**.

The SW-Sheet Scale Property 1:2 is linked to the Title block through the Sheet Format. Later change the Sheet scale to fit the BATTERY dimensions.

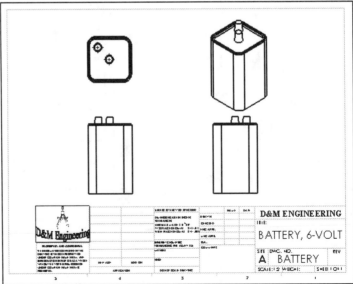

Save the drawing.

95) Click **File**, **Save As** from the Main menu.

96) Select the **PROJECTS** folder.

97) Click **Save**. BATTERY is the default drawing file name.

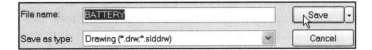

Each drawing has a unique file name. Drawing file names end with a .slddrw suffix in SolidWorks. Part file names end with a .sldprt suffix.

A drawing or part file can have the same prefix. A drawing or part file cannot have the same suffix. Example: Drawing file name: BATTERY.slddrw. Part file name: BATTERY.sldprt.

Text in the Title block is linked to the Filename and description created in the part. The DWG. NO. text box utilizes the Property, $PRP: "SW-File Name" passed from the BATTERY part to the BATTERY drawing. The TITLE text box utilizes the Property, $PRPSHEET: "Description".

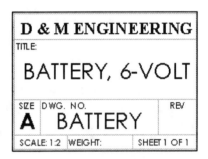

The filename BATTERY is displayed in the DWG. NO. box. The Description BATTERY, 6VOLT is displayed in the Title box.

The BATTERY drawing contains three Principle Views (Standard Views): Front, Top, Right, and an Isometric View. You created the views with the Model View feature. Drawing views can be inserted with the following processes:

- Utilize the Model View feature.

- Click and drag a part into the drawing or select the Standard 3 Orientation view option.

- Predefine views in a custom Drawing Template.

- Drag a hyperlink through Internet Explorer.

- Utilize the Task Pane.

The mouse pointer provides feedback in both the Drawing Sheet 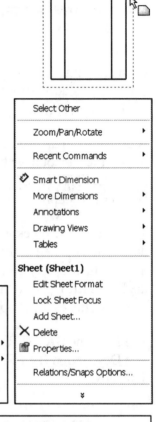 and Drawing View modes. The mouse pointer displays the Drawing Sheet icon when the Sheet properties and commands are executed.

The mouse pointer displays the Drawing View icon when the View properties and commands are executed.

View the mouse pointer for feedback to select Sheet, View, Component and Edge properties in the Drawing.

- Sheet Properties display properties of the selected sheet. Right-click in the sheet boundary.

- View Properties display properties of the selected view. Right-click on the view boundary.

- Component Properties display properties of the selected component. Right-click on the face of the component.

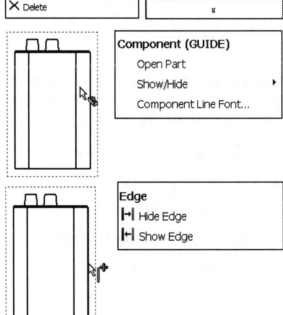

- Edge Properties display properties of the geometry. Right-click on an edge.

The Drawing views are complete. Move the views to allow for ample spacing for the dimensions and notes. Zoom In on narrow view boundary boxes if required.

Detail View

A Detail view enlarges an area of an existing view. You need to specify location, name, shape and scale. Create a Detail view named A with a circle and a 1:1 scale.

A Detail circle specifies the area of an existing view to enlarge. The circle contains the same letter as the view name.

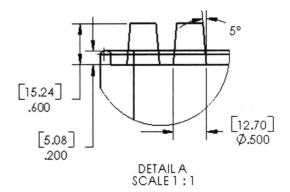

DETAIL A
SCALE 1 : 1

<table>
<tr><td>**Activity: BATTERY Drawing-Detail View**</td></tr>
</table>

Add a Detail view to the drawing.

98) Click **Detail View** View from the Drawings toolbar. The circle sketch tool is selected.

Sketch a circle with the center point located between the two terminals in Drawing View1 (Front).
99) **Sketch** the circle as illustrated.

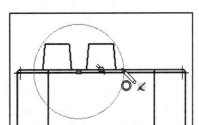

Position the Detail View.
100) Click a **position** to the right of the Drawing View3 (Top).

101) Click the **Use custom scale** box.

102) Enter **1:1** in the Custom Scale box.

103) Click **OK** ⟳ from the Drawing View A PropertyManager.

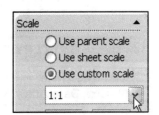

Fit the Drawing to the Graphics window.
104) Press the **f** key.

105) Click **Save** 💾.

Center marks are displayed be default. Center marks and centerlines are controlled by the Tools, Options, Document Properties, Auto insert on view creation option.

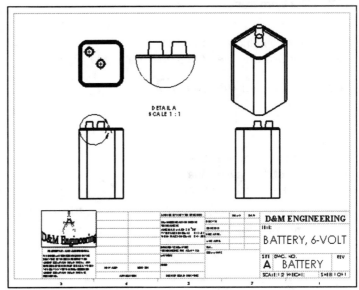

The Drawing View is complete. Allow for spacing of the dimensions and notes. Move the views by their view boundary.

View Display

Drawing views can be displayed in the following modes: Wireframe, Hidden Lines Visible, Hidden Lines Removed, Shaded With Edges, and Shaded mode.

Tangent edges are displayed either in: Visible, With Font or Removed mode. Note: System default is Tangent Edges Visible. Display hidden lines, profile lines and tangent edges in various view modes.

| ✔ Tangent Edges Visible |
| Tangent Edges With Font |
| Tangent Edges Removed |

Activity: BATTERY Drawing-View Display

Display hidden lines in the Detail View.
106) Click **Detail View A** from the FeatureManager.

107) Click **Wire frame** ⊞.

Display the Isometric view Shaded.
108) Click **Drawing View4** from the FeatureManager.

109) Click **Shaded With Edges** ▢.

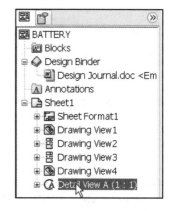

Display Tangent Edges in the Front view.
110) Right-click **Drawing View1** (Front) from the FeatureManager.

111) Click **Tangent Edge**; check **Tangent Edge Visible**.

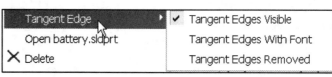

Insert Model Items and Move Dimensions

Dimensions created for each feature in the part are inserted into the drawing. Dimensions are inserted by sheet, view or feature. Select inside the sheet boundary to insert the dimensions into Sheet1. Move the dimensions off the profile lines in each view.

Illustrations for this project are provided in inches and millimeters. The Detailing option and Dual Dimensions Display produces both inches and millimeters for each dimension. The primary units are set to inches. The secondary units are set to millimeters.

Select inches or millimeters for the BATTERY drawing.

Inches
or
Millimeters

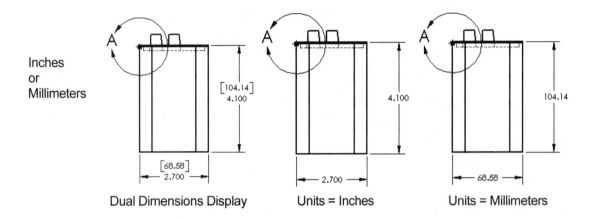

Dual Dimensions Display   Units = Inches   Units = Millimeters

The drawing dimension location is dependent on:

- Feature dimension creation.
- Selected drawing views.

Move dimensions within the same view. Use the mouse pointer to drag dimensions and leader lines to new locations.

Leader lines reference the size of the profile. A gap must exist between the profile lines and the leader lines. Shorten the leader lines to maintain a drawing standard. Use the Arrow buttons in the PropertyManager to flip dimension arrows.

Move dimensions to a different view.

Utilize the Shift key to drag a dimension to another view.

| Activity: BATTERY Drawing-Insert Model Items and Move Dimensions |

Insert dimensions into the Sheet.
112) Click inside the **sheet boundary**.

Model
113) Click **Model Items** Items from the Annotations toolbar.

114) Select **Entire model** from the Source/Destination box.

115) Click **OK** ✅ from the Model Items PropertyManager. Note: Change the Sheet scale to address the dimensions.

Note: Dimensions may appear in different locations. To move a dimension, utilize the Shift key and only drag the dimension text. Hold the Shift key down. Click and drag the dimension. Release the mouse button and then the Shift key.

Move dimensions in Drawing View1 and Drawing View3.
116) Hold the **Shift key** down. Click the horizontal dimension text **2.700**, [68.58] in the Top view.

117) Click and drag the **dimension text** into the Front view. Release the **mouse button**. Release the **Shift key**.

118) Flip the **arrow head** to the inside.

119) Repeat the above procedure for the **other dimensions** as illustrated.

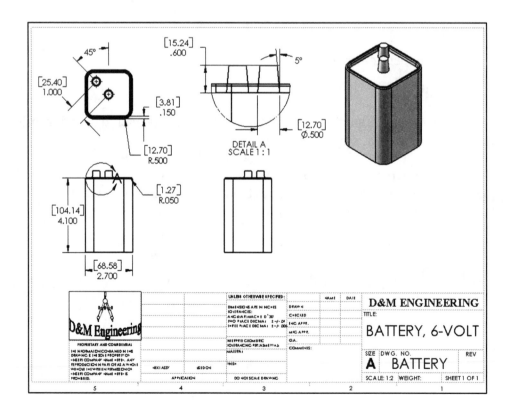

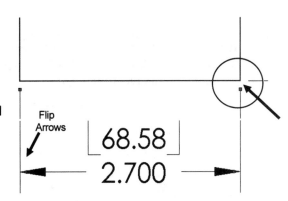

120) Click the vertical dimension text **4.100**, [**104.14**]. Drag the **text** to the right of the BATTERY.

121) Move the **leader line endpoints** if required.

122) The end points of the leader line are displayed as green squares. Drag each **square green end point** to the left until it is off the profile line.

123) Create a **gap** between the profile line and the leader lines.

Modify the diameter text on Drawing View1 and Drawing View3.

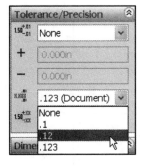

124) Click the ∅.050, [∅1.27] text on Drawing View1. The Dimension PropertyManager is displayed.

125) Select **.12**, 2 places in the Tolerance/Precision box. R.05 is displayed.

126) Click the ∅.500, [∅12.70] text on Drawing View3.

127) Select **.12**, 2 places in the Tolerance/Precision box. R.50 is displayed.

128) Click **OK** ✓ from the Dimension PropertyManager.

Save the drawing.

129) Click **Save** 🖫.

Shorten the Bent leader length.

130) Click **Tools**, **Options**, **Document Properties** tab from the Main menu.

131) Click **Dimensions**.

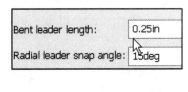

132) Enter **.25in**, [**6.35**] for Bent leader length.

133) Click **OK**.

Activity: BATTERY Drawing-Insert a Note

Insert a Note.

A

134) Click **Note** Note from the Annotations toolbar. Click a **position** in the COMMENTS box.

135) Enter **PROJECT 5**.

136) Click **OK** ✓ from the Note PropertyManager.

Save the BATTERY drawing.

137) Click **Save** 🖫.

There are hundreds of Document Property options. Where do you go for additional information on these Properties? Answer: Select the Help button in the lower right hand corner of the Document Property dialog box.

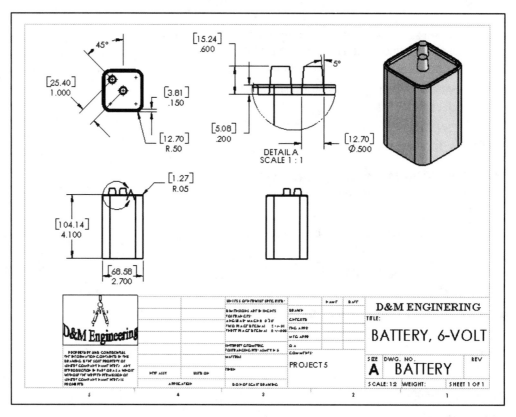

Additional details on Drawing Views, New Drawing, Details, Dimensions and Annotations are available in SolidWorks Help Topics.

Keywords: Drawing Views (overview), Drawing Views (model), Move (drawing views), Dimensions (circles, extension lines, inserting into drawings, move, and parenthesis), Annotations (Note, Hole Callout, Centerline, Centermark) and Notes (linked to properties, in sheet formats, parametric).

 Review BATTERY Drawing

You created a new drawing, BATTERY with the A-IN-ANSI, [A-MM-ISO] Drawing Template. The BATTERY drawing utilized the BATTERY part in the Model View PropertyManager. The Model View PropertyManager provides the ability to insert new views with the View Orientation option.

You selected Front, Top, Right, and Isometric to position the BATTERY views. The Detail view tool inserted a Detail view of the BATTERY. You moved the views by dragging the green view boundary. You inserted the dimensions and annotations to detail the BATTERY drawing. You inserted part dimensions and annotations into the drawing with the Insert Model Items command. Dimensions were moved to new positions. Leader lines and dimension text were repositioned. Annotations were edited to reflect the drawing standard. You modified the dimension text by inserting additional text.

New Assembly Drawing and Exploded View

Create a new drawing named FLASHLIGHT. Insert the FLASHLIGHT assembly Isometric view. Modify the view properties to display the Exploded view.

The Bill of Materials reflects the components of the FLASHLIGHT assembly. Create a drawing with a Bill of Materials. Label each component with Balloon text.

Activity: New Assembly Drawing and Exploded View

Close all parts and drawings.
138) Click **Windows**, **Close All** from the Main menu.

Create a new drawing.
139) Click **File**, **New** from the Main menu.

140) Click the **MY-TEMPLATES** tab.

141) Double-click the **A-IN-ANSI**, **[A-MM-ISO]** Drawing Template.

Insert the FLASHLIGHT assembly.
142) Click **Browse** from the Model View PropertyManager.

143) Select **Assembly** for Files of type.

144) Double-click **FLASHLIGHT** from the PROJECTS folder.

145) Select ***Isometric** for Orientation.

146) Click **Shaded With Edges** from the Display Style box.

147) Click a **position** on the right side of the drawing.

148) Click **OK** ✅ from the Drawing View1 PropertyManager.

🔆 Save parts and assemblies to preview picture thumbnails in the Open dialog box. Utilize the Isometric and Zoom to Fit options.

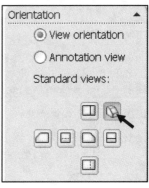

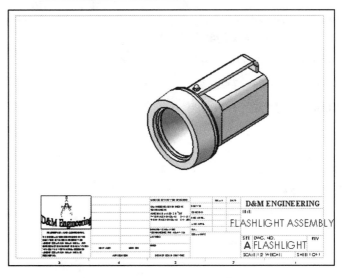

Edit the Title text height.

149) Right-click a **position** in the sheet boundary.

150) Click **Edit Sheet Format**.

151) Double-click the title text **FLASHLIGHT ASSEMBLY**. The Note PropertyManager and the Formatting dialog box are displayed.

152) Enter **.19**in for Text Height.

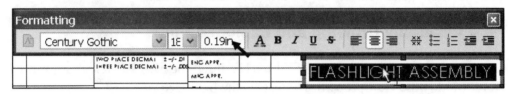

153) Click **OK** ✓ from the Note PropertyManager.

154) Right-click a **position** in the Sheet boundary.

155) Click **Edit Sheet**. The FLASHLIGHT ASSEMBLY text is sized to the Title box.

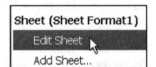

Save the drawing.

156) Click **Save** 🖫.

157) Select the **PROJECTS** folder. FLASHLIGHT is the default File name.

158) Click **Save**.

Display the Exploded view of the assembly.

159) Right-click in the **Isometric view**.

160) Click **Properties**.

161) Check **Show in exploded state** from the Drawing View Properties dialog box.

162) Click **OK**.

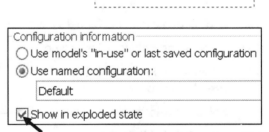

Modify the view scale.

163) Click inside the **Isometric view**.

164) Check the **Use custom scale** box.

165) Select **User Defined**.

166) Enter **1:4** in the Scale box.

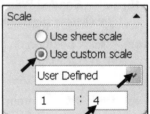

167) Click **OK** 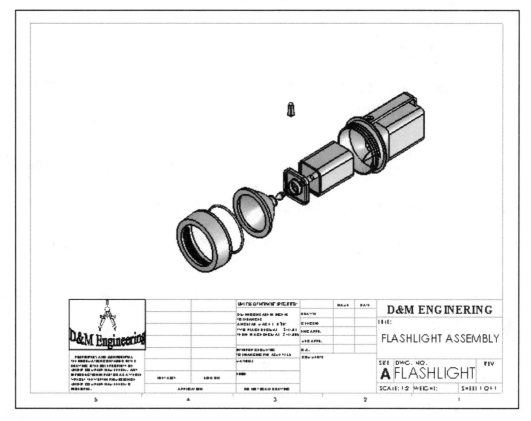 from the Model View1 PropertyManager.

Bill of Materials and Balloons

A Bill of Materials (BOM) is a table inserted into a drawing to keep a record of the parts used in an assembly. The default BOM template contains the Item Number, Quantity, Part No. and Description.

The default Item number is determined by the order in which the component is inserted into the assembly. Quantity is the number of instances of a part or assembly. Part No. is determined by the following: file name, default and the User Defined option, Part Number used by the Bill of Materials. Description is determined by the description entered when the document is saved.

Activity: FLASHLIGHT Drawing-Bill of Materials

Insert a Bill of Materials.

168) Click inside the **Isometric view**.

169) Click **Insert**, **Tables**, **Bill of Materials** from the Main menu.

170) Select **bom-standard** for the Table Template.

171) Click **Parts only** for BOM Type. Accept the default settings.

172) Click **OK** 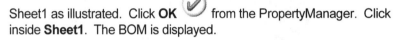 from the Bill of Materials PropertyManager.

173) Click a **position** in the upper left corner of

Sheet1 as illustrated. Click **OK** from the PropertyManager. Click inside **Sheet1**. The BOM is displayed.

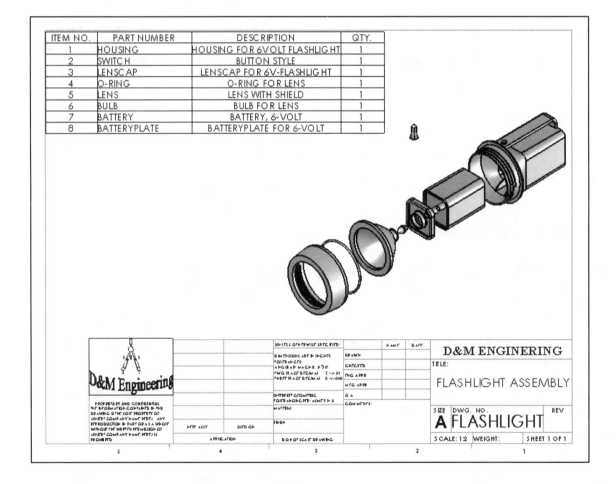

ITEM NO.	PART NUMBER	DESCRIPTION	QTY.
1	HOUSING	HOUSING FOR 6VOLT FLASHLIGHT	1
2	SWITCH	BUTTON STYLE	1
3	LENSCAP	LENSCAP FOR 6V-FLASHLIGHT	1
4	O-RING	O-RING FOR LENS	1
5	LENS	LENS WITH SHIELD	1
6	BULB	BULB FOR LENS	1
7	BATTERY	BATTERY, 6-VOLT	1
8	BATTERYPLATE	BATTERYPLATE FOR 6-VOLT	1

The Bill of Materials requires additional work that you will complete in the next section.

Activity: FLASHLIGHT Drawing-Balloons

Label each component.

174) Click the **Isometric view** boundary. Click **Auto Balloon** AutoBal... from the Annotations toolbar.

175) Click **OK** from the Auto Balloon PropertyManager. Click and drag the **balloons** inside the view boundary.

Insert a balloon for the O-RING.

176) Click **Balloon** Balloon from the Annotations toolbar.

177) Click the **O-RING** in the Graphics window. **Position** the Balloon in the drawing.

178) Click **OK** from the Balloon PropertyManager.

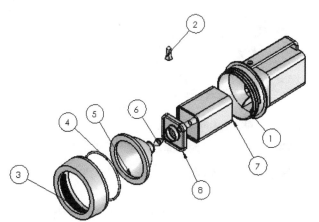

The Balloon note displays an arrowhead on a selected edge and a filled dot on a selected face when the Drawing Standard is set to ANSI. The Balloon note displays a "?" if no edge or face is selected.

Part Numbers

Use the following prefix codes to categories created parts and drawings. The part names and part numbers are as follows:

Category:	Prefix:	Part Name:	Part Number:
Molded Parts	44-	BATTERYPLATE	44-A26
		LENSCAP	44-A27
		HOUSING	44-A28
Purchased Parts	B99-	BATTERY	B99-B01
	99-	LENS	99-B02
		O-RING	99-B03
		SWITCH	99-B04
		BULB	99-B05
Assemblies	10-	FLASHLIGHT	10-F123

The Bill of Materials requires editing. The current part file name determines the PART NUMBER parameter values. The Configuration Properties controls the display of the PART NUMBER in the Bill of Materials. Redefine the PART NUMBER for each part.

Activity: FLASHLIGHT Drawing-ConfigurationManager

Open the BATTERYPLATE part from the drawing.
179) Expand Drawing View1.

180) Expand FLASHLIGHT.

181) Expand BATTERYANDPLATE.

182) Right-click **BATTTERYPLATE**.

183) Click **Open Part**.

Display the Configuration Properties.
184) Click the **ConfigurationManager** tab.

185) Right-click the **Default [BATTTERYPLATE]** configuration.

186) Click **Properties** Properties... .

187) Select **User Specified Name**.

188) Enter **44-A26**.

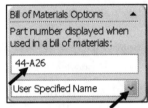

189) Click **OK** from the Configuration Properties PropertyManager.

190) Click the **FeatureManager** tab.

The ConfigurationManager displays the Default [44-A26] configuration.

Return to the FLASHLIGHT drawing.
191) Click **Window, FLASHLIGHT-Sheet1** from the Main menu.

Activity: FLASHLIGHT Drawing-Update the Bill of Materials

Update the Bill of Materials.
192) Click **Rebuild** .

Enter the BATTERY PART NUMBER.
193) Right-click **BATTERY** part from the FeatureManager.

194) Click **Open Part**.

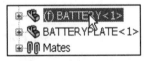

195) Click the BATTERY **ConfigurationManager** tab.

196) Right-click **Default [BATTERY]** from the ConfigurationManager.

197) Click **Properties**.

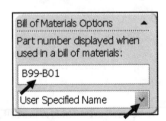

198) Select the **User Specified Name** from the Configuration Properties dialog box.

199) Enter **B99-B01**.

200) Click **OK** ✅ from the Configuration Properties PropertyManager.

201) Click the **FeatureManager** 🗂 tab.

Return to the FLASHLIGHT drawing.
202) Click **Window**, **FLASHLIGHT-Sheet1** from the Main menu.

Update the Bill of Materials.
203) Click **Rebuild** 🔴.

Resize the PART NUMBER column.
204) Drag the **vertical line** between the PART NUMBER and the DESCRIPTION column to the left.

205) Drag the **vertical line** between the DESCRIPTION and the QTY to the left.

Complete the PART NUMBER column. The User Specified Name for the remaining PART NUMBERs is left as an exercise.

ITEM NO.	PART NUMBER	DESCRIPTION	QTY.
1	HOUSING	HOUSING FOR 6VOLT FLASHLIGHT	1
2	SWITCH	BUTTON STYLE	1
3	LENSCAP	LENSCAP FOR 6V-FLASHLIGHT	1
4	O-RING	O-RING FOR LENS	1
5	LENS	LENS WITH SHIELD	1
6	BULB	BULB FOR LENS	1
7	44-A26	BATTERYPLATE FOR 6-VOLT	1
8	B99-B01	BATTERY, 6-VOLT	1

Save the FLASHLIGHT drawing.

206) Click **Save** 💾.

Close All documents.
207) Click **Windows**, **Close All** from the Main menu.

🔍 Additional details on Exploded View, Notes, Properties, Bill of Materials and Balloons, are available in SolidWorks Help Topics. Keywords: Exploded, Notes, Properties (configurations), Bill of Materials, Balloons, and Auto Balloon.

Review the FLASHLIGHT Drawing

The FLASHLIGHT drawing contained an Exploded view. The Exploded view was created in the FLASHLIGHT assembly. The Bill of Materials listed the Item Number, Part Number, Description, and Quantity of components in the assembly. Balloons were inserted to label the top level components in the FLASHLIGHT assembly. You developed Properties in the part to modify the Part Number utilized in the Bill of Materials.

Design Tables and O-RING Drawing

A Design Table is a spreadsheet used to create multiple configurations in a part or assembly. The Design Table controls the dimensions and parameters in the part. Utilize the Design Table to modify the overall path diameter and profile diameter of the O-RING. Create three configurations of the O-RING:

- Small.

- Medium.

- Large.

Save the O-RING part with the Save As Copy option. Create a new drawing for the O-RING. The part configurations utilized in the drawing are controlled through the Properties of the view. Insert the three O-RING configurations in the drawing.

Note: The O-RING contains two dimension names in the Design Tables. Parts contain hundreds of dimensions and values. Rename dimension names for clarity.

Activity: O-RING Part-Design Table

Open the O-RING part.

208) Click **File**, **Open** 📂 from the Main menu.

209) Double-click **O-RING** from the PROJECTS folder.

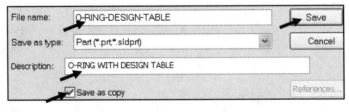

Save a Copy of the O-RING.
210) Click **File**, **Save As** from the Main menu.

211) Check **Save as copy**. Enter **O-RING-DESIGN-TABLE** for File name.

212) Enter **O-RING WITH DESIGN TABLE** for Description.

213) Click **Save**.

Open the O-RING-DESIGN-TABLE part.
214) Click **File**, **Open** from the Main menu.

215) Double-click **O-RING-DESIGN-TABLE** from the PROJECTS folder.

Modify the Primary Units.

216) Click **Tools**, **Options**, **Document Properties** tab. Click **Units**.

217) Select **MMGS**. Enter **2** for Length units Decimal.

218) Click **OK**.

219) Double-click the **face** of the O-RING. The two diameter dimensions are displayed in millimeters.

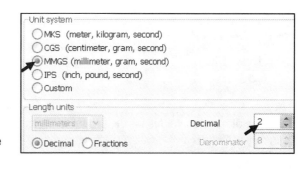

Insert a Design Table.

220) Click **Insert**, **Design Table** from the Main menu. The Auto-create option is selected.

221) Click **OK** ✅ from the Design Table PropertyManager.

222) Hold the **Ctrl** key down.

223) Select **D1@Sketch-path** and **D1@Sketch-profile**.

224) Release the **Ctrl** key.

225) Click **OK**.

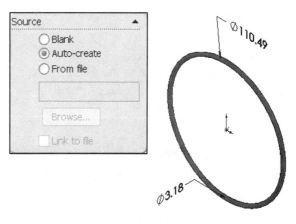

Note: The dimension variable name will be different if sketches or features were deleted. The input dimension names and default values are automatically entered into the Design Table. The value Default is entered in Cell A3. The values for the O-RING are entered in Cells B3 through C6. The sketch-path diameter is controlled in Column B. The sketch-profile diameter is controlled in Column C.

Enter the three configuration names.

226) Click **Cell A4**.

227) Enter **Small**.

228) Click **Cell A5**.

229) Enter **Medium**.

230) Click **Cell A6**.

231) Enter **Large**.

Enter the dimension values for the Small configuration.

232) Click **Cell B4**.

233) Enter **100**.

234) Click **Cell C4**.

235) Enter **3**.

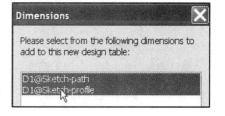

	A	B	C	D	E
1	Design Table for: O-RING-DESIGN-TABLE				
2		D1@Sketch-path	D1@Sketch-profile		
3	Default	110.49	3.175		
4	Small	100	3		
5	Medium	150	4		
6	Large	200	10		

Enter the dimension values for the Medium configuration.

236) Click **Cell B5**.

237) Enter **150**.

238) Click **Cell C5**. Enter **4**.

Enter the dimension values for the Large configuration.

239) Click **Cell B6**.

240) Enter **200**.

241) Click **Cell C6**. Enter **10**.

Build the three configurations.

242) Click a **position** outside the EXCEL Design Table in the Graphics window.

243) Click **OK** to generate the configurations. The Design Table icon is displayed in the FeatureManager.

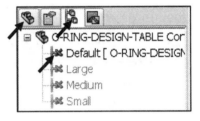

Display the configurations.

244) Click the **ConfigurationManager** tab.

245) Double-click **Small**.

246) Double-click **Medium**. Double-click **Large**.

247) Double-click **Default**.

Return to the FeatureManager.

248) Click the O-RING-DESIGN-TABLE **FeatureManager** tab.

Activity: O-RING Drawing

Create a new drawing.

249) Click **File**, **New** from the Main menu.

250) Click the **MY-TEMPLATES** tab.

251) Double-click the **A-IN-ANSI**, **[A-ISO-MM]** Drawing Template.

252) Double click the **O-RING-DESIGN-TABLE** part from the Part/Assembly to Insert box.

Insert an Isometric view.

253) If required, click *Isometric view from the Orientation box.

254) Click the **left side** of the drawing.

255) Click **OK** from the Drawing View1 PropertyManager.

256) Click **Save**. Accept the defaults.

257) Click **Save**. Note: Adjust the font size in the drawing for the Title box and DWG. No.

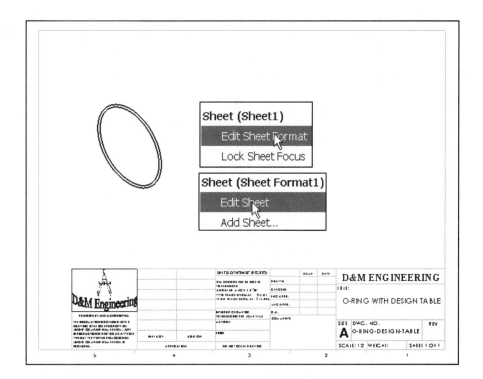

Activity: O-RING Drawing-Design Table

Display the Small configuration.

258) Right-click inside the **Isometric view** boundary.

259) Click **Properties**. Select **Small** from the Use named configuration list.

260) Click **OK** from the Drawing View Properties dialog box.

Copy the Isometric view.

261) Click the **Isometric view boundary**.

262) Press **Ctrl C**.

Paste the view.

263) Click a **position** to the right of the Isometric view.

264) Press **Ctrl V**.

Display the Medium configuration.

265) Right-click the **view boundary** of the second view.

266) Click **Properties**.

267) Select **Medium** from the Use named configuration list.

268) Click **OK** from the Drawing View Properties dialog box.

269) Click **OK** from the Drawing View2 PropertyManager.

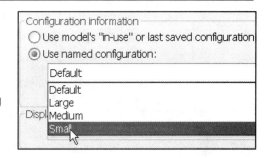

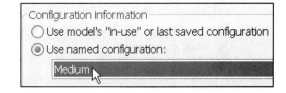

The Large configuration is left as an exercise.

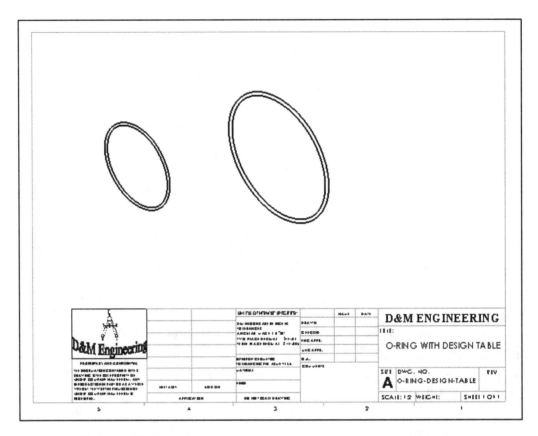

Save the O-RING-DESIGN-TABLE drawing.

270) Click **Save** 💾.

Save time with repetitive dimensioning in configurations. Insert dimensions into the first view. Copy the view. The view and the dimensions are copied to the new view.

Additional details on Design Tables and Configurations are available in SolidWorks Help Topics.

Project Summary

You produced three drawings: BATTERY, FLASHLIGHT and O-RING. The drawings contained Standard views, Detail view, and Isometric views. The drawings utilized a custom Sheet Format and custom Drawing Template. The Sheet Format contained the Company logo and Title block information.

You incorporated the BATTERY part dimensions into the drawing. You obtained an understanding of displaying views with the ability to insert, add and modify dimensions. You used two major design modes in the drawings: Edit Sheet Format and Edit Sheet.

The FLASHLIGHT assembly drawing contained an Exploded view and Bill of Materials. The Properties for the Bill of Materials were developed in each part with a user defined Part Number.

You created three configurations of the O-RING part with a Design Table. A Design Table controlled parameters and dimensions. You utilized the three configurations in the O-RING-DESIGN-TABLE drawing. Drawings are an integral part of the design process. Part, assemblies and drawings all work together to fulfill the design requirements of your customer.

Project Terminology

Bill of Materials: A Bill of Materials is a table that lists the Item Numbers, Part Numbers, Descriptions, Quantities and other information about an assembly.

Center marks: Geometry that represents two perpendicular intersecting centerlines.

Design Table: A Design Table is a table used to create multiple configurations in a part or assembly. The Design Table controls the dimensions and parameters in the part or assembly.

Detail view: A view inserted into a drawing that enlarges an area of an existing view.

Drawing Template: The foundation of a SolidWorks drawing is the Drawing Template. Drawing size, drawing standards, company information, manufacturing and or assembly requirements, units and other properties are defined in the Drawing Template. In this project the Drawing Template contained the drawing Size and Document Properties.

Edit Sheet Format Mode: Provides the ability to: Change the title block size and text headings, incorporate a company logo and add a drawing, design or company text. Remember: A part cannot be inserted into a drawing when the Edit Sheet Format mode is selected.

Edit Sheet Mode: Provides the ability to: Add or modify views, dimensions or text.

Insert Model Items: The tool utilized to insert part dimensions and annotations into drawing views.

Leader lines: Dimension entity that references the size of the profile. A gap must exist between the profile lines and the leader lines for proper drafting practice.

Model View: The tool utilized to insert named views into a drawing.

Note: Annotation tool used to add text with leaders or as a stand-alone text string.

Sheet Format: A document applied to the Drawing Template. The Sheet Format contains the border, title block information, revision block information, company name and or logo information, Custom Properties and SolidWorks Properties.

Title block: The area in the Sheet Format containing vital part or assembly information. Each company has a unique version of a title block.

Questions

1. Identify the differences between a Drawing Template and a Sheet Format. Provide an example.

2. Identify the command to save the Sheet Format.

3. Identify the command to save the Drawing Template.

4. Describe a Bill of Materials. Provide an example.

5. Name the two major design modes used to develop a drawing in SolidWorks.

6. Name seven components that are commonly found in a title block.

7. Describe the procedure to insert an Isometric view into a drawing.

8. In SolidWorks, drawing file names end with a _____ suffix.

9. True or False. Most engineering drawings us the following font: Time New Roman – All small letters. Explain your answer.

10. Describe Leader lines. Provide an example.

11. Describe a Note on a drawing. Provide an example.

12. Explain the procedure to add an Exploded view from an assembly to a drawing.

13. Explain the procedure on labeling components in an Exploded view on an assembly drawing. Provide an example.

14. Describe the procedure to create a Design Table.

15. True or False. You cannot display different configurations in the same drawing. Explain your answer.

16. True or False. The Part Number is only entered in the Bill of Materials. Explain your answer.

17. There are hundreds of options in the Document Properties, Drawings and Annotations toolbars. How would you locate additional information on these options and tools?

Exercises

Exercise 5.1: **SHAFT-COLLAR Drawing**.

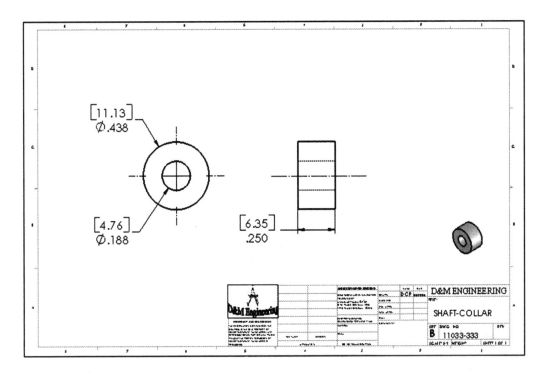

Exercise 5.2: **FLATBAR Drawing**. Add a Smart Dimension to the drawing for the 2X R.250, [6.35] value.

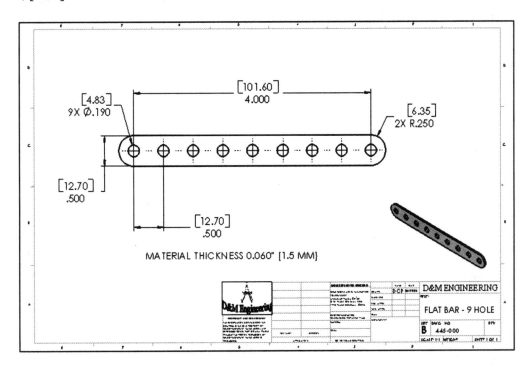

Exercise 5.3: Design Tables.

Utilize the Design Table to create three configurations of the SHAFT-COLLAR:

- Small.

- Medium.

- Large.

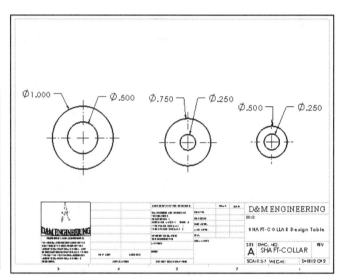

	A	B	C	D
1	Design Table for: SHAFT-COLLAR			
2		D1@Sketch1	D1@Extrude1	D1@Sketch2
3	Default	0.4375	0.25	0.1875
4	Small	0.5	0.25	0.25
5	Medium	0.75	0.375	0.25
6	Large	1	0.5	0.5

Note: The dimension variable name will be different if sketches or features were deleted.

Add a Sheet to the SHAFT-COLLAR drawing. Insert the three different configurations.

Exercise 5.4: Assembly Drawings.

Create an assembly drawing and Bill of Materials for the LINK-AND-HOOK assembly and the BATTERYANDPLATE assembly.

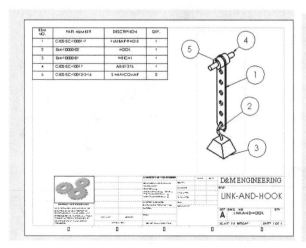

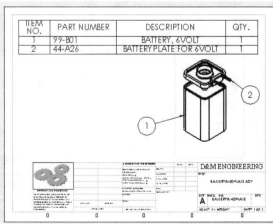

Exercise 5.5: **Industry Collaborative Exercise**.

Utilize the World Wide Web to locate additional parts, assemblies and drawings. Example URLs are given below:

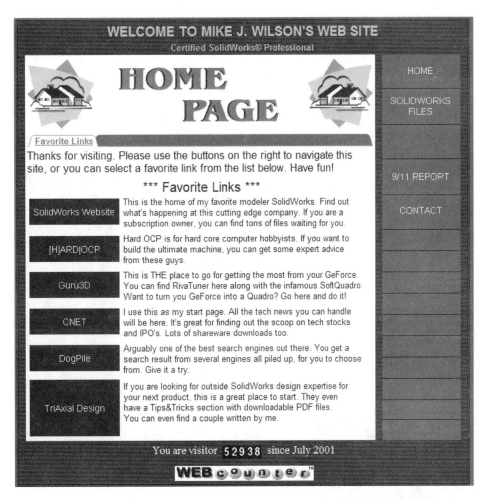

http://www.scottjbaugh.com   Scott J. Baugh

http://www.3-ddesignsolutions.com   Devon Sowell

http://www.zxys.com   Paul Salvador

http://www.mikejwilson.com   Mike J. Wilson

http://www.dimontegroup.com   Gene Dimonte
                                             & Ed Eaton

Online tutorials are for educational purposes only. Tutorials are copyrighted by their owners. Additional models are located at www.3DContentCentral.com or through the SW Design Library/ 3D ContentCentral/Supplier Content.

Notes:

Appendix

Engineering Changer Order (ECO)

D&M Engineering Change Order				ECO # _____ Page 1 of __	
	☐ Hardware			Author	
	☐ Software			Date	
Product Line	☐ Quality			Authorized Mgr.	
	☐ Tech Pubs			Date	

Change Tested By

Reason for ECO(Describe the existing problem, symptom and impact on field)

D&M Part No.	Rev From/To	Part Description	Description		Owner

ECO Implementation/Class		Departments	Approvals	Date	
All in Field	☐	Engineering			
All in Test	☐	Manufacturing			
All in Assembly	☐	Technical Support			
All in Stock	☐	Marketing			
All on Order	☐	DOC Control			
All Future	☐				
Material Disposition		ECO Cost			
Rework	☐	DO NOT WRITE BELOW THIS LINE (ECO BOARD ONLY)			
Scrap	☐	Effective Date			
Use as is	☐	Incorporated Date			
None	☐	Board Approval			
See Attached	☐	Board Date			

This text follows the ASME Y14 Engineering Drawing and Related Documentation Practices for drawings. Display of dimensions and tolerances are as follows:

TYPES of DECIMAL DIMENSIONS (ASME Y14.5M)			
Description:	**UNITS:** **MM**	**Description:**	**UNITS:** **INCH**
Dimension is less than 1mm. Zero precedes the decimal point.	0.9 0.95	Dimension is less than 1 inch. Zero is not used before the decimal point.	.5 .56
Dimension is a whole number. Display no decimal point. Display no zero after decimal point.	19	Express dimension to the same number of decimal places as its tolerance. Add zeros to the right of the decimal point. If the tolerance is expressed to 3 places, then the dimension contains 3 places to the right of the decimal point.	1.750
Dimension exceeds a whole number by a decimal fraction of a millimeter. Display no zero to the right of the decimal.	11.5 11.51		

TABLE 1 TOLERANCE DISPLAY FOR INCH AND METRIC DIMENSIONS (ASME Y14.5M)		
DISPLAY:	**UNITS:** **INCH:**	**UNITS:** **METRIC:**
Dimensions less than 1	.5	0.5
Unilateral Tolerance	$1.417^{+.005}_{-.000}$	$36^{0}_{-0.5}$
Bilateral Tolerance	$1.417^{+.010}_{-.020}$	$36^{+0.25}_{-0.50}$
Limit Tolerance	.571 .463	14.50 11.50

Cursor Feedback

Cursor Feedback provides information about SolidWorks geometry. The following tables summarize cursor feedback. The tables were developed by support engineers from Computer Aided Products, Inc. Peabody, MA. Used with permission.

Sketch Tools:			
	Line		Rectangle
	Circle		Ellipse
	Arc (Centerpoint, Tangent, 3 Point)		Ellipse
	Parabola		Spline
	Polygon		Point
	Trim		Extend
	Split line (not possible)		Split line (here)
	Linear step and repeat		Circular step and repeat
	Modify sketch tool		Modify Sketch (Rotate only)
	Modify Sketch (Move / Flip Y-axis)		Modify Sketch (Move / Flip X-axis)
	Move Origin of Sketch / Flip both axes		

Cursor Feedback Symbols
Courtesy of Computer Aided Products, Inc. Peabody, MA USA

Sketching Relationships:		
Horizontal		Vertical
Parallel		Perpendicular
Tangent		Intersection
Coincident to axis		Midpoint
Quarter arc		Half arc
3 quarter arc		Quadrant of arc
Wake up line/edge		Wake up point
Coincident to line/edge		Coincident to point
3D sketch		3D sketch
3D sketch		3D sketch
3D sketch		3D sketch

Dimensions:		
Dimension		Radial or diameter dimension
Horizontal dimension		Vertical dimension
Vertical ordinate dimension		Ordinate dimensioning
Horizontal ordinate dimension		Baseline dimensioning

Cursor Feedback Symbols
Courtesy of Computer Aided Products, Inc. Peabody, MA USA

Selection:			
	Line, edge		Axis
	Surface body		Select Point
	Select Vertex		Select Endpoint
	Select Midpoint		Select arc centerpoint
	Select Annotation		Select surface finish
	Select geometric tolerance		Datum Target
	Multi jog leader		Select multi jog leader control point
	Select Datum Feature		Select balloon
	Select text reference point	This Field Left Blank	Cursors for other selections with a reference point look similar
	Dimensions		Dimension arrow
	Cosmetic Thread		Stacked Balloons
	Hole Callout		Place Center Mark
	Select Center Mark		Block
	Select Silhouette edge		Select other
	Filter is switched on		

Cursor Feedback Symbols
Courtesy of Computer Aided Products, Inc. Peabody, MA USA

Assemblies:			
	Choose reference plane (insert new component/envelope)		Insert Component from File
	Insert Component (fixed to origin)		Insert Component to Feature Manager
	Lightweight component		Rotate component
	Move component / Smartmate select mode		Select 2nd component for smartmate
	Simulation mode running		

Smartmates:			
	Mate - Coincident Linear Edges		Mate - Coincident Planar Faces
	Mate - Concentric Axes/Conical Faces		Mate - Coincident Vertices
	Mate - Coincident/Concentric Circular Edges or Conical Faces		

FeatureManager:			
	Move component or feature in tree		Copy component or feature in tree
	Move feature below a folder in tree		Move/copy not permitted
	Invalid location for item		Move component in/out of sub assembly

Cursor Feedback Symbols
Courtesy of Computer Aided Products, Inc. Peabody, MA USA

Drawings:			
	Drawing sheet		Drawing view
	Move drawing view		Auxiliary view arrow
	Change view size horizontally		Change view size vertically
	Change view size diagonally		Change view size diagonally
	Align Drawing View		Select detail circle
	Block		Select Datum Feature Symbol
	Insert/Select Weld Symbol		Select Center Mark
	Select Section View		Section view and points of section arrow
	Select Silhouette edge		Hide/Show Dimensions

Standard Tools:			
	Selection tool		Please wait (thinking)
	Rotate view		Pan view
	Invalid selection/location		Measure tool
	Zoom to area		Zoom in/out
	Accept option		

Cursor Feedback Symbols
Courtesy of Computer Aided Products, Inc. Peabody, MA USA

SolidWorks Keyboard Shortcuts

Listed below are the pre-defined keyboard shortcuts in SolidWorks:

Action:	Key Combination:
Model Views	
Rotate the model horizontally or vertically:	**Arrow** keys
Rotate the model horizontally or vertically 90 degrees.	**Shift** + **Arrow** keys
Rotate the model clockwise or counterclockwise	**Alt** + left of right **Arrow** keys
Pan the model	**Ctrl** + **Arrow** keys
Zoom in	**Shift + z**
Zoom out	**z**
Zoom to fit	**f**
Previous view	**Ctrl + Shift + z**
View Orientation	
View Orientation menu	**Spacebar**
Front view	**Ctrl + 1**
Back view	**Ctrl + 2**
Left view	**Ctrl + 3**
Right view	**Ctrl + 4**
Top view	**Ctrl + 5**
Bottom view	**Ctrl + 6**
Isometric view	**Ctrl + 7**
NormalTo view	**Ctrl + 8**
Selection Filters	
Filter edges	**e**
Filter vertices	**v**
Filter faces	**x**
Toggle Selection Filter toolbar	**F5**
Toggle selection filters on/off	**F6**
File menu items	
New SolidWorks document	**Ctrl + n**
Open document	**Ctrl + o**
Open From Web Folder	**Ctrl + w**
Make Drawing from Part	**Ctrl + d**
Make Assembly from Part	**Ctrl + a**
Save	**Ctrl +s**
Print	**Ctrl + p**
Additional shortcuts	
Access online help inside of PropertyManager or dialog box	**F1**
Rename an item in the FeatureManager design tree	**F2**
Rebuild the model	**Ctrl + b**
Force rebuild – Rebuild the model and all its features	**Ctrl + q**
Redraw the screen	**Ctrl + r**
Cycle between open SolidWorks document	**Ctrl + Tab**

Line to arc/arc to line in the Sketch	**a**
Undo	**Ctrl + z**
Redo	**Ctrl + y**
Cut	**Ctrl + x**
Copy	**Ctrl + c**
Additional shortcuts	
Paste	**Ctrl + v**
Delete	**Delete**
Next window	**Ctrl + F6**
Close window	**Ctrl + F4**
Selects all text inside an Annotations text box	**Ctrl + a**

In the Sketch, the Esc key unselects geometry items currently selected in the Properties box and Add Relations box. In the model, the Esc key closes the PropertyManager and cancels the selections.

Windows Shortcuts

Listed below are the pre-defined keyboard shortcuts in Microsoft Windows:

Action:	Keyboard Combination:
Open the Start menu	Windows Logo key
Open Windows Explorer	Windows Logo key + E
Minimize all open windows	Windows Logo key + M
Open a Search window	Windows Logo key + F
Open Windows Help	Windows Logo key + F1
Select multiple geometry items in a SolidWorks document	Ctrl key (Hold the Ctrl key down. Select items.) Release the Ctrl key.

Helpful On-Line Information

The SolidWorks URL: http://www.solidworks.com contains information on local resellers, Partners and SolidWorks users groups.

The SolidWorks URL: http://www.3D ContentCentral.com contains additional engineering electronic catalog information.

The SolidWorks web site provides links to sample designs, frequently asked questions, an independent News Group (comp.cad.solidworks) and Users Groups.

Helpful on-line SolidWorks information is available from the following URLs:

- http://www.mechengineer.com/snug/

  News group access and local user group information.

- http://www.nhcad.com

  Configuration information and other tips and tricks.

- http://www.solidworktips.com

  Helpful tips, tricks on SolidWorks and API.

- http://www.topica.com/lists/SW

  Independent News Group for SolidWorks discussions, questions and answers.

Certified SolidWorks Professionals (CSWP) URLs provide additional helpful on-line information.

- http://www.scottjbaugh.com   Scott J. Baugh

- http://www.3-ddesignsolutions.com   Devon Sowell

- http://www.zxys.com   Paul Salvador

- http://www.mikejwilson.com   Mike J. Wilson

- http://www.dimontegroup.com   Gene Dimonte & Ed Eaton

On-line tutorials are for educational purposes only. Tutorials are copyrighted by their respective owners.

INDEX

Assembly Modeling with SolidWorks 2007

with Multimedia CD

Table of Contents

1. File Management
2. Assembly Modeling—Bottom Up Design
3. Top Down Design—In Context
4. Configurations, Custom Properties Design Tables and References
5. Assembly Drawing
6. Top Down Modeling Techniques

ISBN: 978-1-58503-346-1
555 Pages

Description

Assembly Modeling with SolidWorks was written to assist the intermediate SolidWorks user who desires to enhance their skill sets in assembly modeling. The book provides a solid foundation in assembly modeling using competency-based projects. In step-by-step instructions, you perform the following tasks:

- Explore top-level assemblies that contain hundreds of features, parts, and sub-assemblies.
- Design, create, and modify assemblies, parts, and drawings based on geometric and functional requirements.
- Develop assemblies from a Bottom-up design modeling approach utilizing components from global suppliers.
- Develop a Top-down design modeling approach incorporating a Layout sketch and in-context features.
- Incorporate Configurations, Design tables, Bill of Materials, and Custom properties to represent multiple design options in the part, assembly and drawing.
- Understand external references and features developed In-Context of an assembly; edit and redefine references, features, and components.
- Exercise Shortcut keys, Customize toolbars, and Pop-up menus to build modeling speed.
- Maximize geometric relationships in the part sketch, build symmetry in the part, and reuse components in the assembly.

More Information

For a complete Table of Contents and to download a sample chapter please visit our website at www.schroff.com.

Drawing & Detailing with SolidWorks 2007

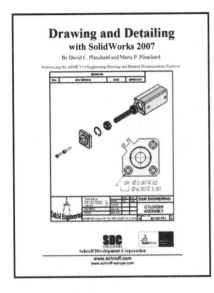

Table of Contents

Introduction

ISBN: 978-1-58503-350-8
426 Pages

Description

Drawing and Detailing with SolidWorks 2006 was written to educate and assist students, designers, engineers and professionals in the following areas:

- A solid foundation using SolidWorks Drawing Options and SolidWorks Detailing Options.
- Applying Engineering drawing standards and practices using SolidWorks tools.
- Building multiple part and assembly configurations that interact with drawings, Bill of Materials and Design Tables.
- A comprehensive understanding of the differences between Drawing Templates and Sheet Formats.
- Increase SolidWorks functionality to create view types with various configurations.
- Combine a series of SolidWorks tools to solve a specific problem using Custom Properties and SolidWorks Properties.

The book utilizes a competency-based approach on five projects. Real world parts, projects and tasks are addressed. Commands are presented in a step-by-step progressive approach. The learning process is explored through a series of design situations, industry scenarios, projects and objectives.

More Information

For a complete Table of Contents and to download a sample chapter please visit our website at www.schroff.com.

Engineering Design with SolidWorks 2007

with Multimedia CD

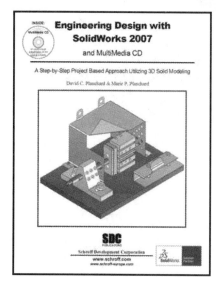

Table of Contents

Introduction
1. Fundamentals of Part Modeling
2. Fundamentals of Assembly Modeling
3. Fundamentals of Drawing
4. Extrude and Revolve Features
5. Sweep and Loft Additional Features
6. Top Down Assembly Modeling
Appendix
Index

ISBN: 978-1-58503-335-5
712 Pages

Description

Engineering Design with SolidWorks 2007 was written to assist students, designers, engineers and professionals. The book provides a solid foundation in SolidWorks by utilizing projects with Step-by-Step instructions for the beginning to intermediate SolidWorks user. Explore the user interface, menus, toolbars and modeling techniques to create parts, assemblies, and drawings in an engineering environment.

Follow the Step-by-Step instructions and develop multiple parts and assemblies that combine machined, plastic and sheet metal components. Formulate the skills to create, modify and edit sketches and solid features. Learn the techniques to reuse features, parts and assemblies through symmetry, patterns, copied components, Design tables, Bill of materials, properties and configurations.

Desired outcomes and usage competencies are listed for each project. Know your objective up front. Follow the steps in Project 1 through Project 6 to achieve the design goals. Work between multiple documents, features, commands and custom properties that represent how engineers and designers utilize SolidWorks in industry.

Review individual features, commands and tools for each project with the Multimedia CD. The projects contain exercises. The exercises analyze and examine usage competencies. Collaborate with leading industry suppliers such as SMC Corporation of America, Boston Gear, DE-STA-CO, Emerson-EPT, Emhart, Enerpac, Reid Tool and Die and 80/20 Inc. Collaborative information translates into numerous formats such as paper drawings, electronic files, rendered images and animations. On-line intelligent catalogs guide designers to the product that meets both their geometric requirements and performance functionality.

More Information

For a complete Table of Contents and to download a sample chapter please visit our website at www.schroff.com.

More books from SDC Publications by David Planchard & Marie Planchard:

SolidWorks 2007 Tutorial
with Multimedia CD

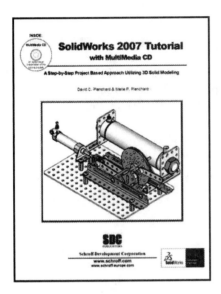

Table of Contents

Introduction

ISBN: 978-1-58503-335-5
712 Pages

Description

SolidWorks 2007 Tutorial was written to assist students, designers, engineers and professionals. The book provides an introduction to the user interface, menus, toolbars, concepts and modeling techniques of SolidWorks to create parts, assemblies and drawings.

Follow the step-by-step instructions and develop multiple assemblies that combine over 80 extruded machined parts and components. Formulate the skills to create, modify and edit sketches and solid features. Learn the techniques to reuse features, parts and assemblies through symmetry, patterns, copied components, design tables and configurations. Review 2 hours of flash movie files that follow the steps in the book.

Desired outcomes and usage competencies are listed for each project. Know your objective up front. Follow the steps in Project 1 through Project 4 to achieve your design goals. Work between multiple documents, features, commands and custom properties that represent how engineers and designers utilize SolidWorks in industry.

More Information

For a complete Table of Contents and to download a sample chapter please visit our website at www.schroff.com.

Notes:

Notes: